The Anglo-Saxon Fenland

Susan Oosthuizen

WIND*gather* PRESS

Windgather Press is an imprint of Oxbow Books

First published in the United Kingdom in 2017. Reprinted in 2017, 2018, 2019, 2020 and 2024 by
OXBOW BOOKS
The Old Music Hall, 106–108 Cowley Road, Oxford OX4 1JE

and in the United States by
OXBOW BOOKS
1950 Lawrence Road, Havertown, PA 19083

Paperback Edition: ISBN 978-1-911188-08-7
Digital Edition: ISBN 978-1-911188-09-4

A CIP record for this book is available from the British Library

Printed in the United Kingdom by CMP Digital Print Solutions

For a complete list of Windgather titles, please contact:

United Kingdom
OXBOW BOOKS
Telephone (0)1226 734350
Email: oxbow@oxbowbooks.com
www.oxbowbooks.com

United States of America
OXBOW BOOKS
Telephone (610) 853-9131, Fax (610) 853-9146
Email: queries@casemateacademic.com
www.casemateacademic.com/oxbow

Oxbow Books is part of the Casemate group

Front cover: Bottisham Lode, viewed towards the north-west along its direction of flow. It carries water from the uplands of east Cambridgeshire to the river Cam, helping to prevent flooding of the intervening fen pastures. The slightly sinuous character of the modern Lode is an index of its age, each slight meander revealing constant maintenance and alteration over the 1000 years or more since it was constructed (© William Blake, reproduced with permission).

Back cover: Aldreth Causeway, an ancient track – perhaps of eleventh-century origin – carrying the major post-Roman land route between Cambridge and Ely across the floodplain of the Old West River, now a course of the river Ouse (© William Blake, reproduced with permission).

Contents

List of Figures

Abbreviations

BL	British Library
Bracton	*De Legibus et Consuetudinibus Angliae*
Cott. Tib.	*Survey of Ely Episcopal Manors, 1222*
DB	*Domesday Book*
ECB	*Ely Coucher Book, 1249–50*
GP	William of Malmesbury, *Gesta Pontificum Anglorum*
Gildas	*Gildas. The Ruin of Britain*
Guthlac	*Felix's Life of Saint Guthlac*
HER	Historic Environment Record
ICC	*Inquisitio Comitatus Cantabrigiensis*
IE	*Inquisitio Eliensis*
JNCC	Joint Nature Conservation Committee
KEPN	English Place-Name Society, *Key to English Place-Names*
LE	*Liber Eliensis*
MP	*Matthæi Parisiensis Monachi Sancti Albani, Chronica Majora*
PAS	Portable Antiquities Scheme
PASE	Prosopography of Anglo-Saxon England
Pet. Chron.	*Peterborough Chronicle of Hugh Candidus*
RABB	*Ramsey Abbey's Book of Benefactors*
RCHME	Royal Commission on Historical Monuments England
e-Sawyer	Electronic Sawyer
VCH Cambs.	*Victoria History of the County of Cambridge and the Isle of Ely*
VCH Hunts.	*Victoria History of the County of Huntingdon*
VCH Som.	*Victoria History of the County of Somerset*

Notes

All dates are AD unless otherwise noted.
All places are in Cambridgeshire unless otherwise noted.

Acknowledgements

This book could not have been written without the support of my family. They have, as is their obdurate custom, forbidden me to mention them but may not notice this brief and wholly inadequate note of my heartfelt gratitude.

I am grateful, too, to Mr Christopher Taylor, Professor Sir Richard Evans, Mr Peter Herring, Dr Christopher Briggs, Professor Sam Turner, Mr Phil Brewin, Mr Tim de Ridder, Dr Alex Woolf, Dr Debby Banham, Dr Keith Briggs, Professor Ian Simmons, Dr Sam Newton, Dr Avril Morris, Dr Willem Dekker, Dr Caitlin Green, Professor Robin Fleming, and Dr Frances Willmoth, who have all discussed aspects of this work with me, corresponded with me about them, or assisted in other ways.

The staff of the British Library Manuscripts Room were generous in assisting with access to the extents of the Bishop of Ely's estates in 1222 (Cotton Tiberius B.ii). Dr Susan Edgington was kind enough to send me copies of her translation of the Ramsey Abbey Book of Benefactors. The Cambridgeshire Archives and the Spalding Gentleman's Society were very helpful in identifying maps and records. Ms Kasia Gdaniec, Senior Archaeologist in the Historic Environment Team at Cambridgeshire County Council, and Ms Sally Croft, Senior Archaeologist on the Cambridgeshire Historic Environment Record, went far beyond any expectations I might reasonably have entertained in assisting with identifying and mapping data on early and middle Anglo-Saxon settlement held in the Cambridgeshire Historic Environment Record.

I am grateful to Mr William Blake for permission to reproduce his photograph of Bottisham Lode on the cover, and of Aldreth Causeway in Figure 6.4; to Cambridgeshire Archives for permission to reproduce a detail from Peylor Smith's 1727 map of the fens (CA R59/31/40/1) in Figure 6.5; to Mr Andrew Crowson for permission to reproduce Silvester 1988, fig. 115 in Figure 4.6; to Mr Richard Mortimer for permission to reproduce Mortimer *et al.* 2005, fig. 3.1 as Figure 2.9; to Dr Sarah Russell, Director of the Norris Museum, St Ives, for permission to reproduce the Museum's photograph of the Abbot's Chair in Figure 4.4; to Dr David Roffe for permission to reproduce his map in Roffe 2005, 185 as Figure 5.6; to Tim de Ridder for permission to reproduce his figure from De Ridder 1999, 13 as Figure 7.7; to Heidi Stoner for permission to reproduce her photograph of the Repton Stone as Figure 3.1; to Wisbech and Fenland Museum for permission to reproduce a detail from the Wisbech Hundred Map as Figure 7.8; and to the Royal Historical Society and Cambridge University Press for permission to reproduce Dr Hart's conjectural map of the Tribal Hidage published in Hart 1971, 137 as Figure 4.2.

Mrs Sarah Wroot kindly drew Figures 1.1, 1.2, 1.3, 2.2, 2.4, 2.6, 2.7, 2.8, 3.3, 3.5, 4.1, 4.3, 6.3, 7.6, and 7.9. Dr Willem Dekker generously recast his fig. 3 from Dekker and Beaulaton (2016), 7, as Figure 6.7 in this volume.

Some of ideas explored in this volume have formed the subject of conference and seminar presentations, public lectures and university courses over the last five years and more, and I am most grateful to discussants and students who have taken the time to talk through them with me. They include papers given at the International Medieval Congress in Leeds in July 2015 and July 2016, public lectures for the GULP programme at Bath University and for the Ouse Washes Landscape Partnership Conference in November 2015, a seminar paper given for the *Medieval Economic and Social History* seminar in the Faculty of History, University of Cambridge in January 2016, and a seminar paper given at the Medieval, Antique and Byzantine seminar at the University of Newcastle in December 2016. Previous work on the Domesday population in fenland, published as Oosthuizen (2014) forms the basis for the discussion of Anglo-Saxon demography in Chapter 2 which extends those arguments considerably. So, too, an exploration of the cultural identity and political organisation of the early medieval fenland, published in Oosthuizen (2016b), contributes to sections of Chapters 4, 5 and 6 where it is discussed in more detail and at greater length.

It goes without saying that remaining mistakes and misapprehensions are (I hope not incorrigibly) my own.

Prologue

So much is known about the centuries between the withdrawal of Roman administration from Britain around AD 400 and the Norman Conquest in 1066 that they are now more often called 'early medieval' than 'dark'. Yet the period still engenders vigorous and sometimes acrimonious debate. The questions under discussion remain the fundamental ones: who *were* 'the Anglo-Saxons'? To what extent were the social worlds and physical landscapes familiar to Romano-Britons still occupied and functional into the fifth and sixth centuries and later? How should the rapid replacement be interpreted of Romano-British artifacts, forms of settlement, burial customs, and agricultural systems by others whose affinity seemed to be with north-west Europe? And, most fiercely contested, the balance between continuity and change, tradition and transformation, evolution and innovation, in the development of the early and middle Anglo-Saxon worlds. This book investigates those questions through the case study of society, political organisation, and economic exploitation in the early medieval landscape of the East Anglian fen basin. In the process, it explores, too, the role of migration in a region that is supposed to have been among the earliest to 'become Anglo-Saxon'.

This introduction briefly discusses the difficulties in using the phrase 'Anglo-Saxon' to describe early medieval England, and the historical and archaeological contexts of modern interpretations of the development of the East Anglian fen basin in the same period. It moves on to the background to, and structures governing, ancient rights of common over the pastures that dominated those wetlands, whose collective exploitation is one of the central themes of this book.

Nomenclature: The phrase 'Anglo-Saxon'

The phrase 'Anglo-Saxon' is commonly used to describe the period between about 400 and 1100. It takes its name from groups of immigrants, said to have arrived in Britain in the fifth and sixth centuries, who were described in some of the earliest post-Roman documents in Britain as 'Angles' and 'Saxons'. That shorthand makes sense: it is brief, to the point and everyone knows what it means. But there are difficulties in using it, especially in its assumptions about what 'Anglo-Saxon' means. First, whether those who arrived in fifth and sixth centuries came in large or small numbers, they did not share a common cultural background and spoke a range of different languages. Their origins lay across a wide geographic region – Francia, the Low Countries, Scandinavia, and what is now Germany, north and west Africa, southern Europe and the eastern Mediterranean. This means that 'calling [them] Anglo-Saxons may give us a sense of their ethnic identity that they did not necessarily share'.[1] Second, the phrase makes no allowance for the inhabitants of post-Roman Britain, the descendants of Romano-British and earlier prehistoric communities, who continued to occupy and farm landscapes familiar to their ancestors across the same period. A third problem lies in increasingly controversial assumption within the phrase that post-Roman immigrants, whatever their number and wherever they came from, were not assimilated into the general population – that groups of 'Anglo-Saxon' newcomers remained sufficient geographically and culturally distinctive for long enough to identify them in archaeological finds and excavations. Some of these issues are discussed in more detail below.

For all these reasons, the phrase Anglo-Saxon, without inverted commas, is used in this book to refer to the period from about AD 400 to about 1100, divided between early (*c.*400–650), middle (*c.*650–900) and late (*c.*900–1100). Where the discussion focuses on scholarly debates and evidence in which the phrase is used to describe a cultural grouping, then 'Anglo-Saxon' is shown in inverted commas to make its contested meaning obvious.

Historical background

Modern narratives of the cultural development of the Anglo-Saxon fenland have generally followed sixth-century and other Anglo-Saxon accounts of what happened in England in the years following the withdrawal of Roman administration in or soon after 400. After all, those who lived during or soon after the events they described were likely to know more about them than any later writers so, for almost as long as histories of the basin have been written, they have been based on those early documents. Gildas, among the earliest, is the most often-cited. Writing in about 540 he described how 'the Saxons … first of all fixed their dreadful claws on the east side of the island' in the mid-fifth century.[2] Bede, the first historian of Britain whose work has survived, drew on Gildas and other sources in 731 to tell how 'the Angles or Saxons came to Britain … and were granted lands in the eastern part of the island'.[3] Those documents and the high proportion of early Anglo-Saxon sites and artifacts found across eastern England underpin the widespread assumption that the region was the first to be settled by post-Roman migrants from north-west Europe.[4]

Many of those groups are considered to have entered the country along rivers which ran through the fens, connecting the North Sea with their large catchments to west, south and east.[5] The fen landscape through which they passed was believed to have been virtually unoccupied, abandoned soon after 400 as the result of 'an increase in wetness that must have been devastating'.[6] That conclusion, too, was based on both documentary and archaeological evidence. The lives of the early saints recounted how Æthelthryth's monastery at Ely in 673 and Guthlac's hermitage in 699 were each located in a wild and empty wilderness.[7] That view was, until the mid 1990s, supported by both the relative dearth of early Anglo-Saxon archaeology, and by the paucity of old English place-names, across the basin.[8]

The first relatively modern review of the archaeology of the Cambridge region, undertaken by Cyril Fox in 1923, was thus unexceptional in concluding that it had been settled by Anglian immigrants as early as 450.[9] The dominance of early Anglo-Saxon material culture across the county – the everyday things that people used, and the homes and settlements they inhabited – was explained in terms of the repopulation of a largely unoccupied landscape area by Germanic immigrants. Modern surveys of the fens continue to suggest, explicitly or by implication, that its early medieval archaeology represents the activities of north-west European colonists in a generally empty countryside.[10]

Both the story and its chronology seems less certain now than either did twenty years ago. The reliability of the early chronology has been reassessed in the light of a growing recognition that the earliest documentary sources were not objective accounts, but written to achieve specific polemical aims. Gildas, surely one of the leading orators of his day, described recent events in Britain in bloodcurdling rhetoric whose principal aim was not to establish an accurate historical record but to relate a series of divine punishments visited by God on sinful kings and communities. The period in which he was writing remains uncertain too, although it is generally believed to have been in the early sixth century, and there is almost no way of identifying the dates of the events that he described, nor of the people of whom he spoke.[11] Nor was Bede, whose narrative appears to have been carefully constructed from available documentary accounts and oral testimonies, free from bias: his objective, not always consistently achieved, appears to have been to establish the primacy of the church of Rome across England by discrediting the legacy and teachings of the Romano-British Celtic Christianity that predated the arrival of St Augustine in the late sixth century.[12] The lists of early Anglo-Saxon kings and their genealogies are also unreliable, apparently constructed more for political ends than for historical record.[13] The use of these early sources to identify specific periods of migration, by specific groups, becomes more doubtful in the light of this research.

Doubts among historians about the chronology that is supposed to have framed early Anglo-Saxon England have been mirrored among archaeologists, stimulated by an unprecedented increase since 1990 in the volume of known archaeological material. New planning guidance issued in 1990 requires archaeological fieldwork to be integrated into the planning process, whether for public, private or commercial developers; the effect has been a five-fold increase in the number of excavations undertaken each year (although sites are not evenly distributed across the country).[14] Finds made by members of the public, either accidently or in the process of private research, are also now recorded through the Portable Antiquities introduced in 1997. The consequent increase in knowledge about the early medieval period, unimaginable a few decades ago, has stimulated a growing realisation that it is impossible to distinguish between 'Romano-British' and 'Anglo-Saxon' communities on the basis of their material culture (the physical evidence of their lives, from the things they used, to their houses, settlements and fields).[15] Settlements, fields and artifacts can be distinguished by status, but not by the cultural background of the people to whom they belonged.[16] Newcomers were assimilated into late British communities; there was no displacement of populations.

The results also stimulated questions about the character of post-Roman migration into Britain. Was the number of people who arrived in Britain in the fifth and sixth centuries greater, smaller or about the same as the numbers who have consistently been moving between Britain and continental Europe over the last 800,000 years? Where did the new settlers come from? And how significant, after all, was their influence on the peoples and culture of late Roman Britain?

More recent genetic research appeared to offer the possibility of a scientific resolution of these questions, through work focused on two particular objectives. First, it was hoped that studies of modern British DNA might identify higher proportions of 'Celtic' and north-west European DNA in different regions of the British Isles, thus confirming the early sources. Second, it was hoped that it might be possible not only to infer the volume and period in which north-west European migration occurred from the proportion of that genetic material in modern Britons, but also to calculate when that admixture took place. There have been some positive results, showing that most Britons can trace their ancestry back into British prehistory.[17] On the other hand, DNA across most of modern England is almost homogenous and reveals no evidence of pockets of Germanic settlement in eastern or central England or of 'Celtic' populations in the west, even in areas like Wales and Cornwall where the latter might be expected.[18]

Other inferences are more contentious. Recent work concluding that between 10 and 38 percent of modern English DNA is derived from the 'Anglo-Saxon' migrations is based on at least three problematic assumptions and methods.[19] The first is that the interpretations of those results are sometimes skewed to fit early medieval documentary evidence whose reliability is, as we have seen, at least questionable. So, for example, a recent major study of modern DNA noted an early medieval migration into Britain from northern Germany, Denmark – *and* from France.[20] Together they appear to have made a substantial contribution to DNA profiles in central and southern England. Yet the evidence of a French input was discounted on the grounds that (unreliable) documentary evidence recorded that 'the Saxon migrations did not directly involve people from what is now France'.[21] A second problem is that the analysis concluded that the most significant genetic contribution made from migrants from north-west Europe occurred in the ninth century, around three or four hundred years after 'the Anglo-Saxons' are supposed to have arrived.[22] An extensive critique of this argument convincingly suggests that the genetic contribution may have been that of ninth-century Scandinavians rather than of fifth- and sixth-century 'Anglo-Saxons'.[23]

The third problem relates to an innovative DNA study of four people buried in an early Anglo-Saxon cemetery at Oakington in about AD 500 and three eighth-century individuals from a cemetery at Hinxton (both Cambridgeshire) – that is, of people actually living in the period under study. Here, the percentage of those individuals' 'Anglo-Saxon' DNA was measured by comparing them with prehistoric Iron Age populations who lived in the area some time between 360 and 1 BC.[24] That is, it measured changes not between (say) 400 and 700 (when the migrations are supposed to have occurred), but between (at worst) 360 BC and AD 700 – a period of nearly a thousand years – or (at best) between AD 1 and 700, from the beginning of the Roman period rather than its end. The results show a significant overall increase in north-west European DNA between the Iron Age and the 'Anglo-Saxon' populations. On the other hand, the period, intensity and number of migratory episodes that shows up in that DNA remain obscure. There is nothing to indicate that it represents people arriving in Britain specifically between AD 400 and 700, rather than immigration across the whole period.[25] A final complication is that the three eighth-century individuals from Hinxton were themselves immigrants from north-west Europe, underscoring the point that migration was a continuous process and making it even more difficult to place the introduction of 'Anglo-Saxon' DNA in in the fifth and sixth centuries.[26]

Both studies show evidence of some relatively recent migration from northwest Europe; however, because each accepts the accuracy of the chronology recorded in the documentary evidence that there *were* substantial migrations from northwest Europe in the fifth and sixth centuries, their conclusions are skewed towards the belief that the DNA *is* a record of that migration. Migration into the British Isles has been continuous since the end of the last Ice Age, and no-one knows whether the numbers of those who arrived in Britain in the fifth and sixth centuries were higher or lower than average, or simply typical. This is not to argue that the DNA does not show the Saxon migrations described by Gildas and Bede. Perhaps it does – but equally well it may not.[27] The case is not yet proven.

The old certainties about the cultural identities of, and the relationships between, 'Romano-British' and 'Anglo-Saxon' individuals and communities are thus more difficult to sustain. The conclusion must be that cultural change across the period does not necessarily reflect the displacement or dominance of indigenous communities by groups of incomers (Fig. 0.1).[28] Those problems are

FIGURE 0.1. Ely Cathedral from the south, across the ruins of its medieval precinct. The seventh-century abbey was at *Cratendune*, a location now lost but believed to be nearby (© Susan Oosthuizen).

discussed again in more detail in the chapters that follow which offer another interpretation of the Anglo-Saxon fenland. They demonstrate that the fen basin shows a degree of early medieval occupation unexpected a few decades ago, representing continuity from earlier Romano-British settlement. The history of these communities appears to show a traditional social order adapting and innovating to new conditions over time. Communities were organised within territorial groups – some subordinate and others dominant, structured as folk-groups, principalities or kingdoms. Their prosperous livelihoods were based on the careful collective control, exploitation and management of the fen, especially the vast natural water-meadows on which their herds of cattle grazed. Their traditions suggest a society with prehistoric origins, which had developed and evolved through the period of Roman control, and which continued to adjust to changing post-imperial circumstances in the decades and centuries after about 400.

The region's most significant agricultural assets were the enormous, rich pastures and other natural resources that lay across the peat wetlands of the central and southern part of the basin. The extent of those resources, the relative prosperity that they brought to those with common rights over them, and the status that those holders derived from those rights, explains why, until drainage began in the mid-seventeenth century, 'in no part of England were common rights more important'.[29] They stood for expectations of community that form a significant thread throughout this book, and make it worth taking a little space to discuss their structure and character.

Rights of common

Common rights are rights allowing defined, limited groups of individuals to exploit specific natural resources within a defined area. Pasture, fishing, hay, peat, reeds, sedge and other wetland resources were all exploited across the fen basin under rights of common (Figure 0.2).

The three most important characteristic of rights of common are first, that they are rights of property, defensible in law – a status that underpins their formal definition, entitlements and enforcement.[30] A legal right of property implies boundaries to the area over which that right extends – which is mine, where I may exercise my right and you may not; and which is thine, where you may exercise your rights and I may not. Figure 4.1 shows how carefully the wetland areas of the basin were sub-divided between groups of intercommoning vills, each (it will be argued in Chapters 4 and 5) representing an early Anglo-Saxon political unit. They have all the appearance of territories divided by known, defined and maintained boundaries, even if the latter were – as often happened – disputed. The old course of the river Nene, for instance, forms the boundary to rights of common exercised by vills on the southern fen-edge, and those on the fen islands. It is highly significant that that boundary was perpetuated not only by that of the seventh-century Abbey of Ely (see Chapter 5), the fenland hundreds, and the tenth-century boundary between the counties of Cambridgeshire and Huntingdonshire.

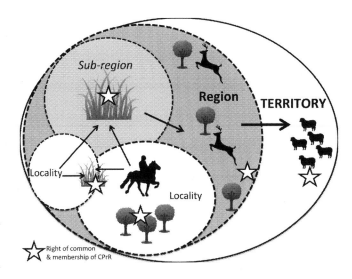

FIGURE 0.2. The exercise of common rights provided an individual with opportunities to meet others of different wealth and status on equal terms (© Susan Oosthuizen). The rider shown above has common rights (shown as a star) in woodland in his own community, grassland shared with a neighbouring community, pasture shared with others from a sub-regional group of communities, wood pasture with regional communities, and grazing with other landholders from the territory as a whole. And he participates in the governance of all the resources in which he has rights of common).

Similarly, the Catswater – also called *Must* – a catchwater running along the fen-edge to the north of Peterborough, separates the rights of common of vills of the Soke of Peterborough, believed to represent Peterborough Abbey's seventh-century estate, and (once more) those of the fen islands to the east; it too is an estate boundary (between the Abbeys of Peterborough and Ely), a hundred boundary, and the boundary between Cambridgeshire and Northamptonshire.[31] As intercommons began to be divided between individual vills in the later Anglo-Saxon period, fen boundaries were recorded in more detail. In 956, for instance, a charter described how the boundaries of fen commons at Yaxley, Huntingdonshire, ran from a catchwater drain on the fen-edge between Yaxley and Farcet to West Fen (now Yaxley Fen), thence to Trundle Mere (now disappeared) and on to a willow-fringed pool, thence to Draymere (now also gone), then along the edges of the mere to Hemmingsbrook, and along the brook to a willow holt, from thence along another stream (the *flyte*) back to the catchwater drain on the edge of the fen.[32] When there was disagreement about boundaries, commoners came to the courts that governed their commons to give evidence about where they lay. Adam of Tydd (Lincolnshire), for example, was summoned in 1218 to testify to the boundaries of the pasture commons on which his cattle had grazed since the later twelfth century. He affirmed that 'he had known these bounds for 40 years and more, and there were no other than these'.[33]

The second central characteristic of common rights is that the resources that they controlled are not public, but restricted to a defined group. By the fifth century (and perhaps much earlier) access to property rights, including rights of common, required the fulfillment of two criteria: first, an individual had to demonstrate full membership of the group within whose territory s/he lived, and had to be of free status (although it should be noted that the definition of 'freedom' ranged along a continuum from those who were indisputably free to others for whom the distinctions between free and unfree were more qualified).[34] Rights of property were made up of two interlocking components: common rights in the shared resources of a territory and enough privately-cultivated land to support an extended household.[35] That early tradition persisted into the middle ages and later in the attachment of rights of common pasture to 'ancient' arable holdings long after the origins of both had been forgotten.[36] In late medieval Spalding, for example, 'the commons contain several thousand acres and belong to ancient commonable messuages'.[37] Property rights were thus marks of status as were their concomitant public, legal responsibilities –

to participate in collective governance at all levels, to contribute to a territorial militia (the *fyrd*), and render characteristic public obligations to lords and kings of goods (*feorm*), services (such as carrying the king's goods or accompanying him locally), and money payments like *gafol*. The obligations may have seemed onerous to some, but their performance was a valued and visible enactment of their social standing. As Rosamond Faith has remarked, 'entitlement to participate in the system, was of paramount importance to personal status'.[38]

The third characteristic of rights of common is the predictability of the framework for their governance and organisation. Those distinctive features have a considerable relevance to the early medieval fenland since each is related to the general principles of collectivity and equity that characterize the organisation of common rights, since every owner of a right of common can expect to have the same access to the shared resource, to take out the same volume of its agricultural products, and to be subject to the same rules for its exploitation. The principle of equity among all right holders is fundamental. It provides for transparency and accountability in the governance and management of their resource, enabling each right holder to monitor the equitable distribution of the resource among members of the group, and the proper application and enforcement of regulations to manage it.

The principle of equity between right holders was reinforced by the expectation that all of them should participate in the governance of their shared resource – not only by attending regular meetings, but also by contributing to discussions and making decisions about how their resource should be managed and their rights enforced. Everyone's assent was required for any changes to the by-laws; in effect, there was an expectation of decision-making by consensus.[39] As the great jurist Henry de Bratton explained in the early thirteenth century, 'unwritten law and custom' was derived from what had been 'approved by the consent of those who use them and confirmed by the oath of kings, they cannot be changed without the common consent of all those by whose counsel and consent they were promulgated'.[40] That principle avoided the potentially disruptive, even destructive, consequences for livelihoods of all the commoners if one right holder claimed that decisions taken by the group did not apply to him because he had not agreed to them, or because he had been absent.

Decisions, including by-laws, made by assemblies of right holders were preserved in oral traditions of custom and practice and recited from one meeting to the next. If everyone remembered the decision, and agreed on what they had remembered, no one individual could, after the event, manipulate that history to his advantage by fabricating it. For this reason, as late as the twelfth and thirteenth centuries, both judges and peasants still regarded public recitations of collective memory as more reliable than the written records of statute law.[41] Generally speaking, by-laws governing commons were not often recorded in writing before the sixteenth century; and quite frequently not even then. A student told me about ten years ago how she had recently moved into a Norfolk parish where the common was managed by the parish council since

FIGURE 0.3. A nineteenth-century pound at Coveney held animals that strayed or were grazing illegally on the commons, the visible embodiment of the enforcement of ancient common by-laws (© Susan Oosthuizen). It stands just above the flood line overlooking across the once-extensive wetlands that separated it from the town of Ely.

there were no longer any commoners. When the Council met to discuss this year's arrangements for leasing the common, she asked where the minutes of the last meeting were so that they could check the arrangements for the previous year; and was told that there was no need for minutes, since all those who had been present last year could remember what had been decided then.

And finally, the rules of equitable allocation of a resource among commoners included the principle of the 'moral economy': no right holder should profit from a common right at the expense of other right holders, beyond satisfying the subsistence needs of his household. Medieval by-laws over common pasture, for instance, frequently stipulated that a right holder could only graze as many beasts as he could support on hay and his home pasture on his own homestead during the winter, a regulation frequently summarised as 'animals *levant* and *couchant*'.[42]

The informal benefits were as important. Access to common rights provided opportunities for individuals to form and maintain bonds of reciprocity with others of different wealth and/or status through gifts in kind, like hay or cheese derived from their shared resources, or through help with tasks like herding, calving or tending sick beasts. It is not surprising, then, that members of early medieval territories described themselves as members of the same kin or folk, descended from the same (real or mythical) ancestor.[43] The mutual obligations, responsibilities and rights integral to the governance of rights of common, as well as their shared oral traditions of custom and practice, are very like those that one finds in extended as well as nucleated families.[44] The ancient legal status of common rights, their integration with early medieval concepts of kinship and rank, and their physical expression in the exploitation of specific early landscapes have convinced generations of historians that areas in which they persisted into the middle ages can be identified with early medieval territorial groups.[45]

That persistence is facilitated by characteristics that predisposed long-term continuity for rights of common and their governance. The longevity of structures for the collective governance of commons was not limited by the lifespans of their individual members; as long as there were two or more people with rights of common in the same resource, the common continued to be collectively governed. Furthermore, because rights of common are legal rights whose amendment requires the agreement of all right holders, their governance and management tends to be intensely conservative and risk averse. And finally, because the principles that framed access to rights of common, the conduct of their assemblies, and the management of their commons were formulated in fairly general terms, they allowed considerable flexibility to communities in adapting their by-laws to local circumstances that changed from one year to the next. For example, the general principle that pastures would be closed to stock for part of the year to allow it to recover its health would not be challenged; but the precise dates at which they would be opened and then, later, closed to grazing could be varied from year to year depending on whether local conditions were wetter or drier.

Common rights were far more, then, than simply a property right. They underpinned a reasonable standard of prosperity for individuals and extended households; they provided a signal of status; they enabled individuals to form personal connections, on an equal footing, across the social hierarchy; and, where there were resources shared across a polity, they framed the governance of whole territories. There is no suggestion, however, that evidence for rights of common property or collective organisation in fenland or elsewhere implies that early or middle Anglo-Saxon society was structured around a utopian egalitarianism, or a lack of conflict, or that such structures were an unsophisticated precursor of 'more complex' social and political hierarchies. The growing development of hierarchical structures across early medieval society is well-accepted and understood: an individual's social position depended on his rank, wealth and access to power. Nothing could have been less equitable. On the other hand, attendance and participation in collective institutions governing rights of common, and the public responsibilities that went with them, were also aspects of status and social identity. They co-existed with, complemented and enriched 'vertical' hierarchies of status, wealth and power by offering individuals carefully controlled opportunities to create reciprocal 'horizontal' relationships with others of different power, wealth and status. When men took their cattle out to their grassland pastures in the spring, or cropped stands of sedge for firing, they took with them their unspoken understanding of the social relationships and standing that those rights represented, the responsibilities they entailed, and their expectations of equity and collectivity in their relationships with other right holders.

The striking characteristics of the early medieval fenland explored in this book are long-term continuities in the nature of its wetland resources, and in the shared property rights through which they were exploited (Fig. 0.3).[46] That underlying persistence in the collective structures that framed daily life, it is argued, offered a secure foundation for smaller- and large-scale changes in other spheres: in the balance between different proportions of grasses, water and other resources from place to place and period to period; in population, rights of private property, economy, social hierarchy, lordship, and in political forms. Only part of that story is dealt with here: the focus of this book is on the individuals and communities who made their living from the collective exploitation of pastoral and other non-arable resources of the fen basin, and their management of those wetlands. Areas on the higher, drier grounds of the fen-edge, silts and islands under the direct control of secular landholders or the early monasteries – settlement, the arable economy, landscape organisation and social structure – where the history of the landscape reflects growing manorialism and intensified agricultural production have been described in earlier work.[47]

Chapter 1 outlines the physical characteristics and ecology of the fen wetlands whose most minute variations might have a striking effect on how the landscape could be exploited and managed, with consequences both for an individual's livelihood and for his social standing. Chapter 2 discusses the degree of occupation of the basin in the decades immediately following the withdrawal of Roman administration. After all, if there were no or few people living in the basin in the four or so centuries after 400 then there would be little impetus for formal political organisation or agricultural management of the early medieval wetland landscape. The third chapter explores the cultural identity (or identities) of the inhabitants of the region between about 400 and 900. Were they late Romano-British communities, or groups of migrants from north-west Europe, or communities that included both, or – yet again – was there deliberate separation of Germanic newcomers and Romano-Britons in different, or even the same, localities? The answers to those questions underpin the likelihood of continuity of agricultural exploitation of the region. Communities who made a living in landscapes that had belonged to their ancestors and in which traditions of husbandry were well-established might be more likely to evolve socially, economically and politically. Colonists entering an uninhabited land or one in which they regarded themselves as separate from, and/or superior to, its indigenous inhabitants might be as likely as not to ignore the traditions they found. Chapters 4 and 5 focus on the political organisation of the region since an individual's ability to make an agricultural living depends on sufficient governmental stability to provide protection for his rights of property. Although the emerging great kingdoms of Mercia and East Anglia increasingly provided that reassurance from the seventh century onwards, little is known of the kingdoms and sub-kingdoms that occupied the region before about 650. A great difference might be expected between communities struggling to support their households in conditions of general disorder and lawlessness, and those located in reasonably secure territorial polities. Chapters 6 and 7 discuss how individuals and households supported themselves in the wet conditions of the fen basin, and the surprising degree of ecological and water management that that exploitation entailed. The Epilogue draws those threads together to provide an overview of the contribution of the Anglo-Saxon fenland to a history of early medieval England in which the limelight rests on a post-Roman society evolving across the millennium from a strong traditional base, and in which population change may have been less influential in the development of new cultural forms than has previously been thought.

Notes

1. Pohl 1997, 25, my addition; see also Gearey 2002, Oosthuizen 2016c.
2. *Gildas* I, 23.
3. *Bede* I, 15.
4. *E.g.* Arnold 1988, 42–3, 54–5, 68, 165.
5. Darby 1934, 193, 185; Fox 1923, 276; Reaney 1943, xxx; Silvester 1988, 158.
6. Hall and Coles 1994, 122; see also Phillips 1970.
7. *Bede* IV, 19; *Guthlac*, XXIV, also XXV, XXX–I.
8. Reaney 1943, xxviii; Davies and Vierck 1974, 156, 283; Silvester 1985, 107; Hall 1987, 11; Hall and Coles 1994, 128; Roberts and Wrathmell 2002, 34, 73–76; Roffe 2005, 286; Williamson 2010, 152.
9. Fox 1923, 276; see also Lethbridge 1931, 81.
10. *E.g.* Hayes and Lane 1993, 213; Hall and Coles 1994, 122; Penn 2005, 299.
11. Sims-Williams 1983; Higham 1994.
12. Higham 1994; Trent Foley and Higham 2007.
13. *E.g.* Dumville 1985; Higham 1992 and 1994.
14. See Evans 2015, for example, for a summary.
15. *E.g.* Hamerow 1997, 33; Lucy and Reynolds 2002, 10.
16. See Hamerow 2012 for settlements and landscape; Oosthuizen 2011a for fields; Lucy and Reynolds 2002, 10, for artifacts.
17. Capelli *et al.* 2003; Weale *et al.* 2002; Leslie *et al.* 2015, 310, 313–14; see also Hughes *et al.* 2014.
18. Leslie *et al.* 2015, 310, 313–14.
19. Leslie *et al.* 2015, 313; Schiffels *et al.* 2016, 1.
20. Leslie *et al.* 2015, fig. 2, 311; Methods, fig. 6.
21. Leslie *et al.* 2015, Methods.
22. Leslie *et al.* 2015, Extended Data, fig. 9.
23. Kershaw and Røyrvik 2016.
24. Schiffels *et al.* 2015, table 1.
25. Schiffels *et al.* 2016, 7.
26. Schiffels *et al.* 2016, 7.
27. See Gearey and Veeramah 2016, 67–71 for a similar, more detailed, methodological critique than is possible here.
28. Penn 2005, 289, 291; see also Hayes and Lane 1993, 68.
29. Darby 1974, 67.
30. Oosthuizen 2013b, ch. 1
31. Reaney 1943, 7–9.
32. e-Sawyer S595; Hart 1966, 159–60.
33. Neilson 1920, xxxv–xxxvi. See Owen 1982 for other examples.
34. Charles-Edwards 1972, 5–9; Gosden 1985, 481; Oosthuizen 2013b, 160–61.
35. Charles-Edwards 1972, 17, 14; Kelly 1997, 447.
36. Neilson 1929, 732, and 1920, xv, lxviii, lxxvi.
37. Cited in Hallam 1963, 41.
38. Faith 1997, 117, see also pp. 116–19.
39. Östrom 1990, 38.
40. Bracton, vol. 2, 22, and vol. 2, 21.
41. Bedell 1999.
42. Neilson 1925, 483, and 1942, 57.
43. See Ensor 2011 for current anthropological approaches to kinship.
44. Reynolds 1983, 381.
45. See Chapter 4, below.
46. Holling 2001, 390.
47. *E.g.* Douglas 1927; Miller 1951; Darby 1974; Biddick 1989; Kelly 2009.

CHAPTER I

The Wide Wilderness

Before drainage in the seventeenth century, the central and southern parts of the East Anglian fen basin supported the largest peat wetland in England, protected from the North Sea by a substantial band of shingle and silt (Fig. 1.1). Four of the major rivers of central England – the Witham, Welland, Nene and Great Ouse – flowed across its flat floor, carrying water to the Wash from a combined catchment of 15,411 km² (5950 sq. miles) that ranged from Buckinghamshire to Lincolnshire, and from Leicestershire to Cambridgeshire. Regionally important rivers like the Cam, Lark, Little Ouse, Wissey and Nar drained Cambridgeshire and parts of north Essex, and the western areas of Suffolk and Norfolk (Fig. 1.2).

The chapter begins with a general description of the physical geography of the early medieval fen basin, from silt fens in the north to peat fens across the central and southern parts of the basin. It describes the processes involved in and the chronology of its formation over the past six millennia and more, and notes the ecological stability – influenced by climatic shifts – that has characterized it at very least since the Bronze Age.[1] It concludes that the character of the fen landscape was already ancient by the time that Roman administration was withdrawn from Britain in about 410.

The fenland environment in the four millennia before drainage

The physical geography of the early medieval fen basin can broadly be divided into three principal zones: coastal salt marsh along the coastline, separated from the peat wetlands to the south by a substantial deposit of sand and silt built up by intermittent episodes of marine flooding over the previous 5000 years; and, behind that barrier, a wetland landscape of natural water meadows, wetlands, and freshwater meres, interspersed with islands of higher ground. Each will be examined in turn.

The southern shores of the Wash form the northern limit of the fen basin. The coastal marshes that line it are constantly shifting. Although the sea consistently replenishes and cleans them, the effects of storms and droughts on the marshes can be extreme. Modern daily tides typically move around 6000 metric tons of sand and silt into the Wash each year; they accrete along the coast in summer and are moved seaward in winter – a process in which mud flats and saltings gradually build up along the foreshore in summer, to be eroded again in the winter.[2] Both sheep and cattle prosper on the mineral-rich

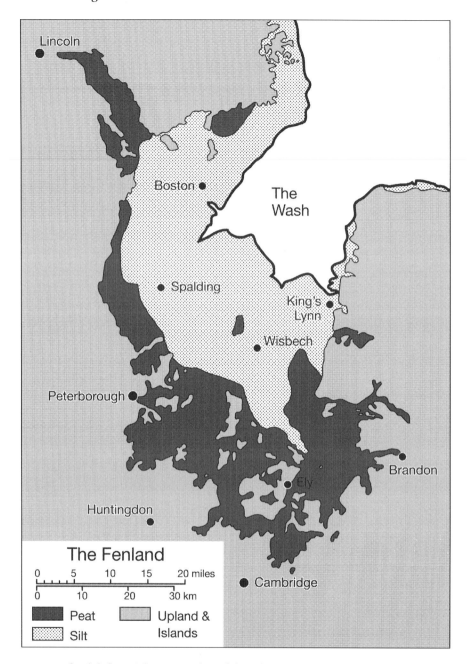

FIGURE 1.1. The geology of the fen basin was divided between the silt fens, built up by successive marine floods, along the coast and peat wetlands in the central and southern parts. Areas of high ground that rose above the flood line appear as islands – sometimes even archipelagos – across the region (© Susan Oosthuizen, after Darby 1940, 5).

grasses of tidal flats. There are plentiful pickings of crustaceans and molluscs; eels, plaice and flounder use the estuary as a nursery; a wide variety of birds exploits the marshes alongside otter, beavers and seals.[3] Coastal grasses include bull and spike rush, as well as eelgrass whose leaves die and float off in mats in autumn, to be dragged ashore and dried. Across the early medieval and later periods, it was not only used as cattle fodder, both fresh and dried, but also as a foundation for low dykes and even for stuffing pillows and mattresses.[4]

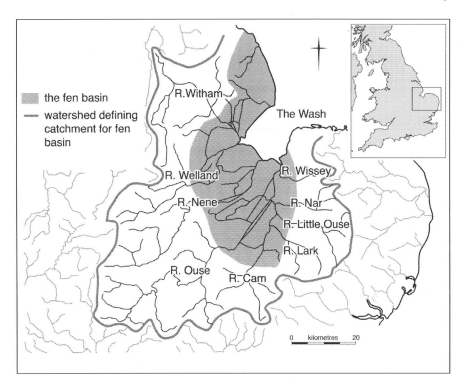

FIGURE 1.2. The catchment of the fen basin, and the sources of the rivers that drained into it, extended far into the central midlands and to the south and east (© Susan Oosthuizen, after Roberts and Wrathmell 2002, fig. 2.2).

The broad band of silt that separates the coastal marshes from the peat-based wetlands to the south offered good grazing for early medieval herds of sheep and cattle and, provided water-levels could be managed and fields protected from the tides, the light silty soils could be ploughed for arable cultivation. It is no accident that these areas had been consistently – sometimes intensively – occupied from the Roman period onwards.[5]

The freshwater landscape to the south of that barrier was quite different. Each of its different geographies and ecologies was a direct response to height above sea level (Fig. 1.3). Areas of dry ground lay where floods could never reach; intermediate fens were flooded in winter and dry in summer; and lakes and meres stood where the basin floor dipped below sea level. Each could be small or extensive; yet the 'complete sequence from aquatic to grassland communities' could be found across a slope of as little as half a metre.[6] Quite minor variations in waterlogging created a multi-patterned and shifting jigsaw of different possibilities for exploitation, depending on whether a location was permanently under water, flooded in winter and permanently damp, or flooded in winter and dry in summer; whether it lay on clay and/or gravel and/or peat; what the season was; and the changing combinations of those conditions over time. One of its most significant natural features was the flood line: the height reached by the winter floods, above which settlement could securely be established. It has consistently stood at around 3.6 m (12 ft) above contemporary sea levels since about AD 800.[7]

Land that rises beyond the highest level of the winter floods offer the same possibilities for human occupation as any other dry location in the English

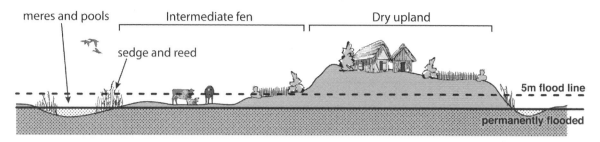

Not to scale.

lowlands. In many places those areas barely top the flood line; only on the island of Ely do they extend as high as 20 m (65 ft) or more above sea level. Forming clay-topped islands in the wetlands, their rich soil is as suitable for dense stands of woodland as for arable farming. They have been occupied at least since Mesolithic hunter-gatherers made their first impermanent camps there around 8000 BC and, from about 4500 BC, by permanently settled communities growing arable crops, managing ancient woods, and exploiting the many resources in the fens below.

An intermediate zone between sea level and the flood line was regularly flooded over the winter months. Its higher areas, lying at, or immediately below, the flood line offered generally safe, if poor, grazing across the year, especially if it lay on a freely-draining cap of gravel, locally called 'hards'.[8] These pastures were particularly important for over-wintering beasts who could be moved down into the lower pastures in summer. The earthworks of Romano-British house-platforms, lanes, paddocks, and a vineyard at Bullocks Haste in Cottenham survive in excellent condition on just such a 'hard' because the site was high enough to provide early medieval and medieval winter pasture, but not sufficiently secure from flooding to risk ploughing it for arable crops.[9]

The best grassland of the basin lay in those zones that were low enough to be flooded in winter but sufficiently high that the water did not linger too long into spring. Purple moor grass (*molinia caerulea*) was the dominant cover, its dense tussocks growing to 90 cm (just under 3 ft), in which curlews, lapwing and snipe nested. Interspersed in it were a wide range of subordinate plant species, up to 50 in every m^2.[2] They included clumps of common tormentil (*potentilla erecta*), the meadow thistle (*cirsium dissectum*) with its dark purple flowers in June and July, clumps of small sedges, wild angelica and 'pungent meadowsweet', and other wild flowers.[10]

In the blurred and shifting areas where the ground becomes wetter, being damp for most of the year, grasses gave way to wider, rougher pastures of rushes (*junculus subnodulosus*) mixed with dense stands of fen saw sedge (*cladium mariscus*), growing up to 3 m (10 ft) tall, with an undercover of mosses and liverworts, yellow flag and great water dock (Fig. 1.4). Ungrazed, the landscape appears 'as a rank sward', an intermediate landscape between fen pastures above and reedbeds below.[11] The Ely chronicler painted it graphically when recounting

FIGURE 1.3. Making the fen ecology: as sea levels rose to their modern levels, the degree of waterlogging in different areas of the fen was critically dependent on their height above sea level – lakes and pools in the lowest areas, below sea level; reed and sedge in areas that were permanently wet; natural water-meadows between sea-level and the flood line, and areas that lay above the flood line (© Susan Oosthuizen). Although the medieval flood line stood at around 3.6 m above OD, it is conventionally referred to as lying at 5 m to enable easier cross-referencing with 5 m contours on modern Ordnance Survey maps.

the difficulties faced by William's the Conqueror's troops as they tried to pass into the Isle of Ely: Underfoot, what appeared to be solid, turned liquid as soon as one stood upon it, the land 'collapsing like chaos into a whirlpool of solid matter into which, when loosened by the slightest rain, flow [waters] in streams and rivers, disguised all the time by the hazardous beds of flag-iris'.[12]

The lowest-lying areas were the freshwater pools, lakes and meres that filled smaller and larger hollows lying below sea-level. They were fringed by beds of common reeds (*phragmites australis*) that also form islands in open water. Now all drained, the names of many of those meres can still be found on modern Ordnance Survey maps. The small modern settlement of Ramseymereside, Huntingdonshire, self-evidently preserves the location of Ramsey Mere, whose medieval 'fishers and fowlers cease neither by day nor by night to frequent it, yet there is always no little store of fish', now completely disappeared.[13] Whittlesey Mere was the largest fresh-water lake in southern England. By 1786, when fen drainage was well underway, it was still around 635 ha (1570 acres) in extent, and had a depth of between 0.5 and 2 m (2–6 ft).[14] It is likely to have been considerably larger in the medieval period. Camden noted in 1610, just a few decades before drainage began, 'that cleere deepe and fishfull Mere' measured about 9 × 5 km (6 × 3 miles) – which, if accurate, suggests an area of over 4653 ha (11,500 acres), about ten times greater than its late eighteenth-century extent.[15] Other large meres in the south-west of the fen included Trundle Mere (in Yaxley) and Ugg Mere (also in Ramsey, Huntingdonshire); Willingham, Stretham and Soham Meres, the latter around 554 ha (1370 acres) in extent, lay in the south-east of the basin.[16] There were many more – like *Weremere* in Doddington, *Brademere* in Ely, or *Ethelmere* in Littleport, all invisible today.

FIGURE 1.4. The vast expanse of Wicken Sedge Fen, the long-term sustainability of its sedge carefully preserved over centuries by maintenance of 4–5 year cropping cycles (© Susan Oosthuizen).

It was a rich environment. In the mid-twelfth century Hugh *candidus* described how the fens around Peterborough were 'very valuable to men because there are obtained in abundance all things needful to them that dwell thereby'.[17] Ramsey, said its chronicler, 'is garlanded beautifully roundabout as much with alder thickets as reedbeds, indeed, with a luxuriance of reed and rush... The same place is encircled by eel-filled marshes, by far-reaching meres and by still pools sustaining a variety of fish and swimming birds.'[18] The wetland landscape supported an almost unimaginably varied fauna. The twelfth-century *Liber Eliensis* lists 'stags, little roe-deer, goats and hares', as well as 'otters, weasels, stoats and polecats'.[19] It described how 'innumerable eels are netted, large wolf-fish and pike, perch, roach, burbot and lampreys which we called water-snakes … salmon and likewise the royal fish, sturgeon, are occasionally caught', as well as carp, tench, bream, chubb, roach, dace and gudgeon.[20] Birds ranged from 'the crane, the heron, the wild duck, teal and most savoury snipe, the swallow-kite, the swarthy raven, the hoary vulture, the swift eagle, the greedy goshawk' to swans, bittern, bustards and heronshaws, as well as 'countless geese, chiff-chaffs, coots, divers, cormorants … [and] … vast numbers of ducks'.[21] The open waters of large and small lakes, wide slow-flowing rivers, winding streams and narrow ditches provided such a wide range of habitats to so many 'leaping and swimming' fish and water birds that 'for one halfepenny and under, five men at the least may not only eat to slake hunger and content nature, but also feed their fill of fish and fowl'.[22] Chapter 6 shows that early medieval fen communities lived in and exploited the same landscape and the same resources.

Risk and opportunity across fenland

Each specialised micro-landscape in the wetland fen represented a sensitive, natural response to different, changing, and intensely-localised interactions between fresh or salt water, height above sea level, climate, drainage, and surface geology; human intervention over many millennia added another layer of complexity. Of all those influences, volumes of water were, for two reasons, the most critical. The first is that much of the floor of the basin lies at, or only barely above, sea levels that have remained *relatively* constant for the last three millennia.[23] The gradients between the floor and the sea were so slight that water that collected in the basin flowed slowly into the sea. Second, the basin floor slopes so gradually towards the Wash that a fall of just one or two metres can sometimes extend over a number of kilometres. Both conditions allow slow-moving water to accumulate in low areas, and encourage water coming into the basin along the rivers, from groundwater and from rainfall, to accumulate when it is unable to drain freely.

When sea levels are low, as they were around 11,000 years ago, water can flow at a reasonable pace along the fen rivers. When sea levels rise to levels closer to those of the modern period, as they did over a period from about 5500 and 2000 BC, the burdens of the rivers take much longer to reach the sea.[24]

Heavy rainfall and high sea levels respectively bring a greater threat of fresh water or marine inundation. The risk from marine surges is especially intense when strong onshore winds and low air pressures coincide with spring tides after prolonged periods of heavy rain. The catastrophic salt-water floods of 31 January 1953, when the sea broke through flood defences around the Wash (and in other parts of eastern England and Holland), was the result of just such a combination of factors: Force ten northerly winds blew hard against the east coast and a reduction in air pressure raised sea levels to unusual heights. South of the Humber estuary sea levels rose by more than 2 m (6 ft), and waves rose to nearly another 5 m (15 ft) above this level.[25] Many hundreds of people were drowned, thousands of hectares were flooded, buildings and roads destroyed, and innumerable crops and livestock washed away. The maximum height that the sea is currently likely to reach on the Wash under similar conditions is at present around 4.7 m (15 ft) above modern sea levels, well above the flood line that has stood at 3.6 m (12 ft) across the basin since about AD 800.[26]

The formation of the fen landscape has a long and dynamic history. Around 12,000 years ago sea levels were 30 m (98 ft) or more lower than they are today, and the basin supported a dryland landscape.[27] Water flowed along broad rivers up to 1.5 km (0.9 miles) wide, ancient tributaries of an ancestor of the Great Ouse that met the sea at a coastline that lay far out into the modern North Sea.[28] They wound through huge deciduous forests where middle Stone Age (Mesolithic) communities camped seasonally as they followed migrating red deer, Irish elk and auroch (giant wild cattle), or foraged for fruits, berries, nuts and – on the coast – shell-fish.[29]

Sea levels rose rapidly between about 8000 and 5000 BC, and continued to rise, albeit more slowly thereafter. They had reached about 1 or 2 m (3–6 ft) below modern levels by about 1500 BC.[30] The coastline, where habitable land met salt marsh, previously hundreds of kilometres out on Doggerland, now ran *relatively* near its modern line – although it is difficult to be certain of its precise alignments over the past 2500 years since that evidence is buried under successive later layers of silt. The earliest feature to provide a relatively certain date for the medieval coastline is the Sea Bank, a massive eleventh-century earthwork that runs continuously from west to east along the southern shore of the Wash.[31]

Fresh water began to back up along their tributaries and then in the main channels, an effect made worse in times of flood. Lakes and meres filled previously-dry depressions that now lay below sea level. The huge forests of oak, lime, beech, elm and ash that covered the basin were not suited to such damp conditions. Trees nearer to rivers began to fall over, many impeding the flow of water yet further. Their massive trunks have been preserved in astonishing numbers in the anaerobic conditions of the peat that began to form around them – like the remains of a 13.4 m (43 ft) tall Fenland Black Oak discovered at Methwold Hythe in Suffolk in 2012, which had toppled into the water over 5000 years ago (Fig. 1.5).[32] The region became increasingly waterlogged as large,

FIGURE 1.5. Bog oaks at Holme Fen: A fragment of ancient bog oak, preserved in the anaerobic peat, speaks to the enormous trees that wooded the basin when sea levels were 30 m or more lower than they are today (© Susan Oosthuizen). It can be seen with many others in the car park at the Great Fen Information Point, New Decoy Farm, near Holme Fen (Huntingdonshire).

volumes of dead leaves and other plant matter accumulated and rotted in the shallow waters, not only obstructing the course of rivers but also encouraging the development of peat. Forming along the banks of sluggish, congested watercourses in places like Holme Fen, in the south of the region, and Welney Washes, in the north, from around 5100 BC, and expanding across the landscape at a rate of about 10 m per year, the peat had colonised almost the entirety of the southern and central parts of the fen basin by about 800 BC.[33] Nearly two millennia later, the oldest peat beds were between 4 m and 5 m deep.[34]

The process of peat formation was intermittently interrupted, particularly between about 3000 and 2000 BC, by extended periods of marine flooding that deposited thick layers of sea-borne silts and gravels on top of earlier peats. After the sea receded, the new silts were colonised in turn by new peat growth, creating an interleaved geology of peat, silts and gravels in proportions that reflected localized variations in the intensity of such episodes.[35] Sir William Dugdale vividly described evidence for the ferocity and intensity of such inundations, recording in 1662 how he had seen 'xvii feet deep, diverse furze bushes, as also nut trees, pressed flat down, with nut sound and firm lying by them; the bushes and trees standing in solid earth, below the silt, which hath been brought up by the inundations of the sea, and in time raised to great thickness' in the Marshland fens along the Wash.[36]

The risk of inland flooding from the sea was gradually reduced from about 1000 BC onwards by the emergence of a wide silt and shingle bar along the coastline, built up by successive episodes of marine inundations. In about 500 BC a major flood deposited a vast amount of silt on top of the bar, raising it to a height of about 3 m (10 ft) above contemporary sea levels (at that time still a metre or so below modern levels).[37] For the first time, a sufficient barrier stood between the sea and the peat wetlands that protected the latter from all but the most severe marine floods.[38] On the other hand, the silt bar also formed a new impediment for rivers, in that it restricted opportunities for their waters to find an outlet to the sea. In an iterative process river beds gradually silted up with soil particles carried in their waters, the latter flowing too slowly for natural scouring to occur. Growing beds of reeds and then sedge along their banks constricted their channels and gradually obstructed the remaining flow. Once silt, reeds and sedge had reduced a river to a narrow, shallow channel, peat was able to form within it, and the riverbed was eventually blocked. Fresh water gradually backed up into the basin, causing widespread flooding. Volumes of water accumulated until their pressure was sufficient to force a new route towards the sea – and the cycle began again. As time went on, practicable routes for new river courses became increasingly limited as waters had to find a route around and between the silted-up beds (locally called roddons) of earlier watercourses, islands of higher ground, and the peat beds (Fig. 1.6). At the end of the Iron Age, for instance, the river Nene flowed north towards its outfall at Wisbech, to the west of the Doddington/March archipelago. By the Roman period the northerly section of that course had become silted, and the river's waters were forced eastwards towards Elm, limited on the west by peat beds and the roddon of its earlier course and, on the south, by an outcrop of gravel that rose almost 3.6 m (12 ft) above modern sea levels.[39] The process was repeated for millennia in larger and smaller watercourses across the region.

FIGURE 1.6. Ancient watercourses: Silted creeks and their tributaries interrupt the road surface along the B660 west of Ramsey St Mary (Huntingdonshire), standing proud of the peat that has shrunk around them (© Susan Oosthuizen). The instability of the peat is visible, too, in those leaning telegraph poles that have been planted in it.

The period of Roman administration of Britain coincided with a climatic upturn during which sea levels fell by about 1.5 m (5 ft). The height of the winter floods fell too, and Romano-British populations were able to move into areas of the basin that had previously been too low for permanent settlement. Fenland was intensively occupied and exploited.[40] Along the shore, sea water that filled small brackish creeks across the coastal marshes on an in-bound tide was trapped and evaporated to produce salt – sometimes naturally, sometimes in containers over peat fires.[41] Salterns were so densely distributed across the coastal marshes that, on a still day, the haze of peaty smoke from fires under their evaporation tanks may have been visible for kilometres.[42] Large numbers of cattle grazed on the wetlands in summer and overwintered on higher ground in extensive farmyard paddocks, while arable fields were laid out and planted wherever grain was likely to be able to grow to maturity.

These conditions remained more or less constant until about AD 600, when a significant deterioration in climate led to a rise both in sea levels and in the heights achieved by fresh water floods in the peat fens, the latter increasing by about 1.5 m to stabilise at around 3.6 m (12 ft) above sea level by about AD 800.[43] Settlement in the lower parts of the peat fens now became unsustainable, but the islands and fen-edge continued to be occupied. The western, Lincolnshire, coastal silts were continuously inhabited throughout the period; the eastern, Norfolk, silts may have been abandoned for permanent settlement in the fifth and sixth centuries, and were occupied only for summer grazing. By 650, however, they too had become sufficiently built up by further episodes of marine flooding to be dry enough once more for permanent occupation.[44]

Environmental and ecological stability

The varied and complex ecology of the undrained fen basin has remained remarkably stable over the six millennia since the wetlands first began to form. From the Neolithic period onwards, it has principally been a landscape of open grassland studded with occasional stands of shrub and trees, and including areas of water sufficiently deep to support reeds and sedge.[45] That constancy is significant as, without human intervention (provided sea levels remain relatively stable), the vegetation of the fen gradually follows the natural succession to evolve into a dryland landscape. Uncropped beds of reeds in standing water build up ground levels at a rate of about 1 mm each year by drawing vast volumes of water from the fen and contributing each winter's leaf-fall to that of previous years. As the water around their roots becomes shallower, they are gradually replaced by sedge and other wetland grasses that continue to extract water, drop their leaves and contribute to a rise in the land surface. Eventually the fen becomes dry enough to support species-rich grasslands, tolerant of seasonal flooding. Shrubs like buck thorn, guilder rose and sallow appear, and then woodlands – first of water-tolerant alder and willow, and then of birch, oak and ash.[46] It is of particular interest, then, that there is little evidence anywhere or in any period of any large-scale natural succession to woodland in the fen basin. That ecological continuity is a strong indication of its intentional, careful maintenance and management by generation upon generation of fen men over hundreds – if not thousands – of years.

Early medieval farmers and stockmen, peasants and lords – just like the prehistoric and Romano-British farmers who preceded them, and the medieval and early modern communities who came after – were able to make good livings from this watery landscape only because they had mastered the detailed expertise required to manage wetlands and marshes, lakes and meadows sustainably. They knew where the flood line lay above which permanent settlement was safe from flooding; they knew that the different kinds of rich grazing that fed their herds depended on episodic winter flooding, to different depths, of the fen's natural water meadows – and how to maintain them; they managed stands of reed and sedge to prevent natural succession to woodland; they extracted peat without exhausting turbaries; and they snared sustainable volumes of fish and waterfowl in small and larger watercourses, ditches and lakes. The physical character of the fenland and the responses of generations of fen men to its attributes provide a continuous underlying accompaniment to the story outlined in this book.

Notes

1. Hall and Coles 1994; Behre 2007; Natural England 2013.
2. Kestner 1975, 391–3.
3. Brandt *et al.* 1984, 10.
4. Van der Meer 2009, 100–103; see also Thirsk 1953a, 14–19.
5. *E.g.* Hallam 1954; 1965; Philips 1970; Frere and St Joseph 1983, 210–15; Hall 1987; Silvester 1988; Hayes and Lane 1992; Green 2012.
6. Rothero *et al.* 2016, 56.
7. Hall 1987, 11; Shennan 1986. Since the Ordnance Survey conventionally maps contours at 5 m intervals, 5 m above modern sea levels offers a fair approximation.
8. Ravensdale 1974, 67.
9. Frere and St Joseph 1983, 208–11.
10. English Nature 2004, 6; see also JNCC 2001, 50, 52.
11. JNCC 2001, 48.
12. *LE* II, 109. *Iris pseudacorus* is a colourful invasive water plant, with bright yellow flowers at eye level or above,
13. Cited in Darby 1974, 30.
14. VCH Hunts. III, 187.
15. Camden 1610, 'Huntingdonshire', 6.
16. VCH Cambs. X, 500.
17. *Pet. Chron.*, 2.
18. *RABB* 1, 5–6.
19. *LE* II, 105.
20. *LE* II, 105.
21. Mason 1984, 9, and *LE* II, 105, respectively.
22. *LE* II, 105 and *GP* IV, 183 respectively; translation of the latter is by Camden 1610, 'Cambridgeshire', 13.

23. Shennan 1986; Waller 1994.
24. Godwin and Clifford 1938; Godwin 1940; Godwin and Vishnue-Mittre 1975; Waller 1994; Brew *et al.* 2015, 81.
25. Baxter 2005.
26. Waddelove and Waddelove 1990, 255.
27. Hall 1987, 4; Shennan and Horton 2002, 512–14; Behre 2007, 98.
28. Hall 1987, 4, 84; Waller 1994; Shennan and Horton 2002; Behre 2007.
29. Hall and Coles 1994, 25–37.
30. Shennan 1986, 170; Hinton 1995, 103–108; Shennan and Horton, 2002, 512–14; Shennan *et al.* 2006, 595–96; Behre 2007, 98; Smith *et al.* 2010, 260.
31. Silvester 1988, 160–61.
32. Hall and Coles 1994, 25–37; Waller 1994; BBC Regional News, Norfolk, 26 September 2012 'Fenland Black Oak: 5,000-year-old-tree found in Norfolk', http://www.bbc.co.uk/news/uk-england-norfolk-19722595, accessed 3 March 2017.
33. Godwin and Clifford 1938; Godwin and Vishnu-Mittre 1975; Hall and Coles 1994, 28 and 92; Waller 1994, 138, 186, 225.
34. Hall 1987, 8.
35. Shennan 1986; Hall and Coles 1994, ch. 2; Waller 1994.
36. Cited in Halls and Cole 1994, 27.
37. Hall 1987, 8; Shennan 1980; Behre 2007.
38. Hall 1987, 4.
39. Hall 1987, 40–41.
40. *E.g.* Philips 1970; Hall 1987; 1992; 1996; Silvester 1988; Hayes and Lane 1992; Crowson *et al.* 2005.
41. Hall 2000.
42. Hall 1987, 42–45.
43. Hall 1987, 11; Shennan 1986.
44. Silvester 1988, 156–60.
45. *E.g.* Godwin 1940, 299; Pryor 1998, 284–92; 2001, 368–73; French 2001, 403; Evans 2003a, 212–13; 2003b, 83 and 121; see also Ballantyne 2004, 189; Evans and Hodder 2006, 5; Gibson and Knight 2006, 129; Evans and Serjeantson 1988, 365–68; Malim 2010, 72; Oosthuizen 2016a. See Chapter 6 below.
46. English Nature 2004; Natural England 2008; 2013.

CHAPTER 2

One of the Loneliest Pieces of Country

The Anglo-Saxon fenland is usually described as wild and unmanaged, under-populated and under-exploited. As Sir Clifford Darby, the great historical geographer, explained, 'It is not difficult to understand that many parts [of the fens] in the eighth century could still be described as a "wide wilderness", devoid of settled habitation'.[1] Such judgements were consonant with early documentary sources which described a frighteningly wild and isolating landscape, penetrated only by a few explorers who liked it too little to stay. In 731 Bede described Ely 'surrounded on all sides by sea and fens'.[2] St Guthlac is said to have founded his late seventh-century hermitage at Crowland in 'a most dismal fen of immense size', remote, untilled, uninhabited, and infested by demonic spirits.[3] That view, it might be said, persisted into the mid-twentieth century when a young researcher for the Victoria County History plaintively described the fens north and east of Littleport as 'one of the loneliest pieces of country within a hundred miles of London'.[4] Yet by 1334 the fen basin was among the wealthiest and most populated regions of England (Fig. 2.1).[5] Only in London did more people in each community pay the lay subsidies of 1327, 1332 and 1334 – a tax paid

FIGURE 2.1. St Clement's church, Terrington St Clement (Norfolk), is around 51 m long, one of the largest in the fens (© Susan Oosthuizen). The current building, a masterpiece of Perpendicular architecture, was constructed in the fourteenth century, replacing a Norman church. The settlement within which it stands was established in the mid-seventh century.

only by the better off. In 1334 Ely (raising £358), Wisbech (raising £410) and almost every silt fen vill were in the top 20% of English settlements that each contributed more than £225. And that wealth was relatively widely dispersed: more than 60 people in each community paid the subsidy, each generally paying between £2 10 s and £3.[6]

The contrast across the fen basin between late eleventh-century poverty and early fourteenth-century wealth was firmly established by the mid-twentieth century. Darby's iconic *Medieval Fenland* outlined what became the dominant interpretation: that monastic houses, newly founded or re-established in the late tenth century, had by 1250 transformed the fen economy through an intense focus on management for profit.[7] Net annual income from estates belonging to the Abbey of Ely in 1086 (and transferred to the Bishop in 1109), for instance, rose from £484 in the late eleventh century to £2550 in 1298–99.[8] Nor was all innovation driven by manorial lords. Groups of lay tenants, many individually enfeoffed with just a few acres, were collectively able to transform substantial areas of rough fen into meadows and pasture on which immense herds of cattle grazed 'horn under horn'. First-hand accounts told the same story. Matthew Paris reported in the mid-thirteenth century how 'a wonder has happened in our time; for in the years past, beyond living memory, these places were accessible neither for man nor for beast... This is now changed into delightful meadows and also arable ground'.[9] It was, said Darby, 'a great revolution in economic geography'.[10] That consensus persists today: 'The Fenland and Fen-edge economy that supported these extraordinary taxpayer numbers was largely a product of widespread colonization and reclamation during the previous 250 years [before 1334]' – that is, after the Norman conquest.[11]

This chapter explores the principal assumption underlying that argument: that new colonists were attracted to an empty region after the re-foundation of the monasteries from around 970 onwards. In exploring whether the Anglo-Saxon fenland was abandoned or under-populated, it begins by taking two approaches to establishing population density in the fenland in 1086 – our earliest relatively reliable benchmark: it shows that maps of eleventh-century population density in the basin significantly underestimate the size of local communities; and it argues that at least 30% of the population was not recorded in *DB*. It moves on to compare the intensity of settlement across fenland in the later eleventh century with evidence for equally high Romano-British occupation. Having discussed evidence for settlement across the basin at the beginning and at the end of the Anglo-Saxon period, the chapter moves on to explore evidence for occupation of the region in the intervening centuries, concluding that it was intensively occupied across the early middle ages.

Mapping population densities in fenland in 1086

Professor Darby's conclusion that fenland was still all but abandoned in the eleventh century was based on his maps of data from *DB*. His map of

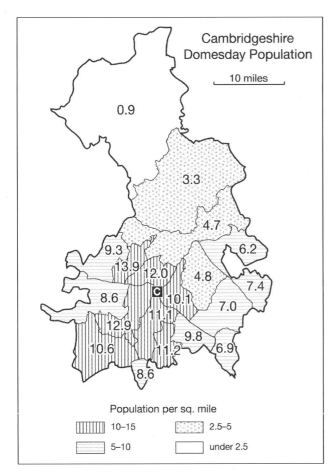

Cambridgeshire
Domesday Population

10 miles

0.9

3.3

4.7

9.3   6.2

13.9 12.0

8.6   4.8   7.4

[C]   10.1   7.0

11.1

12.9

10.6   11.2   9.8   6.9

8.6

Population per sq. mile

|||||| 10–15   2.5–5

5–10   under 2.5

FIGURE 2.2. Professor Darby's calculation of population density in the fen basin in 1086 was based on the entire area of the basin, even though large tracts were uninhabitable. The results showed only 0.9 tenants per square mile in the two northern hundreds of the Isle, and 3.3 in the two southern hundreds – compared with an average of 9 tenants per square mile in the Cambridgeshire uplands south of the modern river Ouse (© Susan Oosthuizen, after Darby 1971, fig. 80).

distributions per square mile of the numbers of tenants per square mile across the country showed which English regions were more densely occupied than others. The results for fenland were startling: they were so low that a mappable result could only be achieved by combining the four hundreds of the Isle of Ely into two pairs rather than using his conventional base of individual hundreds. His calculations revealed just 0.9 tenants per square mile in Wisbech and North Witchford Hundreds, and around 3.3 tenants per square mile in Ely and South Witchford Hundreds (Fig. 2.2). These figures were remarkably low compared with those for upland Cambridgeshire south of the river Ouse where there were, on average, around nine tenants per square mile, leading him to conclude that 'the sparse distribution of Domesday villages ... suggests that the Fenland was an area of comparative poverty in the eleventh century'.[12]

The central problem for fenland, of course, is that Darby's calculations took no account of its extreme physical geography, where – unlike the uplands that surround it – there is no middle ground between land that *can* and land that *cannot* be permanently inhabited. For fenland at least, this is a substantial flaw. Darby treated the fenland as if the whole area were as habitable as the uplands of south Cambridgeshire when this was clearly not the case. It was impossible to establish any permanent settlement below the flood line, and a glance at the map shows how large that uninhabitable area was (see Fig. 1.2). No-one in their right minds would settle here, and the homes and fields of anyone mad enough to try would have been submerged as soon as the waters began to rise, as they predictably did several times each year. Permanent settlement was only safe if it was located above the flood line on the fen islands and on the silt fens. On the Cambridgeshire upland, by contrast, farms, hamlets and villages could, in geographical terms at least, be located almost anywhere. The number of tenants per square mile in fenland was low because the flood line placed an absolute restriction on where they could live in that wetland landscape.

Darby himself appears to have been bullish in his 'belief in the descriptive objectivity and explanatory power of maps' to the extent that 'the map *bestowed objectivity*'.[13] What stood out for him from these maps was the poverty of the eleventh-century fenland basin. He was sure that 'here is no vague generalization about the comparative values of fen and upland, but *definite statistical evidence'* for the impoverished condition of fenland in 1086.[14] This may have been a step further than the evidence warranted. Whether or not the maps of population density in fenland do actually reflect poverty and under-exploitation is yet to be shown. All they can really be said to demonstrate is the restriction placed by the flood line on the area available for settlement. The same point has already been made convincingly in relation to the silt fens, where around 40% of the Norfolk parishes was marsh and fen and where, if these were taken into account, fen men were no poorer or wealthier than their upland neighbours.[15] What might be revealed if population density in the peat fens were re-calculated in the same way? If the fenland really was under-populated in 1086, then Darby's argument for Anglo-Saxon abandonment would be confirmed; if, on the other hand, there were plenty of people living in the region in the late eleventh-century then the story about what happened in fenland between about 400 and 1086 may need to be rewritten.

Re-calculating Domesday population densities across fenland

The calculation of population density is straightforward: it is worked out by dividing the *number of people* living in an area (specified in, for example, acres, square miles or square km) at a known date *by the area in which they live* at the same date (or its nearest approximation). For the later eleventh century, for example, the sum will be 'number of *DB* tenants in a hundred/area of the hundred'. Because permanent settlement in the fen basin was only possible *above* the flood line, the measure of population density on land capable of supporting settlement there should be: '*DB* tenants in the hundred/[area of the hundred – area of fen in the hundred = land available for habitation]'.

There are, however, problems with the reliability of all three elements in that calculation. The information recorded in *DB* depended on the questions that the *DB* commissioners asked. First, they were counting tenanted landholdings rather than individuals and, in most cases, did not record the names of the tenants. Extrapolating the numbers of tenants from *DB* may thus lead to some unintentional double-counting as there is no way of telling whether an anonymous individual held two (or more) landholdings and was thus counted as two (or more) people instead of as one. Second, *DB* did not record each person in a household; it was not a census. Third, the *DB* commissioners seem only to have recorded those heads of households who were also manorial tenants of one sort or another – freemen, sokemen, *villani* (peasants), *bordarii* (demesne workers), *cottarii* (cottagers), and *servi*. They do not seem to have included unmanorialised day labourers, living by their wits at the bottom of the social scale, and selling their services at a daily rate across the seasons. Nor did they record many others, often the local holders of Norman estates, who were important enough locally to attest the accuracy of information from their hundreds when the commissioners collected their evidence. Some had Norman

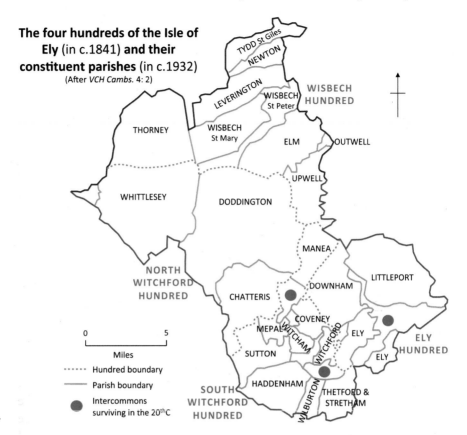

The four hundreds of the Isle of
Ely (in c.1841) **and their
constituent parishes** (in c.1932)
(After *VCH Cambs.* 4: 2)

FIGURE 2.3. Parishes and hundreds in the Isle of Ely. Note: Boundaries are as they were in the nineteenth century (© Susan Oosthuizen, after VCH Cambs. IV, 3).

names – Gilbert of Linden, Osmund of Stretham, Reynold of Downham, and Tancred of Sutton; others had English names, like Alnoth of Sutton, Ælfwine of Hinton, Huna of Ely, or Loedmær of Witchford.[16] We know about them only by chance, since they were listed in a local draft of information to be sent to the commissioners, and it is likely that many others who were similarly omitted.

If it is difficult to be sure of the accuracy of the information in *DB*, the second element in the calculation – the area of each medieval hundred calculated by combining that of its constituent parishes – is as problematic. It is almost impossible to know the medieval acreages of most parishes. Changes to parish boundaries were often unrecorded before the later eighteenth century; in many cases, the first firm statement of parish acreages came with Parliamentary enclosure. And it is especially difficult in fenland to extrapolate backwards from modern parish acreages to those of the middle ages because large areas of previously extra-parochial, intercommonable pastures were added to existing parishes like Littleport, March and Outwell in the nineteenth century. In other cases, completely new parishes were established largely from those commons: Welches Dam was created in 1883 from an extensive area of intercommonable fen; and Manea, previously a hamlet of Coveney, also received parochial status in 1883 when an additional 1618 ha (4000 acres) of the same intercommon was allotted to it.[17] It made sense to use the hundred as the base unit of area, then, although their boundaries, too, were subject to change (Fig. 2.3).

The third part of the calculation, that of the area of medieval fen in each hundred, is as fraught. The earliest known survey of the peat fen was undertaken by the great cartographer William Hayward in 1636.[18] Hayward was an accurate, professional surveyor so, when he recorded 90 ha (224 acres) of fens at Throckenholt, he was probably right.[19] But it is difficult to be sure for our own purposes how reliable those figures might be. First, Hayward did not explain how he decided what was and what was not fen, so it is impossible to know whether or not he included everything that we would call fen, or even if he applied the same rules to every fen he surveyed. Second, he was inconsistent in including some areas of improved fen, but not others. Third, he listed areas of extra-parochial intercommon under the names of modern parishes whose area is often smaller than the total acreage of the fens that he attributed to them. And lastly, his survey was undertaken almost 350 years after the *DB* when average summer and winter temperatures were respectively between 1.4 and 1.7 °C lower than they had been in 1086 – the area of wetland in the basin was therefore probably a little larger in the mid-seventeenth century than it had been at the end of the eleventh.[20] The area of a wetland changes from season to season and year to year. Even relatively small changes in volumes of rainfall could have a noticeable impact: the *ECB* noted in 1249–50, for example, that there were 4 acres in West Meadow in Willingham 'which can also be gained for certain in very dry years'.[21] The range of that seasonal variation might, furthermore, be exacerbated by climate change: areas liable to freshwater or marine flooding tended to become more extensive during downturns, like that between 600 and 800, and to shrink in the upturns, like that between 800 and 1300.[22] More or less catastrophic episodes of marine flooding along the eastern coast of the Wash in the seventh and eighth centuries were discussed in the previous chapter.[23] The monk recording the Bishop's demesne at Leverington in 1249–50 will have empathised, describing 'another fen called *Northale* containing 40 acres, but sea flooding sometimes reduces it and sometimes increases it'.[24] Under these conditions the area that could be counted as fen pasture in, say, 1086 was likely to have been smaller than that available three or four centuries earlier. The combined influences of seasonal variation and climatic change make it problematic, to say the least, to infer that (for example) Grunty Fen covered 517 ha (1280 acres) in the drier conditions of 1086, or the wetter ones of 786, simply because that was its area in the seventeenth century.[25]

All three elements of the calculation 'population density = DB tenants/(area of the vill – area of the fen)' are thus problematic. The DB tenants may have been under-enumerated, and in any case represent only heads of household; the area of each medieval vill can only be roughly calculated; and the area of fen wetland in 1086 is likely to have been somewhat less than it was in 1636. On the other hand, this is all the data available. Given the choice between abandoning the venture for lack of solid ground and proceeding warily, recognizing the

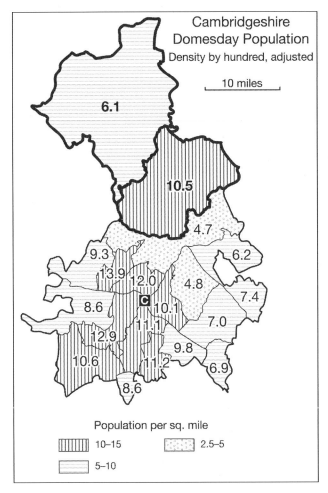

Cambridgeshire Domesday Population
Density by hundred, adjusted

10 miles

6.1

10.5

4.7

9.3   6.2

13.9 12.0

4.8   7.4

8.6   10.1

7.0

11.1

12.9

9.8

10.6

11.2

6.9

8.6

Population per sq. mile

|||||| 10–15   ·····: 2.5–5

5–10

FIGURE 2.4. A recalculation of population density in the fen basin in 1086 using only the area of land capable of supporting permanent settlement suggests that the population density of the two southern hundreds of the Isle of Ely was similar to the average across the southern uplands; population density in the silt fens remained lower than that average but not outlandishly so (© Susan Oosthuizen).

fuzziness of the result, the second option was chosen: DB tenant figures were used; the total acreage of peat fen in each hundred was calculated from Hayward's survey; the total acreage of each hundred was calculated from modern parish acreages; and population densities were calculated per square mile across each of the hundreds which were then paired to provide direct comparability with Darby's maps.

As may be expected, the results show that there was more dry land in the parishes on the Isle of Ely itself than in other parts of the fen basin. Places like Haddenham, Wilburton and Little Thetford came in at the high end of the range with between 40% and 60% of the parish lying above the fen, while 96% of the parish area at tiny, landlocked Wentworth was habitable. There was, predictably, less land available for settlement in the central and western parts of the fen basin where the peat was more extensive: only 16% and 21% respectively of Chatteris and the Doddington archipelago lay above the flood line. When population densities are re-calculated only for the habitable land within the fen basin, they show around 10.5 tenants per square mile in Ely and South Witchford Hundreds in 1086, around three times greater than Darby's figure of 3.3. The difference for Wisbech and North Witchford Hundreds is more than six-fold, with around 6.1 tenants per square mile there compared with Darby's figure of 0.9 per square mile. These densities are directly comparable with the more affluent uplands of Cambridgeshire south of the fens. The stark contrast between fenland and upland shown on Darby's maps has disappeared (Fig. 2.4). However, two thirteenth-century documents indicate that even those adjusted population densities may be an underestimate.

Ancient Anglo-Saxon holdings missing from the *DB* accounts

The details of landscapes and holdings recorded on the Bishop of Ely's manors in 1222 and 1249–50 indicate the remarkable survival of ancient landholdings and traditions into the medieval period, a theme taken further in the next chapter.[26] They report the names and other details of individual landholders who paid public dues to the hundred. These obligations were an archaic relic of rights of property whose origins were almost certainly associated with landholdings in fifth- and sixth- century territories, and which were transferred to the hundreds, probably in the tenth century.[27] They were a form of landholding so ancient that no new holdings of this kind can have been created since before the Norman Conquest.[28] Some remained independent of the manorial system in 1249–50; others were gradually being absorbed under lordly authority, but retained some relics of their earlier status in these payments. They were only recorded because, although the sums were collected by the Bishop's reeves, they did not contribute to the Bishop's income, but were instead transmitted to the hundred.[29] Their significance in this context is that they suggest that the *DB* significantly under-represented of the population of the basin, since at least 176 of these holdings were omitted from its account.

The evidence for these ancient landholdings falls into three groups (Fig. 2.5). The first group is made up of individuals described as *hundredors* at Wilburton, Doddington, Somersham and Lyndon (now in Haddenham). They were men whose holdings were held from the hundred to which they contributed public obligations in money renders. Such holdings were straightforwardly identifiable not only by their name, but also by their distinctive payments of *sextithepeni* and *wardpeni*, and by specific early Anglo-Saxon public obligations attached to their holdings, including attendance at the hundred court that met every three to four weeks. *Sextithepeni* was a public obligation to pay 60d. from each hide; *wardpeni* represented the commutation of the public obligation from each hide to contribute to the construction and maintenance of fortifications, and to perform guard duties.[30] Robert at the chapel and Geoffrey *le sokeman* (both *hundredors* at Haddenham), for instance, owed ½d and 1¼d *sextiethpeni* respectively, and paid 1d *wardpeni* each.[31]

The second group is made up of holdings that were called *ware* acres, holdings that owed the ancient public obligations of fortification and guard.[32] Many also made the distinctive payments of *sextithepeni* and *wardpeni* mentioned above and were recorded in Ely, Wilburton, Lindon (Haddenham, Hill Row and Linden End), Littleport, and Stretham. Some of these holdings remained free in 1249–50; others were becoming absorbed into customary tenancies but were still being described as *ware* acres.[33] Nicholas son of Elias and William *le hale*, for instance, were free tenants of the Bishop who jointly held 18 *ware* acres in Ely. Their public obligations included undertaking the role of coroner, if required, in addition to attendance at the hundred courts, and accompanying the bailiff of the hundred in enforcing public order in the Isle. Robert of Sproutun, who was also a free tenant, held ten *ware* acres in Stretham, 'paying 1d for *sextithepeni* and 1d for *wardeselver*', while Philip de Lisle, a free tenant at Wilburton, held 16 *ware* acres and owed 'suit to the court of Ely, Wilburton court and to each hundred (court) throughout the year. He owes *sixthepeni* and *wardpeni*'.[34] Others, those of customary tenants paying labour services in 1249–50, appear as *villani* (villeins) in Domesday Book. They included 15 tenants at Littleport described as *villani* in 1086 whose holdings, then described as customary lands,

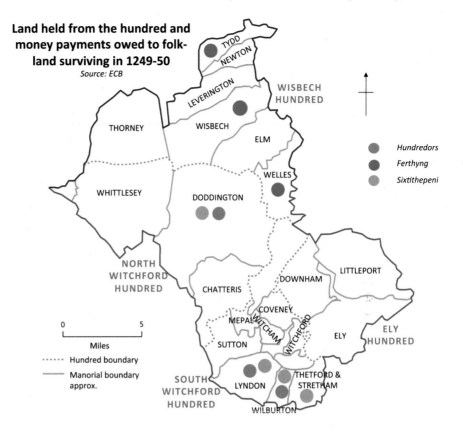

Land held from the hundred and money payments owed to folk-land surviving in 1249-50
Source: ECB

FIGURE 2.5. Land held from, and money payments owing to, the hundreds (rather than to the manors) across the Isle of Ely in 1249–50 provide evidence for the survival of public obligations to render money payments to early Anglo-Saxon folkland. They provide evidence for a large number of non-manorial individuals who appear to have been omitted from *DB*. Note: Boundaries are as they were in the nineteenth century (© Susan Oosthuizen, after VCH Cambs. IV, 3).

were described as *ware* acres in 1249–50; or the 13 *villani* recorded in *DB* at Wilburton, almost identical in number to the 14 holding customary lands in 1249–50, also made up of *ware* acres.

The third group is that of holdings that owed an equally archaic payment called *ferthyng*, a contribution to an early Anglo-Saxon territory from one of the quarters into which it was divided.[35] By the mid-thirteenth century these payments only survived in Wisbech Hundred, albeit in substantial numbers: 34 in Wisbech, 15 in Tydd, 44 in Elm and 28 in Welles (Outwell and Upwell).[36] John Uncle of Wisbech, for example, held 'a messuage and half of *Ninemannedale* for 16d each year, [and] 2½d for *ferthing* at the Annunciation of the Blessed Mary'; 'Emma sister of Aspelon holds a messuage and appurtenances for 2½d *ferthing* at Easter'.[37]

Around 179 of these holdings appear to have been omitted from *DB*. Three examples illustrate the point. The 22 manorial tenants documented at Wilburton in 1086, for instance, can almost certainly be identified with the 24 listed in 1249–50; yet eight *hundredors* were also recorded in the mid-thirteenth century and must therefore be missing from the *DB* account.[38] There were 52 manorial tenants at Doddington in 1086, and 51 in 1249–50 – when 14 *hundredors* were also recorded.[39] And there were 47 manorial tenants (including two fishermen) on the Ely manor at Wisbech in 1086, and 44 in 1249–50, as well as a further 87 holdings, not included in those numbers, that paid *ferthyng*.[40]

Many of these manors do, of course, show a significant increase in their overall population across the period, but that change can be accounted for in two ways: by the subdivision of full villein holdings into half holdings, and, more importantly, by an significant increase in the number of rent-paying tenants who did *not* owe rents to the hundred.[41] The expansion of the post-Conquest population at Littleport is typical: by 1249–50 eight of the 15 villein tenancies documented in 1086 had been subdivided into half-lands; a further 59 rent-paying tenancies had been created, often of small pieces of land in the fen.[42]

Stability in the numbers of hundredal holdings between 1222 and 1249–50 may indicate that their mid-thirteenth-century numbers were not far off those in *DB*: 132 holdings paid *ferthyng* in Wisbech Hundred in both thirteenth-century extents, for instance.[43] The overall increase (from 312 to 323) of 11 in holdings paying rents to the hundred between those dates can almost entirely be accounted for by the subdivision of full customary *ware*-land holdings into half holdings. Detailed notes in the mid-thirteenth century extents suggest that any other form of subdivision of these ancient holdings was so unusual that it needed a full explanation. For example: Ralph son of Hugh was a *hundredor* at March in 1222; the *ECB* noted that, by 1249–50, his son Roger and daughter Margaret had divided his holding between them, one paying the *sixtipeni* it owed and the other the *bregesilver*. He had retained the larger part of the holding, 5 acres (2 ha), while she held one rood 'formerly belonging to this messuage'.[44] The apportionment of the payments between them, though, indicates that both they and the scribe still regarded the subdivided holding as a single entity and its subdivision as informal. No new *hundredor* holdings could, it seems, be created.

That long-term stability makes it possible to estimate the degree to which the fenland population was under-recorded in 1086. *DB* listed 339 tenants across the basin as a whole; the 1222 and 1249–50 extents indicate that around 176 holdings may have been omitted. It is possible, then, the population across the whole of the Cambridgeshire fenland may have been around 34% higher in 1086 than was previously thought. Those numbers are skewed, though, by the very high proportion of holdings that were not recorded in Wisbech Hundred. Here, 87 holdings that paid *ferthyng* in the mid-thirteenth century were not accounted for in *DB*, suggesting that it omitted around 65% of the late Anglo-Saxon landholders in Wisbech Hundred. The last is particularly intriguing since *DB* only listed a single vill in Wisbech Hundred – Wisbech itself; none of the other vills was mentioned, although archaeological evidence makes it plain that they were present, and the evidence of the *ECB* indicates that it was as well settled in 1086 as any other part of the fen basin.[45]

If the 47 tenants listed in Wisbech in 1086 are subtracted from the total number of tenants in DB, and the 87 additional holdings in 1222 and 1249–50 are subtracted from total number of those holdings (176), then the proportion of

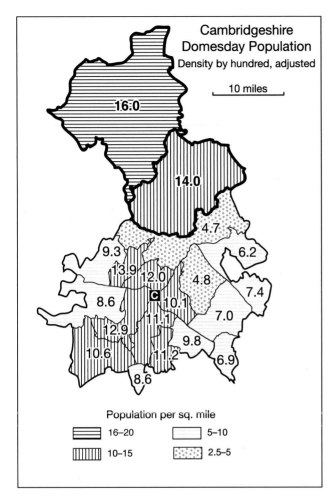

Cambridgeshire
Domesday Population
Density by hundred, adjusted

10 miles

16.0

14.0

4.7

9.3

6.2

13.9 12.0

4.8

8.6

C 10.1

7.4

12.9

11.1

7.0

10.6

9.8

11.2

6.9

8.6

Population per sq. mile

16–20   5–10

10–15   2.5–5

FIGURE 2.6. When population density on habitable land in the fen basin in 1086 is adjusted to take account of the non-manorial (hundredal) holdings omitted from *DB*, the results indicate an unexpectedly high population of the region by the later eleventh century (© Susan Oosthuizen).

landholders omitted from *DB* across Ely and the two Witchford Hundreds may have been around 31%. Darby's population densities can therefore be adjusted further. The population density of the southern two hundreds might increase to around 14 men per square mile; and if those in North Witchford Hundred were also under-calculated by around 31%, but those in Wisbech Hundred by 65%, the population density across their combined area increases to around 16 tenants per square mile – bringing the silt fens into line with the Isle as a whole (Fig. 2.6). The difference in Darby's maps between the two northern and the two southern hundreds disappears and so, too, has the distinction between fenland and south Cambridgeshire. Instead, it appears to have been as true in 1086 as it was in the fourteenth and seventeenth centuries that the late Anglo-Saxon fenland supported populations as large as, or even larger than, those on the uplands.

Was the substantial late eleventh-century occupation of the basin a recent phenomenon, or a continuous tradition? The discussion that follows explores this question first, by outlining evidence for extensive Roman settlement across the region, and then by asking whether that settlement n, relatively intense at the beginning and end of the Anglo-Saxon period, was interrupted or continuous across the centuries that intervened.

Romano-British and Anglo-Saxon occupation of the fenland

For at least the last 300 years historians, antiquarians and others have known that the Romano-British fen basin was as well-occupied and exploited as anywhere else in Britain, whose late fourth-century population appears to have reached between two and five million.[46] The fen landscape was occupied by men and women as canny as their medieval successors in their exploitation of local resources (Fig. 2.7).[47] Their farms, fields, droveways and paddocks survived into the twentieth century in many places on the silt fens. The islands and fen-edge of the peat fens were as intensively used, being 'more densely settled than at any time previously'.[48] The enormous Romano-British settlement at Chatteris covered 10 ha (just under 25 acres), four times the area of its late Iron Age predecessor.[49] These were landscapes dominated by pastoral husbandry:

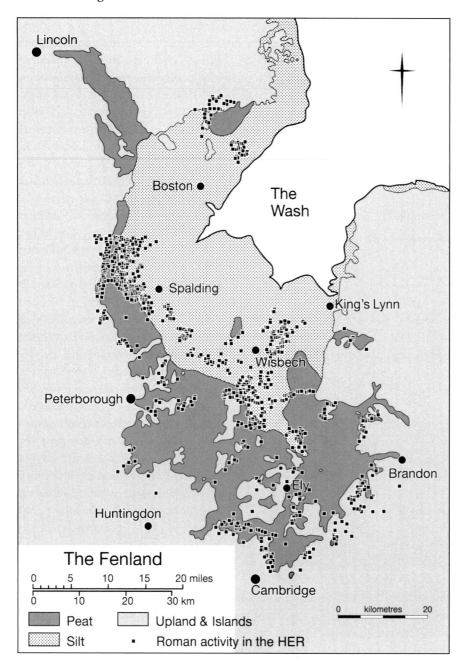

FIGURE 2.7. Romano-British sites and finds across the fen basin in about 100 (© Susan Oosthuizen, data from Hall and Coles 1994, fig. 68).

small rectangular fields and paddocks on the higher ground near the flood line, connected by droves with settlements above and the lower wetland grazing. Every hilltop on the Isle of Ely was the site of a bothy 'for a shepherd or grazier, placed on a local high spot giving a good view and suitable for controlling stock' across the extensive grazing of the rich peat grasslands below.[50]

If the population of the fen basin was high in 1100, and in about 400, was it continuously settled across the intervening centuries, or had it been abandoned and then re-colonised? Before the mid-1990s the Anglo-Saxon fen basin was assumed to have been almost deserted. The English Heritage Fenland Survey map of the region in about 700 showed just eight early and middle Anglo-Saxon sites across the peat fens: four on the Isle of Ely, two on the fen edge just north of Cambridge, one on Whittlesey, and one on the Northamptonshire fen-edge just north of Peterborough.[51] That paucity had previously led Darby to imagine the fenland as 'a frontier region … the resort of brigands and bandits'.[52] Small numbers of Old English place-names suggested to Reaney that 'by the fifth century, it seems clear, the general abandonment of the [fenland] district was inevitable', leaving a region only 'sparsely settled'.[53]

That abandonment was believed to have been driven by rising sea levels between about 600 and 800 which led to a 'catastrophic' rise of 1.5 m in the level reached by winter floods across the basin.[54] This was a period, too, of climate change that saw substantial increases in annual rainfall and in mean winter temperatures.[55] That is, the fens became significantly wetter and warmer in the seventh and eighth centuries. Yet changes in climate were not restricted to fenland. They affected other parts of Britain, too. Were early and middle Anglo-Saxon fen men and women likely to have been any less resilient in the face of such conditions than their upland counterparts?

The case is not immediately obvious. The agricultural economy of the fenland region was primarily focused on pastoralism, since arable cultivation was necessarily restricted to those areas that lay above the flood line. Fen communities were already experienced in making adjustments to water levels that varied in their local fens from one season and one year to the next. Permanently inundated lakes and mere expanded in area; the limits of the natural water meadows in intermediate fens, flooded in winter and grazed in summer, were gradually moved onto somewhat higher ground; low-lying settlements, now at or below the flood line, were no longer viable – but settlement remained possible on the fen islands and upland verges. The flood line that rose 1.5 m higher between 600 and 800 than that in the Roman period has, after all, remained more or less stable ever since, yet – as we have already seen – the wetland landscape was nonetheless still regarded as an immensely rich resource throughout the middle ages. There can be little doubt that adjustment to new conditions was required, but there is no reason to think that the new environmental conditions were any less promising for economic exploitation in 600 or 800 than they were in 1086 or 1250.

This is not to say that the early Anglo-Saxon communities who lived in the fens faced no hurdles in responding to climate change; simply that it is difficult to argue that the problems that they did have to resolve were *so much* harder than on the uplands that they were forced to abandon the basin. The scale of climatic change and increases in the height of the winter floods should not be underestimated; but they did not make the fenland *un*inhabitable. There is a growing recognition, too, that the desertion of some sites and the new foundation of others, alongside continuity of occupation of yet others, is unlikely to have been significant in signaling abandonment of an area. The appearance and desertion of farms and hamlets, and their movement from one location to another, has been typical of settlement history across all English landscapes in all periods.[56]

Archaeological excavation, field survey and stray finds, especially over the past quarter century, have revealed early and middle Anglo-Saxon farmsteads, hamlets and settlements across large areas of the silt fens on every fen island, and along the fen-edges. The Lincolnshire silt fens were inhabited along their entire length in the seventh century by settlements that appear to show no break with the Romano-British settlements that preceded them. Those at Quadring, Pointon and Sempringham, Gosberton, Pinchbeck, and at Thurley, where another huge settlement covered at least 2.2 ha (just over 5 acres), are typical.[57] For some time – perhaps a number of decades, perhaps one or two centuries – seasonal grazing replaced permanent settlement across the Norfolk silt fens. Then seven settlements were laid out along them at regular intervals of 1.5 and 2 km in the mid-seventh century, landscape planning on a considerable scale that indicates existing territorial control over the area.[58] They included a 7 ha (17 acres) site at Hay Green in Terrington St Clement, so large as to be 'truly remarkable', two equivalently large sites at Walpole St Peter, and others at West Walton.[59]

There is as little evidence of post-Roman abandonment of the wetland fens. Modern mapping reveals a landscape as densely settled as in any other period (Fig. 2.8). The life of many Romano-British settlements (some with Iron Age origins) continued without a break into the Anglo-Saxon period. Most farms and hamlets lay dispersed across the landscape, scattered from south to north, west to east, across the Isle of Ely, its satellite islands, and along the fen-edge. The post-holes of early medieval wooden buildings just north and south-east of Chatteris church provide just one example of such long-term continuity of occupation;[60] others include an early Anglo-Saxon sword found in the hypocaust below the *tepidarium* in the bath house of a Roman villa at Little Oulsham in Feltwell, and the early Anglo-Saxon houses in a palisaded enclosure that gradually replaced Romano-British structures at the Iron Age earthwork at Stonea Camp just west of March.[61]

Stray finds of early and middle Anglo-Saxon rings, pendants and weapons as well as consistent evidence across the basin for middle Anglo-Saxon Ipswich ware confirm that impression of established early medieval communities.[62] Much evidence comes from burials, like the weapons and a glass goblet at Somersham Ferry, Chatteris, or the many brooches and other objects from a large early Anglo-Saxon cemetery at Elm.[63] There were at least two large cemeteries at Ely, one including a young woman whose burial appears to have been a religious focus of some kind, and which included (among other things) rich jewellery, blue palm cups, and a wooden chest.[64] A couple buried together at Haddenham were accompanied by weapons and jewellery; there was a large early cemetery at Little Downham, and finds of three brooches hint at another

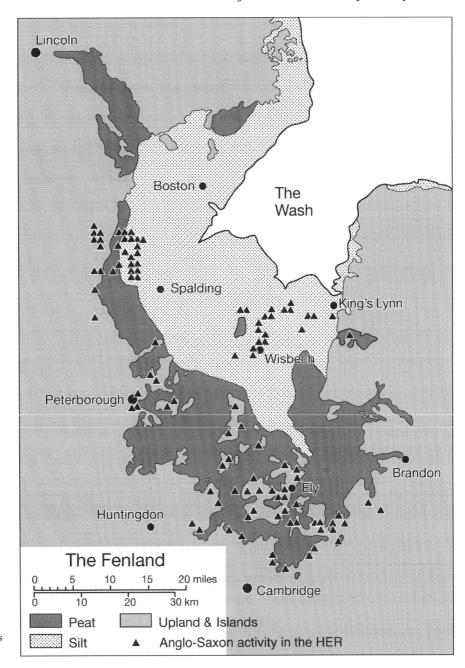

FIGURE 2.8. Early and middle Anglo-Saxon sites and finds across the fen basin (© Susan Oosthuizen, data from CHER and PAS, excluding multiple entries for the same sites).

at Little Thetford; a skeleton discovered in Manea Fen in 1838 had with it a necklace of north European amber and European glass beads; similar burials have been discovered at Sutton, Tydd St Giles, Wentworth, Whittlesey and Witchford; and so on.[65]

Archaeological investigation at West Fen Road, Ely, between 1999 and 2000 revealed the rare example of a middle Anglo-Saxon fen landscape lying in close

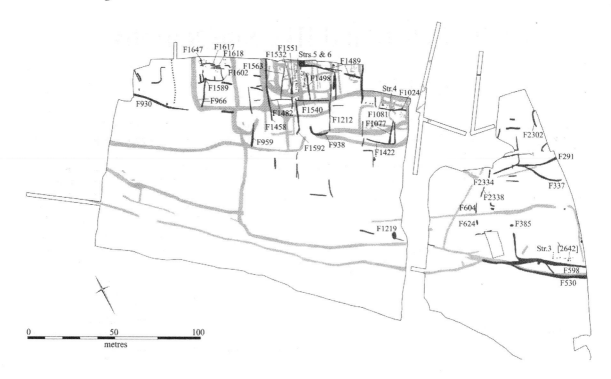

proximity to the large area of damp pasture that separated it from the modern settlement at Coveney (Fig. 2.9).[66] Established in the eighth century – dated from a silver coin of around 730–40 – and persisting into the eleventh, this large settlement and its fields lay on a site above the flood line that had been continuously inhabited since the Iron Age. Extensive exploitation of the fenland was clearly an important part of the livelihood of its early medieval inhabitants, who left behind over 16,000 bones of both cattle and sheep, a substantial body of evidence for weaving and for some small-scale bone-working.

The high population density of the late eleventh century fenland was, it seems, not a new phenomenon. It appears to have been simply the latest manifestation of continuous, extensive settlement across the fen basin in the centuries after 400.

FIGURE 2.9. The ditches (dark grey) of a planned middle Anglo-Saxon settlement at Ely re-using or following the alignments of earlier Iron Age and Romano-British (mid-grey) banks and ditches. Clusters of post holes (shown as collections of dots) in the lower right-hand, middle top, and centre top left of the settlement suggest the sites of houses (© Richard Mortimer, reproduced with permission)

Notes

1. Darby 1974, 8.
2. *Bede* IV, 19.
3. *Guthlac*, XXIV, also XXV, XXX–I.
4. VCH Cambs. IV, 96.
5. Campbell and Bartley 2006, maps 18.3, 18.8, 18.9d, 18.13.
6. Glasscock 1975, 28, 107, 168–69, 181–83; Glasscock 1976. See Thirsk 1953a, 42 for a similar profile in the sixteenth-century Lincolnshire silt fens.
7. Darby 1974, 141–42.
8. Miller 1951, 94.

9. *MP* V, 570.
10. Darby 1974, 141–42.
11. Campbell and Bartley 2006, 331.
12. Darby 1974, 122.
13. Harley 1989, 81 and 84 respectively, my emphasis.
14. Darby 1936, 44, my emphasis.
15. Silvester 1985, 111.
16. Lewis 1993, 31; *IE*, f.39a(1); *ICC*.
17. VCH Cambs. IV, 164–65, 136, 138.
18. Wells 1828–30, ii , 141–233.
19. Wells 1828–30, ii, 207.
20. Lamb 1985, 153, 154, 155; Pfister *et al.* 1998; Patterson *et al.* 2010; Büntgen *et al.* 2011, 581.
21. *ECB,* f.58r(2).
22. Shennan 1986; Hall 1987, 10–11; Waller 1994; Behre 2007.
23. Shennan 1986; Hall 1987, 10–11; Waller 1994; Behre 2007.
24. *ECB,* f.39d(1).
25. Wells 1828–30, ii; 194.
26. *BL* Cotton Tiberius B.ii; CUL EDR G.3.7.
27. Faith 1997, 90–101.
28. Douglas 1927, 145ff.; Miller 1951, 117-9; Faith 1997, 89–125.
29. Miller 1951, 117.
30. Neilson 1910, 159–61, 131–37; Faith 1997, 90–101.
31. *ECB,* f.20d(2)–f.21r(2).
32. Neilson 1910, 12; Faith 1997, 90, 115.
33. Miller 1951, 117–18.
34. *ECB,* f.14d(2) and f.17d(2) respectively.
35. Neilson 1910, 107;
36. *ECB,* f.48r(1)–f.48d(1).
37. *ECB,* f.34d(2) and f.35r(2) respectively.
38. *DB* Cambs. 5, 51; *ECB,* f.18r(1)–f.19d(1); Oosthuizen 2006, 116, n.10. The *DB* also lists 8 *servi* on the manor in 1086. They are excluded here because they and their labour formed part of the manor's demesne assets (Faith 1997, 59–70).
39. *DB* Cambs. 5, 45; *ECB,* f.26d(1)–f.31d(1).
40. *DB,* Cambs. 5, 55; *ECB,* f.33d(2)–f.38d(2).
41. For a detailed example, see Oosthuizen 2013a.
42. *ECB,* f.11d(1)–f.13d(2).
43. Forty-five of them can be identified with the *DB* tenantry of the manor, leaving 87 in both thirteenth-century accounts unaccounted for in 1086.
44. Cott. Tib. F.100r; *ECB,* f.26d(1)–f.27r(2).
45. Hayes and Lane 1992; Crowson *et al.* 2005.
46. *E.g.* Miller and Skertchley 1878, 454–91; Phillips 1970; Hall 1987; 1992; 1996; Silvester 1988; Hayes and Lane 1992; Hall and Coles 1994, 105–21.
47. See McCarthy 2013, 35.
48. Hall and Coles 1994, 111.
49. Hall 1987, 93.
50. Hall and Coles 1994, 111.
51. Hall and Coles 1994, 123, fig. 77.
52. Darby 1974, 9.
53. Reaney 1943, xxviii and xxx respectively (my addition).

54. Hall and Coles 1994, 122.
55. Lamb 1985, 146; Patterson *et al.* 2010; Büntgen *et al.* 2011, 581; Pfister *et al.* 1998. Barrow and Hulme (1997) do not cover the period between AD 1 and 1200.
56. *E.g.* Taylor 1983, 109–24.
57. Hayes and Lane 1992.
58. Crowson *et al.* 2005, 292; Silvester 1988, 158.
59. Silvester 1988, 37, 76, 92.
60. Adams 2013, 6.
61. Silvester 1991, 38; 1993; Hall and Coles 1994, 128.
62. Fox 1923, chapter 6; Cherry 2001, 200–203; Blinkhorn 2005, 62–65; see also Hall 1987, 103.
63. Cambridgeshire HER.
64. Lucy *et al.* 2009.
65. Cambridgeshire HER; Fox 1923, 262–3; Hall and Coles 1994, 128–31.
66. Mortimer *et al.* 2005.

CHAPTER 3

Cultural Identity
in the Early Medieval Fenland

The chapter begins with a review of evidence and arguments for the cultural background of the people and communities who occupied the fenland between about AD 400 and 700. It asks who they were: the descendants of prehistoric and Romano-British communities or, as is commonly supposed, fifth- and sixth-century immigrants from north-west Europe? The problem is explored in most detail in this chapter through evidence for the languages they spoke, preserved in its place-names. If all or most of those place-names are Old English in origin, then – despite difficulties in attributing cultural background to the language that was spoken at the time – perhaps most early medieval people across the basin were either immigrants from, or dominated by colonists from, north-west Europe. If, instead, all or most were rooted in Brittonic, then one might conclude that the fenland population of the period was indigenous in origin, and that immigrants to the region had become fully assimilated into late Romano-British society. If, on the other hand, place-names originating in both languages can be found, then cultural background becomes unattributable. The results appear to show that, although more early fen place-names with Brittonic elements survive than those rooted in Old English, there is no difference in their distribution in the region. Both can be found across the basin. It concludes that, like the results from archaeological and genetic, early fen place-names indicate that early medieval communities across the basin were largely Romano-British in descent, that incomers – whatever their origins – were assimilated into those existing local communities, and that most individuals were almost certainly bilingual in both languages.

The identification of 'Anglo-Saxons' in fenland: archaeology and genetics

The underlying problem at the heart of this chapter is the significant change after 400 in material culture across England, including fenland, as both everyday and expensive artifacts and lifestyles were adopted that seemed to have more in common with those from north-west Europe than the Mediterranean. Does that change reflect the wholesale replacement of indigenous communities by groups of migrants, the forcible imposition of Germanic material culture on an existing population, or simply a change in lifestyle adopted by existing post-Roman communities?

For many years archaeologists concluded that the rapid adoption of apparently north-west European forms of pottery, jewellery, dress, and weaponry in the fifth and sixth centuries offered physical evidence for the Germanic migrants mentioned by Gildas and Bede. Maps of the distribution of distinctively 'Anglo-Saxon' artifacts, it was argued, might reveal the areas of where north-west European immigrants first settled, perhaps even enabling the identification of the regions from which different groups had originated.[1] That assumption was based two further beliefs: that post-Roman communities and Germanic immigrant groups were so indefatigable in their refusal to use each other's goods that the cultural identity of each could be identified in their different material cultures; and that, whether from choice or because it was imposed upon them, incomers from north-west Europe lived in settlements at a distance from existing Romano-British communities.

Those preconceptions have been eroded by more recent research. Even if their numbers were sufficient to make a difference to the cultural life of early medieval England (and no-one knows if they were), fifth- and sixth-century immigrants did not share a common background or even a common language: they travelled from different parts of northwest Europe, spoke different languages, and came from communities with a wide range of cultural traditions.[2] Cultural identity is, too, a contested concept since it can be deliberately or unconsciously constructed. Depending on their ages, gender and status even people within the same household may speak different dialects, eat dissimilar foods, and have diverse social traditions; the greater the geographic range, the greater the variation between households, communities and regions. Such identities are, moreover, learned either during childhood – people are not born speaking a particular language, or practicing specific social customs – or by assimilation; migrants do not, by and large, tend to introduce their native languages into the societies in which they settle.[3] So neither material culture, birth nor language are certain indicators (or predictors) of an individual's origins.

Archaeological evidence is as unhelpful. Fifth-, sixth- and seventh-century communities so uniformly used the same kinds of goods, lived in the same kinds of houses in the same kinds of place, and made their livings in the same ways as their neighbours that it has become 'increasingly difficult ... to continue to think about the fifth and sixth centuries in eastern Britain as consisting of highly-distinctive ethnic communities'.[4] Those studies are confirmed by recent

FIGURE 3.1 *(opposite)*. The 'Repton Stone' is a fragment of an early eighth-century cross that once stood outside the royal Mercian mausoleum at Repton (© Dr Heidi Stoner, reproduced with permission). The figure – perhaps that of Æthelbald, king of Mercia, who died in 757 – represents a confident amalgam of cultural references. The movement of the horse, its saddle, and the rider's stance upon it, his full-face portrait, pleated skirt, neat hair and diadem are all drawn from late Roman imperial models; the moustache is an inheritance from both Celtic and Germanic traditions; the figure's hose and shirt may be Germanic, like the Anglo-Saxon *seax* carried at his waist (Biddle and Kjølbye-Biddle 1985).

genetic studies that show that assimilation of migrants was the norm: there is no distinctive Celtic DNA in those parts of western Britain that are dominated by Celtic cultural traditions and language; nor are there pockets of 'Anglo-Saxon' DNA in eastern England.[5] Cultural differences between those with a local ancestry and those who were incomers remain invisible in genetic and in archaeological evidence (Fig. 3.1).

The identification of 'Anglo-Saxons' in fenland: place-names

Linguists and place-name scholars adopted a different approach. They suggested that, even where archaeological evidence indicated that people, whatever their background, were using the same kinds of goods in their daily lives, indigenous Romano-British communities might still be distinguished by the languages they spoke: British Celtic (Brittonic), which had evolved from an older form of Celtic spoken across Britain in the prehistoric period, and Late Spoken Latin, a vernacular language that had emerged during the Roman administration of Britain, both spoken by indigenous Romano-British communities. Similarly, immigrants from north-west Europe might be identified because they were speakers of Old English, whose origins lie closest to the Germanic languages of Frisia, Jutland and Saxony.[6] The hypothesis was thus developed that the geographic distributions of the two groups could be identified because Germanic migrants will have named places in Old English, while place-names created by existing communities were more likely to use elements drawn from Brittonic or Late Spoken Latin.

The second part of that proposition appears to be supported both by place-name studies and by archaeology. The strikingly widespread number of Latin loanwords in modern Welsh, Scottish Gaelic and English place-names, for instance, reflects how widely Late Spoken Latin was spoken in post-Roman Britain.[7] Many examples of elements drawn from a colloquial form of Latin and Brittonic survive in just those parts of eastern England where north-west European incomers are supposed to have settled first, including the fen basin. Elements from Latin Spoken Latin survive at (Castle and Shudy) Camps in Cambridgeshire (1086, *campus*, 'field'), and at Wicken Bonhunt in Essex (1086, *funta*, 'a specialised spring').[8] Many may have persisted in the everyday speech of the seventh or eighth centuries when the place-names were coined, at least in part because the secular and religious institutions that they named also often continued to thrive: (West) Wickham in Cambridgeshire is just one of many to include the word *vicus*, 'a small town'; the last element of Brancaster (Norfolk) and the whole of Caistor by Norwich (also Norfolk) are based on *castra*, 'a Roman fortification'; *colonia*, 'formally-established civilian settlement' persists in Lincoln; and religious belief is indicated by the two Eccles in Norfolk, both named from *ecclesia*, 'church'.[9] Latin inscriptions continued to be carved in those parts of south-west England, Wales and Scotland where stone is plentiful well into the eighth century. Many were memorial stones for people with Latin

FIGURE 3.2. The middle Anglo-Saxon cross base from Haddenham, now in Ely Cathedral, is doubly rare: it is one of only three pieces of Anglo-Saxon stone sculpture in East Anglia, and it has a literate Latin inscription in good lettering (© Susan Oosthuizen). The inscription reads '*Lucem tuam Ovino da. Deus et requiem Amen*', that is, 'O Lord, give thy light and peace to Ovin. Amen'. Because a high status East Anglian man called Ovin had managed Æthelthryth's household before about 670, the stone is usually associated with him but there is no evidence to support the connection (Bede IV, 3).

names or whose Brittonic names were presented in Latin form.[10] There are one or two even in the east of England, where there is no naturally-occurring stone, like the mid to late seventh century cross base found in Haddenham, near Ely, which solicits God's grace for Ovin (Fig. 3.2). Brittonic also continued to be spoken throughout early Anglo-Saxon England. Large numbers of early medieval memorial stones across Britain were dedicated to people with Celtic names, often within Brittonic inscriptions; and, even though the number of English place-names that incorporate Brittonic elements is restricted, a community speaking Brittonic is preserved in the place-name at Comberton (1086, *Cumbre*, 'Britons') in Cambridgeshire.[11]

The neatness of the contrast between the existing languages of post-Roman Britain and the origins of English in the languages spoken by fifth- and sixth-century immigrants from north-west Europe is, however, untidy by the recent suggestion that a West Germanic dialect may already have been spoken in eastern Britain by the late Iron Age, five or more centuries before the Anglo-Saxons are supposed to have arrived. The evidence is derived from names and titles of office inscribed on first century BC Iron Age coins from Norfolk, the pre-Roman Iron Age kingdom of the Iceni. Nash-Briggs has argued that 'ECEN', for example, is almost impossible to translate meaningfully if a Brittonic origin is sought; on the other hand, she suggests, the Germanic interpretation of 'Lord of the oaks' is at once obvious to place-name experts, although the suggestion remains controversial.[12]

It may, then, be worth comparing the distributions in fenland of place-names with Late Spoken Latin or Brittonic roots against those making use of Old

English elements. Recent research indicates that around 70% of major place-names recorded in England by 700 have survived, especially those of the larger estates; that, in turn, suggests that many with Romano-British or prehistoric names had been renamed in Old English by that date.[13]

If Gildas and Bede were accurate in their descriptions of the conquest and domination of eastern England by incomers from north-west Europe in the fifth and sixth centuries, one might expect to find that most early medieval fen place-names carry names in Old English, and that there are few, if any, rooted in Brittonic or Late Spoken Latin. There are, after all, many places in the New World named after the European places where early modern colonists were born or had lived before they emigrated: New York – and its earlier name New Amsterdam – are obvious derivations from Britain and the Netherlands respectively; Perth in Australia was named after Perth in Scotland by its Scottish founder. If, on the other hand, fenland had been continuously occupied by largely indigenous communities into which relatively small numbers of newcomers were soon assimilated, it would be reasonable to expect the survival among them of at least some Brittonic place-name elements and/or of names recording the presence of Brittonic-speaking communities.

Old English place-names

There are only around twelve reliably-identified Old English place-names in fenland, and most of them can securely be located in the early Anglo-Saxon period (Fig. 3.3). That small number is especially remarkable given that most people across the east of England had switched from a predominantly Romano-British to a predominantly Germanic material culture by the mid-fifth century: although the things that people used appeared to be almost exclusively north-west European in character, they do not seem to have been using Old English in naming local places.

Three of those names – Ely, Mepal and March – are particularly ancient. All were formed from archaic elements that went out of use very early in the Anglo-Saxon period. Ely was the first to be recorded – by Bede, who noted in 731 that it had been given to Æthelthryth, an East Anglian princess, in the mid-seventh century, so the name is at least as old as the gift.[14] It is believed to be 'a name of high antiquity' since it incorporates elements – *æl* or *ēl* + *gē* – that soon became obsolete.[15] The second element, *gē*, may represent an archaic Old English element meaning a territory, district or province, perhaps from the same root as modern German *gau*.[16] The meaning of the first element, *æl* or *ēl*, is uncertain. Even Bede did not seem to have been quite sure what it meant. Because it sounded like 'eel' he simply glossed it as named from the many eels in fenland and, while that is as good an explanation as any, its actual interpretation remains unknown. The other two names include similarly archaic elements, although the names themselves were not first recorded in documents for centuries after they had been coined. The origins of Mepal's place-name –

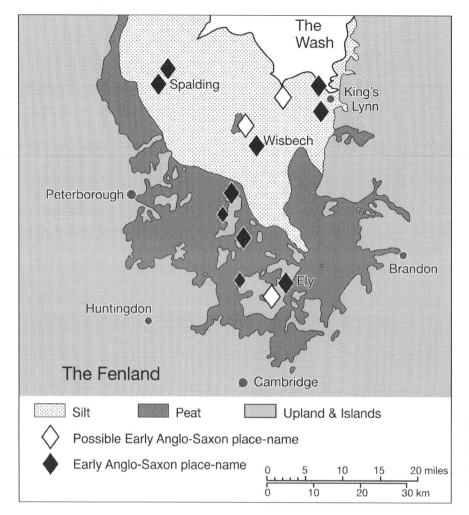

FIGURE 3.3. Old English place-name elements are distributed across the fens. There is no sign that they were confined to particular regions of the basin (© Susan Oosthuizen).

first recorded as *Meahala* in the twelfth century – remain enigmatic, although it is believed to refer to a folk group of some kind.[17] March (first recorded as *Merch* between 995 and 1001) takes its name from *mearc,* 'a boundary'.[18]

Six other early Old English place-names in the fens incorporate the element *-ingas,* 'a small, sixth-century, folk-controlled territory'.[19] The *Bilsingge* (thirteenth century) were located around Beezling Fen in Doddington, and the *Beorningas* (1285, *Berengal(e)*) at Brangehill Drove in Sutton, on the western slopes of the Isle of Ely.[20] On the Lincolnshire and Norfolk silt fens they are respectively represented by Spalding (late seventh century, **spald,* 'stream or ditch', *-ingas*) and Islington (1086, *elesa,* personal name, *-ingas, tūn*).[21] Terrington (1086, *Tir(a),* '?personal name', *-ingas, tūn*) and Quadring (1086, *cwead,* 'mud', *hæfer,* 'higher ground', *-ingas*) seem likely to have had similar origins.[22] It is possible that Leverington (*c.*1130, *Leofhere, -ingas, tūn*) may also be an *–ingas* place-name, but, if it is, it refers to a small local polity, like the *Bilsingge*.[23] Clenchwarton (1086, *clenc,* 'a hill', *ware,* 'public land', *tūn*), on the east of the

Norfolk silt fens, carries a similar meaning – a small community occupying a hill that had formerly been folk land – although it expresses it through a different linguistic element.[24]

It is remarkable how few of these Old English place-names there are in the fens given the supposed dominance of north-west European migrants in the region. If there was early Anglo-Saxon settlement in the region, the incomers were not, it seems, naming their settlements in Old English.[25] Stenton acknowledged the problem as long ago as 1940 when he noted in a letter to Darby that 'the local names of the Fens are very difficult' since their small numbers were at odds with his belief that they proved that 'this whole country had been explored … and had been named far back in the Anglo-Saxon period'.[26] Stenton's conclusion was not controversial when the Anglo-Saxon archaeology of the fenland was also regarded as minimal. At that time, both archaeology and place-names were at least consistent with the view that the fen basin had been abandoned in the fifth and sixth centuries, and only sparsely settled thereafter. Now, however, there is good evidence from a range of sources to indicate that there were plenty of people living in the fens in the early Anglo-Saxon period. But they were *not* using Old English to name their communities, nor is there any sign of isolated clusters of migrants within a wider receiving society in the distribution of those place-names – Old English names, although relatively few, are found across the

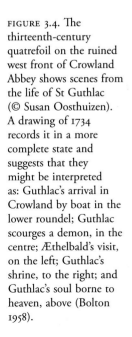

FIGURE 3.4. The thirteenth-century quatrefoil on the ruined west front of Crowland Abbey shows scenes from the life of St Guthlac (© Susan Oosthuizen). A drawing of 1734 records it in a more complete state and suggests that they might be interpreted as: Guthlac's arrival in Crowland by boat in the lower roundel; Guthlac scourges a demon, in the centre; Æthelbald's visit, on the left; Guthlac's shrine, to the right; and Guthlac's soul borne to heaven, above (Bolton 1958).

fen basin. How, then, is the discrepancy between archaeology and place-names to be resolved?

Christopher Taylor presciently suggested in 1973 that changes in the archaeology of the fifth and sixth centuries were not the result of migration, but instead represented a cultural shift on the part of local people, most of whose ancestors had been born and brought up in Britain. The growing use of Old English in forming place-names was rather, he thought, an indication of growing bilingualism as Old English began to be used alongside other languages.[27] If he was right, one would expect to find at least some evidence that local communities across the early Anglo-Saxon fen basin continued to speak Brittonic and Late Spoken Latin.

Documentary evidence for Brittonic speakers

There is good evidence that Brittonic were indeed spoken across the fenland well into the eleventh century. St Felix recorded the presence of Brittonic-speaking communities who tormented St Guthlac at his Crowland hermitage in the early years of the eighth century, and there are three reasons to think that his history can be relied upon. First, it was written between 730 and 740, less than a generation after the saint's death in 714, when Felix was still able to consult many of the people who knew Guthlac and may even have participated in or observed some of the events he recorded. The second reason is that there is enough prosaic detail recorded about some incidents in the *Life* to suggest that those at least were based on actual events. From our point of view, one of the most significant is the story of the attack on Guthlac by a British army whose 'sibilant speech' he could understand (Fig. 3.4).[28] It stands out because it has two unusual characteristics: it is the sole focus of the chapter in which it occurs (most chapters are made up of a number of stories); and it was set within a short and particularly specific time-frame, the brief reign of King Cœnred of Mercia (704–709) – in contrast to most stories about Guthlac which are not attributed to any date. The third reason is that Felix, who was himself East Anglian and knew the fens, took it for granted that Brittonic-speaking communities could still be found there in the seventh and early eighth centuries.

Felix also assumed that many people were bilingual in Old English and Brittonic. He explained that Guthlac could understand Brittonic 'because some time previously he had been in exile' among communities speaking the language.[29] It is even possible that the saint may have been fluent in both languages from childhood. His father, *Penwealh*, was a prince of Mercia, one of highest ranking members of the Anglo-Saxon – and presumably Old English-speaking – kingdom; yet -*wealh*, the last element in his name, means 'someone with a Romano-British cultural background', a trait he shared with other apparently 'Anglo-Saxon' kings.[30] If the 'Anglo-Saxon' prince *Penwealh* was untroubled by the overtly Romano-British connotations of his name, then the specific association that is believed to have existed between language and cultural tradition in early medieval England may have been less significant than has previously been thought. The possibility that many communities and individuals were bilingual in the seventh and eighth centuries is supported by recent research which suggests that the structures of English sentences, which have more in common with late Brittonic than any other Germanic language, indicate that English evolved as a second language spoken by large numbers of people whose first language was Brittonic.[31]

Brittonic was still being spoken in the Cambridgeshire region three centuries after Guthlac's death. The regulations of a late tenth- or early eleventh-century guild of Cambridge thegns distinguished between 'English' and 'British Celtic' members, suggesting that there were sufficient numbers of high status men living in or near Cambridge who identified themselves with Romano-British traditions for the regulation still to be worth retaining in about 1000.[32] The implications of that regulation are supported by two stories recorded in the twelfth-century Ramsey Chronicle. The first told of an event said to have taken place between 1015 and 1035: a Danish lord of Therfield (Hertfordshire) was so unpopular that his Anglo-Saxon retainers had to guard him while he slept. He woke up one night to overhear one asking the other, 'How long are we going to keep nightly watch for this foreign fellow, who deserves to be handed over to the Britons to murder?'[33] (The Dane prudently left for London the next day.) The second tale recorded ravages by 'wild and untamable British people' (*fera et indomita gens Britonum*) around St Ives (Huntingdonshire) some time between 1002 and 1090.[34] Both accounts are problematic: they are secondary, their primary sources are not listed, they are uncorroborated, and they were written down at least a century after the events were supposed to have occurred. The fact that the Chronicle includes two stories about eleventh-century Britons in the region might, on the other hand, give pause for thought. One story might be fanciful; but that there are two suggests that, whether or not the events described actually occurred, both writer and readers thought they were at least plausible. Brittonic may just, it seems, still have been spoken in Cambridgeshire in the early eleventh century.

In predominantly monoglot modern Britain, we forget how everyday bilingualism – the ability to speak two languages reasonably well – was in these islands even in the recent past, when many people spoke a local language (whether Welsh, Gaelic or an English dialect) as well as standard English, just as many continue to do today. Indeed, more than half of the world's modern population speaks at least two languages on a daily basis. There are 41 million native speakers of Spanish, and another 11.6 million people bilingual in English and Spanish, in the United States of America, for example.[35] There are *three* official languages in Belgium (French, Dutch and German) and, in 1990, nine other indigenous minority and regional languages were recognised by its French Community.[36] The possibility of a bilingual – or even multilingual – 'Anglo-Saxon' past should not be surprising.

Brittonic or Late Spoken Latin place-name elements in the fens

Three sets of place-names, larger in number than those based on Old English, demonstrate the continued use across the early medieval fen basin of elements drawn from Brittonic, Late Spoken Latin and even pre-Celtic: river names, place-names that include a range of different elements drawn from Brittonic or Latin, and a subset of Old English place-names that refer to communities or individuals as Britons (Figure 3.5). Together they suggest that both Brittonic and Late Spoken Latin continued to be spoken in the region through much of the Anglo-Saxon period.

River names

The most common British Celtic, and sometimes earlier, place-names to survive across England are those of rivers, including almost every major river flowing through the fens. That persistence may be due to the obvious regional dominance of waterborne communications. Here the infrastructure of trade, transport, travel, messages, and connections of all kinds depended almost exclusively on the rivers. Whatever the reason, the retention of names, some of which might even be pre-Celtic, is remarkable in a region where Germanic material culture was believed to be dominant at such an early date. By the time they were first mentioned in documents most of these river names were already a millennium old, and possibly much older. The earliest to be recorded was the Granta (*Gronte*, *c.*745) a Celtic name interpreted as 'muddy or fen river', mentioned in passing by St Felix in his *Life of St Guthlac* in around 730–40.[37] This is the old name for the full length of the river now generally called the Cam – and, in its more northerly reaches, the Ouse – which drained south-west and south-east Cambridgeshire, as well as north Essex.[38] The name of Grunty Fen, a large area of intercommoned wetland almost entirely surrounded by the Isle of Ely, may be a derivation from the Granta, in the same way that Grantchester (1086, *Grantesæte*) to the south is now the only survivor of the late Romano-British territory, the *sæte*, that controlled the river's upland catchment.[39]

Green has suggested that the name of the river Glen, which flows to the Wash through the Lincolnshire silt fens near Spalding, may also have a British Celtic root dating from the eighth century, perhaps derived from Brittonic **glanos* 'pure, clear water'.[40] The name for the Ouse was derived from another British Celtic or even pre-Celtic name; it may simply have meant 'water'.[41] There are two rivers Ouse flowing through fenland. The first, the fourth longest river in England, is now called the Great Ouse; it was first recorded in 880 as (*on*) *Usan* and reaches the fens at Earith.[42] The second is the Little Ouse which flows westward into the fens at Littleport from its source almost 65 km to the east.[43] Although Ekwall discounted the possibility that the name of the river Wissey, which enters the fens just south of Downham Market, also from the east, may be another form of the Ouse, his arguments have since been eroded. He argued that, despite its earliest form, Wissey could not be a derivative of Ouse because the Ouse did not run

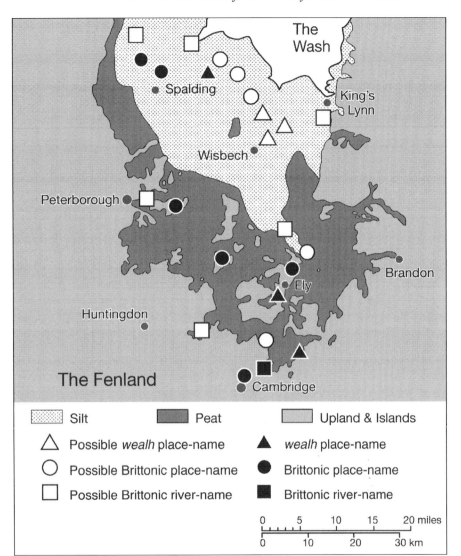

FIGURE 3.5 The distribution of Brittonic and Late Spoken Latin place-name elements across the same stretches of the fen basin as those with Old English elements may indicate the presence of multilingual communities (© Susan Oosthuizen).

to Wisbech.[44] The work of the Fenland Survey, however, has since demonstrated that the courses of the early medieval Nene and Ouse, of which the Wissey was a tributary, met just south of Wisbech before debouching into the Wash.[45] The confluence of the Wissey and the Ouse was still called *Wysemuth* in 1249–50, and Wisbech (1086, *Wisbece*) itself may have been named from the Ouse.[46] The river Welland – another of the great rivers to drain the English midlands – is generally agreed to have a pre-British Celtic name, though its meaning is unknown. Its earliest form, *Weolud,* was recorded in the *Anglo-Saxon Chronicle* in 921.[47] The name of the Nene, one of the longest English rivers, is Celtic or pre-Celtic.[48] The first element of *Camhale,* an alternative name given for the winding course of the Old Croft River (1249–50, *Wellenhe*) at Littleport, also appears to be derived from British Celtic – in this case (appropriately) *cam,* 'crooked'.[49]

There are thus eight rivers flowing through the fens whose names were already ancient by the time that Roman administration was withdrawn from Britain. At least three (the Great Ouse, the Nene, and the Welland) are among the great rivers of England, connecting the Wash with the western reaches of Northamptonshire, Nottinghamshire, Buckinghamshire and Bedfordshire and a further four (the Cam, the Glen, the Little Ouse, and the Wissey) are regionally significant. As we shall see, they were not the only fenland features to retain their ancient names.

Place-names including Brittonic elements

There are three definite, and four less certain, Brittonic elements that survive in fenland place-names. Woodland (*cēto-*) could once be found on the fen islands at Chatteris, at Chettisham (*c.*1170, *Chetesham*) just north of Ely and, perhaps, at Chittering (1426), between Stretham and Waterbeach.[50] The pool, *linn*, was the distinctive feature of (King's) Lynn (1086).[51] The names of Tydd (1086), northwest of Wisbech, and of Lutton (1086) in Holland may also have had Brittonic origins.[52] *Penhenorte* (1249–50, now called Wood Fen) in Littleport is a tantalising name: it is just possible that, like Penge (Kent), it incorporates Brittonic **penno-* 'most important, high'.[53] Nowhere in the fen basin was ever likely to be considered high, but it may just be an ironic reference to a slight eminence in the fen or, perhaps, a locally important place.

Two place-names preserve elements of Late Spoken Latin. Funthams Farm (thirteenth century, *Funtune*) in Whittlesey is based on *funta*, 'a particularly Roman spring or well, perhaps one with special technology for drawing water'.[54] Since the site lies on the edge of wetland where drawing water would have been neither difficult nor unusual, the name may have referred to specialized technology for managing rather than accessing water. A lost settlement of *Wykeham*, a place-name derived from Latin *vicus,* 'a Romano-British administrative centre', was recorded just north of Spalding.[55]

-Wealh *in fen place-names*

Some Old English place-name elements in fenland were used to refer to speakers of Brittonic: *-brettas*, 'British' and *-wealh*, 'someone with a Romano-British cultural background'.[56] The first is represented by just one example, a small settlement called *Bretlond* recorded in Fleet (Lincolnshire).[57] There are rather more examples of the second element, some of which refer to individuals and others to communities. Three fenland place-names record the land holdings of individuals locally identified as Brittonic either by the language they spoke, the late Romano-British customs they followed, or both: *Walewrth* (thirteenth century) in Ely, *Waleuort* (1249–50) at Horningsea, and *Walecroft*, at Fleet (Lincolnshire).[58]

The first two place-names combine *-wealh* and *-worthig*, a name that survives in the modern landscape as Walworth. Both elements of Walworth place-names have come under intense scholarly scrutiny. The most recent summary of what contemporaries understood by -*wealh* concluded that the term continued to be applied as late as the tenth century to groups and individuals who still thought of themselves as part of, or descended from, the Roman world.[59] Many were men of rank. A *wealh* who owned an estate of five hides in the late seventh century had the same status as an Anglo-Saxon thegn, and 200 years later King Wulfric's elite troop of horse was led by a *wealh gerefa*, a Briton of royal status. The prevalent misconception that the term was used to mean unfree peasants, tied to the land, was dismissed in 1975 in the most searching investigation of the term which concluded that '*wealh* meaning slave does not seem to have been widely adopted', even by the time of the Norman conquest.[60] The punitive fines applied in the early Anglo-Saxon laws for assault or murder of *ceorls* (while crimes again *wēalas* were assessed more lightly) may have been intended to discourage conflict with Old English speakers in established communities speaking Brittonic. A similar rationale has been adopted in modern laws that attempt to reduce alcohol consumption by applying taxation that becomes progressively more punitive as the proportion of alcohol in the drink increases. Instead, the high status accorded to men perceived as *wealh* may explain why apparently impeccable royal genealogies record the foundation of the Anglo-Saxon kingdoms by kings whose names were either entirely Brittonic or included a Brittonic element, like *Cenwealh* of Wessex (d. 672), *Merewalh* of the *Magonsæte* (d. late seventh century) and *Ædelwealh* of the south Saxons (d. *c.*685).[61]

Landholdings called *worthigs* were also indicators of rank. They were first mentioned in the late seventh-century laws of King Ine of Wessex which stipulated that 'a *ceorl's* homestead [*worthig*] must be fenced winter and summer'.[62] That is, a *worthig* was enclosed in some way, whether by ditches, hedges, banks or walls or a combination of them; and, second, its owner was an individual of some status.[63] Other sources make it clear that *worthigs* were those parts of his holding that a landholder managed directly (his inlands), in contrast to other parts of his estate that were leased out to tenants. The curvilinear outer ring fences of surviving worthys have been identified on Dartmoor, still surrounded by upland common pastures.[64] The two fenland *wealh worthigs* were probably, then, the enclosed demesne farms of gentry perceived by their contemporaries as Romano-British in their cultural background.[65] The survival of the place-name at Ely and Horningsea – both the locations of early royal minsters and both important central places – confirms the solid status implied by both elements in the name, and the evidence in the Cambridge guild regulations that such men were leading members of wealthy communities.

A second group of *wealh* place-names can be found in four contiguous parishes on the silt fens immediately east of Wisbech: Walsoken, Walpole (St Peter, and its daughter settlement, St Andrew), and (West) Walton (Figs 3.5 and 4.6). All three names were first recorded between the late tenth and late eleventh centuries. Walsoken (*Walsokne*) was listed in a charter of 974 in which

Ealdorman Æthelwin gave an estate there to Ramsey Abbey; its second element is *sōcn,* 'a large estate or district'.[66] Although doubts have been expressed about the authenticity of the charter, which was confirmed in about 1062, the form of the place-name has not been queried.[67] Walpole (*Walepol*, second element is *pōl*, 'pool') was first recorded in 1016 in a charter of Bishop Ælfwine; although the surviving copy of the charter (a confirmation dated 1042 x 1066) is generally regarded as a reworking of an earlier original, the form of the place-name is regarded as genuine.[68] Walton first appears in *DB* as *Waltuna*, its second element being *-tūn*, 'a small estate or community', a commonplace suffix.[69]

The common first element of the place-names and the tight geography of the three communities is significant, since it is generally accepted that, where two or more contiguous medieval parishes share the same prefix or suffix, they represent fragments of an older, once larger, estate.[70] The example of a large early Anglo-Saxon royal holding around Micheldever, just north of Winchester in Hampshire, is well-known: it is has been reconstructed from the *worthig* place-names of the contiguous medieval parishes of King's Worthy, Abbot's Worthy, Martyr Worthy and Headbourne Worthy.[71]

How is the shared prefix of Walsoken, Walpole and Walton then to be interpreted? None of the place-names survives in a sufficiently early form for a certain translation. Could the prefix of each be derived from *wealh,* indicating someone with a Romano-British cultural background? Neither of the earliest authorities considered that was likely: Smith was explicit that all three names were based on *weall*, 'wall', and Cameron seems to have agreed as he did not include any of them in his gazetteer of names in *wealh*.[72] Faull interpreted Walsoken as '*weall*', but did not discuss the other two.[73] By the later twentieth century, however, there had been a small but significant shift in the scholarship. Silvester, in his survey of the landscape history of the Norfolk silt fens, noted that the possibility of 'the survival of a Celtic-speaking community, cannot entirely be dismissed'.[74] A few years later Hall and Coles were more definitive in concluding that 'a more likely explanation of the name forms, in view of the Roman activity in the area, is from the Anglo-Saxon *w(e)alh*'.[75] Some limited support for that view has come from Gelling and Cole, who suggested that *Walepol* 'indicates the gen[itive] pl[ural] of *Walh*' 'Britons'', although they did not comment on Walsoken or West Walton.[76]

If there is doubt that these place-names are based on *-wealh*, how reasonable is it that instead they include *weall*, 'wall', as Smith suggested? The 'wall' in question is generally accepted to be the Sea (sometimes called 'Roman') Bank, a substantial, continuous earthwork around the shore of the Wash that protects inland settlements and fields from marine flooding (Fig. 3.6).[77] The argument that there 'must have been' a pre-Conquest earthwork of some size *because* the place-name means 'wall' is circular and should be dismissed. If it was built after the settlements were founded or named, then the Sea Bank cannot have given its name to them; conversely, if it predates the settlements then they may have been named from it. It is, then, important to establish the period in which the Sea Bank was constructed.

FIGURE 3.6. The Sea Bank between West Walton and Walpole St Peter. The road runs along the top of the Bank which, when it was constructed, separated coastal salt marshes (on the right of the photograph) from reclaimed arable land (on the left) and protected the latter from floods from the sea (© Susan Oosthuizen).

Until the end of the ninth century, there were no defences against the sea around the Wash, and most arable fields on the eastern silt fens were regularly subject to marine flooding. In the mid-tenth century separate, small-scale systems of drains and sluices were dug in each, administratively distinct, community to keep the sea water out. Their upcast formed low banks around each group of fields, but were not linked a continuous earthwork around the Wash. The Sea Bank was appears to have been constructed no earlier than the mid-eleventh century. It connected and significantly heightened the earlier, separate, sets of low, tenth-century banks previously constructed in each community to create the first unbroken, regional barrier against the sea.[78] There were, furthermore, large permanent settlements in all three communities by the mid seventh century, and the Sea Bank respects those earlier landscapes: it was constructed around existing middle Anglo-Saxon fields at West Walton, and overlies a middle Anglo-Saxon settlement at Tilney.[79] The earliest references to Walsoken (974) and Walpole (1016) were recorded at least half a century before the Sea Bank was built. The archaeological evidence extends that gap, and Dr Owen added a further argument, suggesting that 'the normal [Anglo-Saxon] term for a sea bank was *dic'* (dyke) rather than 'wall', so – if Walsoken, Walpole and Walton really were named from the Sea Bank – they should have been called *Dic-sōcn, Dic-pōl* and *Dic-tūn*.[80] Place-name and archaeological evidence indicates that the three settlements were well-established long before the Sea Bank was built, and it seems unlikely that any of them was named from it. In that case, their shared place-name element seems most likely to be *wealh*, a conclusion that, combined with their cohesive geography, may mean that they represent an early Anglo-Saxon territory whose origins were identified with the traditions of Roman Britain.

Conclusion

Where does a survey of the surviving place-names of the region leave the question of the cultural background of early medieval fen communities? Speakers of Brittonic, Late Spoken Latin and Old English appear to have been relatively uniformly distributed across the fen basin from the early middle ages until, perhaps, the eleventh century. Most were, moreover, communities who defined themselves in terms of their locality (a topic to which the next chapter returns): The *hæfer-ingas* were the people who were settled on the 'higher ground' of the silt fens around Quadring (Lincolnshire); the *clenc-wara* were those who held rights over higher ground at Clenchwarton (Norfolk). There is no indication in the distribution of the place-names that the region was divided between groups speaking different languages.

Those observations suggest that fen place-names simply record which language was most useful in a particular place at the particular moment in which the name was coined, most people being able to speak Old English and at least one of the other languages of Roman Britain. The possibility is consistent with recent research suggesting that bilingualism was common across much of southern Britain during the Anglo-Saxon period.[81] That should not be surprising, since being able to speak two or more languages is a social strength. An individual able to converse with another in his/her native tongue has considerable advantages over a person able to speak just one language – in making and reinforcing social relationships, and in having the flexibility to adjust his/her social identity to each of the many specific contexts that make up daily life. The place-name evidence from the early medieval fenland indicates that the attribution of cultural background may have been similarly blurred for individuals who were able – perhaps even as late as the eleventh century - to switch from one language to another depending on who they were talking to and the context in which the conversation took place.

That conclusion brings us back to the question with which this chapter began: whether these communities were primarily Romano-British or 'Anglo-Saxon', or an admixture. There are three models through which such evidence might be explained. The first, favoured here, follows archaeologists and geneticists in suggesting that most 'Anglo-Saxons' across the basin were the descendants of late Romano-Britons, among whom incomers from north-west Europe had been assimilated, and who had collectively adopted artifacts made in new forms, materials and styles within a generation of the removal of Roman administration from Britain. It has the advantage of simplicity, since it is based on three assumptions, discussed both in the *Prologue* and above, each of which has a reasonable degree of support: demographic continuity from Roman into Anglo-Saxon England (confirmed by genetic studies); uninterrupted agricultural activity across the period in which the migrations are supposed to have taken place (confirmed by pollen analysis and by the lack of evidence for woodland regeneration); and assimilation of incomers into existing communities (confirmed by genetic and isotopic research, and by the impossibility of distinguishing between 'Romano-British' and 'Anglo-Saxon' communities in archaeological evidence).

The two other possible models – political and social dominance of late British communities by speakers of Old English, or vice versa – are not only based on four flawed assumptions (discussed in the *Prologue* and above), but also require more complicated explanations. The assumptions are, first, that people arriving from north-west Europe shared a common language when they did not; second, that an individual's genetic descent can be identified through the language s/he speaks; the third is that such immigrants refused to speak anything other than their mother tongue, or variants of it; and the fourth is that the ubiquity of 'Anglo-Saxon' artifacts reveals their refusal to use anything that was not Germanic in origin. In other words, they assume that Old English place-names record the locations of 'Anglo-Saxon' colonists; and the widespread adoption of their material culture is evidence for their political dominance, social exclusivity, and cultural intransigence. Explanations for how those conditions were achieved are complicated. There have been suggestions, for example, that Old English was the language of the elite, or that 'Anglo-Saxons' and Romano-Britons were so formally separated in physical terms that all access to livelihoods and influence depended on being able to speak Old English.[82] These models need also to overcome the serious objection that there is no contemporary evidence for them.

The principle of Occam's razor – that the explanation that requires the fewest assumptions is most likely to be the most reliable – offers a useful way through the morass. That explanation was, as we have seen, suggested by Taylor in 1973: the rapid adoption of north-west European cultural forms seen in the archaeology of the fifth and sixth centuries reflected social choices made by largely indigenous communities, and the increase in the number of Old English place-names was evidence of a growing bilingualism.[83] In other words, fenland continued to be occupied throughout the Anglo-Saxon period by communities whose ancestors could largely be traced into British prehistory, and among whom smaller and larger groups of incomers had, across most millennia, been assimilated.

Notes

1. For examples, see Arnold 1988, 165, and Roberts and Wrathmell 2002, 76.
2. Pohl 1997, 25; see also Ravenstein 1885; Burmeister 2000; Brugman 2011; Oosthuizen 2016c, 202–204.
3. *E.g.* Hills 2011; Goffart 2006; Pohl 1997.
4. Lucy and Reynolds 2002, 10; see also Brather 2005.
5. Leslie *et al.* 2015; Schiffels *et al.* 2016; see *Prologue* for a more extended discussion of the DNA results.
6. Tristram 2007; Schrijver 2013, 33–34, 48.
7. Gelling 1974, 66–85.
8. Reaney 1935, 544–45; Baker 2006, 173–81; Charles-Edwards 2013, 75.
9. Gelling 1974, 85.
10. Smith 1980, 33, 36; Higgitt 2006, 64.
11. Reaney 1943, 73–74. See also Gelling 1974, 88; Coates 2006, 336; Higgitt 2006, 64.
12. Nash Briggs 2011, 86–87 and 99.
13. Hall 2012, 124–25.
14. *Bede* IV, 19.
15. Reaney 1943, xxx.
16. Dr Alex Woolf, personal communication.
17. Reaney 1943, 237.
18. Reaney 1943, xviii, 253; Hart 1966, 46.
19. Dodgshon 1966, 2; Gelling 2010, 1015.
20. Reaney 1943, 252, 239–40.
21. Roffe 2005, 282; Green 2012, 170; *KEPN*.
22. Roffe 2005, 282; Green 2012, 170; *KEPN*.
23. Reaney 1943, 271.
24. Reaney 1943, 30, 271, 252.
25. See Reaney 1943, xxx.
26. Cited in Darby 1974, 8.
27. Taylor 1973, 50–52.
28. *Guthlac* XXXIV.
29. *Guthlac* XXXIV.
30. Gray 1911; PASE; Gelling 1974, 89; Charles-Edwards 2013, 75; Dumville 1985.
31. Tristram 2007.
32. Whitelock 1979, 658; Gray 1911.
33. Gray 1911; Brady 2010, 681.
34. Gray 1911; Brady 2010, 681.
35. Instituto Cervantes, *El Español, Una Lengua Viva*, cited in Burgen 2015.
36. 'Belgium', European Federation of National Institutions for Language, http://www.efnil.org/projects/lle/belgium/belgium (accessed 21 March 2017).
37. *Guthlac*, XXIV; Ekwall 1928; Reaney 1943, 6.
38. Smith 1980, 36–37; Reaney 1943, 6.
39. Reaney 1943, 75–76; Gelling 1992, 82; Smith 1980, 36–37.
40. Green 2012, 178, 182.
41. Ekwall 1928, 313–17; Reaney 1943, 11–14.
42. Ekwall 1928, 313–17; Reaney 1943, 11–14.
43. Ekwall 1928, 313–17; Reaney 1943, 11–14.
44. Ekwall 1928, 466.
45. Silvester 1991; Hall and Coles 1994.

46. Reaney 1943, xxx, 12–13, 291–2; translated by Miller as Wysenniye, *ECB* f.33r(2).
47. Mills 2011.
48. Ekwall 1928, 288–300; Coates and Breeze 2000, 366; Mills 2011.
49. Reaney 1943, 9–10 and 226.
50. Reaney 1943, xix, 247–48, 217; Schram 1950, 430; see Coates 2005 for an alternative interpretation for Chatteris.
51. Schram 1950, 430.
52. Coates and Breeze 2000; Green 2012, 178; Reaney 1943, 283–84 offers an OE interpretation of Tydd.
53. Reaney 1943, 228; Smith 1956, ii, 61–62.
54. Parsons 2011, 125; see also Reaney 1943, 260; Baker 2006, 173–81.
55. Green 2012, 178.
56. Gelling 1974, 89; Charles-Edwards 2013, 75.
57. Green 2012, 178.
58. Reaney 1943, 218; Penn 2005, 298.
59. Charles-Edwards 2013; see also Faull 1975, 25.
60. Faull 1975, 35.
61. Gray 1911; Faull 1975, 35; Cameron 1979–80, 5; PASE.
62. Whitelock 1979, 403, my addition.
63. Cameron 1979–80, 5; Faith 1997, 32; 2004, 76.
64. Faith 1997, 32–34; Faith 2012.
65. Reaney 1943, 218.
66. Hart 1966, 79 and 241; PASE; *KEPN*.
67. e-Sawyer S798; e-Sawyer S1030.
68. e-Sawyer S1051; PASE; Hart 1966, 214; *LE* II, 75; Gelling and Cole 2000, 28; Fairweather 2005, 172.
69. *DB* Norfolk 15,4; 8,21; 20,4; 66,21; *KEPN*.
70. *E.g.* Rackham 1987, 158; Bassett 1997; Faith 1997, 11–14; Aston and Gerrard 2013, 135–39.
71. Faith 1997, 32–34; Lavelle 2003, 69–71
72. Smith 1956, ii, 244; Cameron 1979–80.
73. Faull 1975, 32.
74. Silvester 1985, 108.
75. Hall and Coles 1994, 127.
76. Gelling and Cole 2000, 28, my additions.
77. First recorded in 1221 (Reaney 1943, 206–207).
78. Silvester 1988, 160; Penn 2005, 295.
79. Silvester 1988, 76, 84, 92; Hall and Coles 1994, 126–28; Crowson *et al.* 2005, 204–205; Penn 2005, 295. See Owen 1984, 47, for similar arguments concerning the Sea Bank along the coast of Holland, Lincolnshire.
80. Cited in Silvester 1988, 160, my addition.
81. *E.g.* Tristram 2007; Schrijver 2013, 15–72.
82. *E.g.* Scull 1993; Tristram 2007; Härke 2011.
83. Taylor 1973, 50–52.

CHAPTER 4

Brigands and Bandits?

Previous chapters have argued that the early and middle Anglo-Saxon fenland landscape cannot have been as lonely and as haunted by 'manifold horrors' as St Felix suggested. Instead, the evidence of place-names and archaeology indicates a region full of people. How were these communities organised? Darby, the first modern historian to consider this question, believed that there had been a dramatic fall in the population of the region in the 200 or so years following the withdrawal of Roman administration in the early fifth century. The 'marshy wastes' of the basin now became, he argued, a permanent, natural barrier between the emerging kingdoms of Mercia and East Anglia.[1] Since the wetlands were incapable of supporting arable fields and the potential for arable cultivation on the islands was limited, he assumed that the region as a whole was of little interest to early Anglo-Saxon settlers. He concluded that fenland remained unoccupied, uncultivated and unexploited except for lawless 'brigands and bandits' for whom isolation offered an attractive refuge.[2]

As earlier chapters have shown, the assumptions underlying Darby's attractively colourful characterisation were mistaken. Yet persistent settlement does not necessarily imply the presence of, let alone continuity in, formal structures of governance, so he may have been right, albeit for other reasons than those he cited. What, then, were the political conditions within which early medieval fen communities lived? *Was* the region an anarchic wilderness inhabited only by bands of outlaws and solitary hermits, or is there instead evidence of communities living within continuous, stable political territories? This chapter explores those questions through two principal sources: the geography of rights of common across the region which demonstrate its subdivision between territories, each controlling access to a specific area of fen grazing; and through early documents, especially the Tribal Hidage, a (probably) late seventh-century tribute list that names early polities across much of England. It draws two conclusions: first, that by about 700 the fringes of the region were, and had for a considerable time already been, controlled by a number of small, but stable, political units of varying scales who shared similar characteristics in the ways that they identified themselves and very governed; and second, that there is a *lacuna* in the evidence for governance of the central and southern fenland.

The evidence of common rights

Neilson was the first to grasp the significance of rights of common, recorded for the first time in the middle ages, for the history of political organisation in the early Anglo-Saxon fenland. She noticed that clusters of vills, forming cohesive geographic units, intercommoned in discrete areas of the fen and that each was also a distinct administrative unit.[3] Figure 4.1 maps those rights of common as 'pins': the head of each 'pin' represents a medieval vill (essentially, a named community), and the sharp end of the 'pin' the area in which men of that vill had rights of common grazing. Each group of 'pins' is focused on a separate, identifiable area of fen common. Vills on the silt fens of south Lincolnshire in the Wapentake of Elloe, also called south Holland, for instance, had exclusive rights to common in Great Postland and South Holland Fens (Lincolnshire); only men from vills in the two Northamptonshire hundreds of Nassaburgh had rights to common in Borough Fen.[4]

Neilson also noticed that the organisation and management of the fen pastures belonging to each group of intercommoning vills were based on the same characteristic principles (see *Prologue*):

- Boundaries of manorial holdings were invisible in the geography of each group of intercommoning vills. Some manors straddled two or more groups, and/or some groups contained a number of manors, yet this was not reflected in the organisation of each group of intercommoning vills;
- Rights of common were legally-recognised property rights; this meant that the governance, management and regulation of each area of fen common was enforceable in law;
- Each common was collectively governed by a court made up of all those with rights of common in it, whose powers of governance, justice and taxation took precedence over manorial courts;
- All commoners, regardless of status – whether they were tenants or manorial lords – had equal rights in the governance and exploitation of their commons; this meant that lords were as susceptible as any other commoner to challenge for breach of the regulations governing a common.
- Rights of common were attached to ancient land holdings.[5]

She drew two important conclusions from this evidence, both still accepted today. First, that the focused geography of each group of vills, their rights of common in specific fen pastures, the legal status of their rights of common, the primacy of courts of the commons over manorial courts, the invisibility of manorial holdings in the organisation of an intercommon, and the equity between holders of rights of common even when they stood at opposite ends of the social scale, all suggested that the origins of common rights not only predated the emergence of manor but preserved early Anglo-Saxon polities.[6] The origin of these 'ancient administrative arrangements', she suggested, lay in 'time out of mind', a period so distant that it went back at least 'to the early days of settlement' in the fifth or sixth centuries.[7]

FIGURE 4.I.
Intercommons in the
medieval fenland:
the head of each pin
shows the location of a
settlement, and the sharp
end the fens in which
its men intercommoned
with those of other
vills in their group.
The map reveals how
intercommoning
communities formed
geographic clusters, each
with their own, exclusive
areas of fen pasture
(© Susan Oosthuizen,
after Neilson 1920).

Neilson's second conclusion also formed subsequent scholarship. Noting the close relationship between clusters of intercommoning vills and pre-conquest units of public administration like hundreds, or commoners' courts, she suggested that the identity of early medieval folk groups was based on their rights to and governance of shared non-arable resources rather than on lordship or kingship.[8] It was not unusual for stretches of open or wood pasture to be so important to early Anglo-Saxon folk groups that they named themselves from them. The fens from whom the *Gyrwe* (see below) took their name covered large areas that later belonged to the Abbeys of Peterborough and Crowland; fragments of the *feld* (more like African *veld* than an English 'field') belonging to the *Hæslingas* at Haslingfield were preserved in the nineteenth-century Offals, the 'old *feld*', of the land-units into which their territory had by then been sub-divided.[9] Half a century later, Davies and Vierck built on her work in suggesting that 'it is groups and associations of people that form the raw material of early political development, not the carving up of territory.'[10] Twenty-five years later still, Faith explained that 'one of the shaping influences in the formation of early land-units was their rights to grazing';[11] in the same year Lewis, Dyer and Mitchell-Fox were unequivocal that 'local communities were fundamentally defined by their shared rights in the territory that they occupied'.[12] Fowler concluded in 2002 that for 'much of the [first millennium AD] it seems that pasture was defined as much by the right to feed animals over certain areas of land as by definitions of land itself', while Roberts wrote in 2008 that 'at first [commons] were shared by the whole territory of the shire, but were gradually appropriated to individual parishes or townships. The question is not of the presence of manors or estates in early Anglo-Saxon times, but of the emergence of rights in land and rights over land'.[13] Examples of those generalities can be found in the moors, woods or pastures from Devon to Northumberland in which freemen from whole shires had rights of common.[14]

Territories were thus defined in terms of the groups of individuals who held property rights in them, of which the most significant were their rights of common property in a polity's shared resources. Rights of common property connect an individual with other land holders across the largest area in which he has such rights. The territorial ambitions of a man who only has rights of common in a pasture in his own community are more limited, for example, than those of an individual whose rights of common lie in a resource shared by men from an area as large as a hundred or a kingdom. The significance of Neilson's map of clusters of intercommoning vills is thus that it provides a proxy for the political organisation of the early Anglo-Saxon fenland. A document called the Tribal Hidage adds a little more detail.

The Tribal Hidage, and other sources

The Tribal Hidage is the earliest surviving, and most extensive, post-Roman document to describe the early medieval political geography of central and

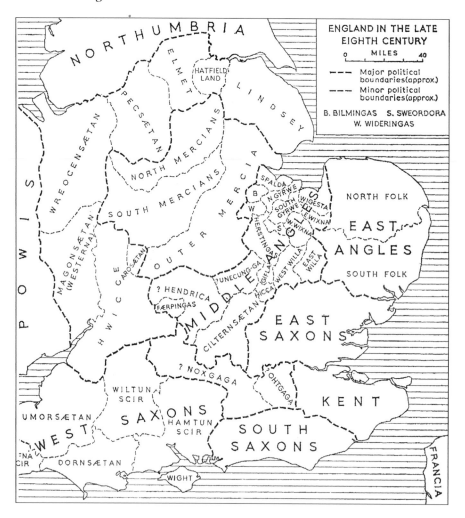

FIGURE 4.2. The Tribal Hidage conjecturally mapped across central, southern and eastern England by Dr C. R. Hart in 1971 (© Royal Historical Society and Cambridge University Press, reproduced with permission).

southern England in any detail (Figure 4.2).[15] It appears to be a late seventh-century list of kingdoms and smaller territories that includes the number of hides at which each was valued. Despite its detail, the objectives behind the compilation of the Tribal Hidage remain opaque; its provenance and even the period of its origin are, too, the subject of debate. There is a tremulous consensus that it describes those territories south of the Humber that owed fealty or paid tribute to one of the major Anglo-Saxon kingdoms, most likely Mercia or Northumbria, and that it was probably compiled between the seventh and eighth centuries. If the purpose of the Tribal Hidage was to note tribute and/or fealty then those who commissioned it had every reason to wish it to be comprehensive. Yet it was not a definitive list. Other sources, either contemporary with it or recording events of its general period, document other territories that, for one reason or another, it omitted. The venerable Bede, writing in around 731, for instance, described polities like the province of Ely (*regione quae vocatur Elge*) that was not in the Tribal Hidage.[16] And St Felix's

Life of St Guthlac, written in the 730s or 740s, mentioned 'the kingdom of the *Wisse*' (*in provincia Wisse*) which was also left out.[17]

There are a number of other problems with the Tribal Hidage. First is the notable imbalance between big players like Mercia (assessed at 30,000 hides), Wessex (assessed at 100,000 hides) and East Anglia (assessed at 30,000 hides); middle-ranking kingdoms like the *Lindes-farona* (assessed at 7000 hides), the south Saxons (assessed at 7000 hides), and the *Chilternsætene* (assessed at 4000 hides); and a number of smaller territories assessed at between 300 and 600 hides, like the *Spalde* (assessed at 600 hides), the North and South *Gyrwe* (each assessed at 600 hides), the West and East *Wixna* (assessed at 600 and 300 hides respectively) and the West and East *Willa* (also assessed at 600 hides each). Scholars generally agree that many of the smaller polities, of different sizes and more fragmented than anywhere else in England, appear to have been located around the fen basin.[18] Dumville offered two possible explanations for this apparent geographic and political anomaly.[19] First, he proposed, perhaps there simply *were* more small units around and within fenland than elsewhere in late seventh-century England, having not yet coalesced or been absorbed into one of the Anglo-Saxon kingdoms then in the ascendant; or second, perhaps the compiler was more familiar with the fen basin and thus able to describe in more detail the minor polities that were sub-units of the larger kingdoms. Others have suggested a third explanation: that these small polities together formed the principality of the Middle Angles, a sub-region of Mercia that had been established some time before 653, and, for some unknown reason, the author of the Tribal Hidage preferred to list these constituent communities one by one rather than include them under a single heading.[20] On balance, opinion generally veers towards the first explanation, that is, that the region, disputed between East Anglia and Mercia, had yet to come firmly under the control of either. By the late seventh century it remained 'an agglomeration of formerly independent peoples of very varying sizes and relative importance', perhaps offering an insight into the vestiges of an earlier political landscape that had by that time almost disappeared from other parts of England.[21]

A second problem with the Tribal Hidage is that it is a good example of that historical truism, a snapshot in time. Place-names and other evidence for England between about 400 and 700 show that, over that period, kingdoms of all sizes appeared and disappeared, expanded and contracted, absorbed their neighbours and/or were assimilated into – perhaps even partitioned between – them. Some, once dominant across a small or wider region, may already have arrived, flourished and disappeared by the time that the Tribal Hidage was written while others were still in the ascendant. In fenland, some of these polities are recorded in place-names that include the *-ingas* ('a folk or clan group') suffix discussed in the previous chapter. The wider history of many is invisible today. All we can say is that they existed at some time between about 400 and 800, that they may have been too insignificant to feature in the Tribal Hidage and paid their tribute through one of the larger groupings it listed, or that they had already disappeared by the time it was compiled. We have no idea whether the Tribal Hidage records the majority or the minority of those territories that existed in the period in which it was drawn up, or even whether those on its list were representative of the range of political groupings at the time.

A third problem lies in how to describe the hierarchy of such political units, partly because the precise meaning of many of the words Bede and others used to differentiate between them has been lost, and partly because our perceptions of kings and kingdoms may be very different from those of the fifth, sixth and seventh centuries.[22] Some – like the kingdoms of Wessex, Kent, Northumbria or East Anglia – were large and powerful by the later seventh century. Others, ruled by princes, appear to have been self-governing units that nonetheless owed some form of fealty to the larger, more established kingdoms. Yet others were small, sometimes very small; many appear to have been too small to have a king, being subordinate in some way to territories that did, but still independent enough to be assessed on their own. Of yet others we know nothing more than their name. Whatever the character of their rulers, whether kings, princes or other leaders, the political identity of each territory was defined in terms of the shared property rights held in its resources by all its free inhabitants, the 'folk' who rationalized their collective identity in terms of (a claimed) shared descent from a common ancestor. To paraphrase Faith, kings ruled the people – they did not rule the land.[23]

The sixth- and seventh-century political geography of the fen-edge

Despite Roffe's view that 'on its own the Tribal Hidage is just a series of names… Pushing the names around on a map is of little help', historians have consistently explored the possibilities inherent in place-names and documentary evidence for locating the political groupings it listed.[24] There is now sufficient consensus among them for the location and extent of many – but not all – of those polities to be described with reasonable certainty.[25] This chapter builds on that work to describe the early and middle Anglo-Saxon political geography around the upland edges of fenland. It outlines that political landscape in an anti-clockwise direction, beginning on the Lincolnshire silt fens in the north-west, then moving respectively around the western, southern and eastern borders of the basin, before heading north towards the Norfolk silt fens that lay along the south-eastern shores of the Wash. Patterns of intercommoning across the basin appear to offer a close overlap with evidence drawn from documents and place-names which, in a number of cases, appear to indicate that the origins of these polities might be sought in the fifth or sixth centuries, or even earlier (Fig. 4.3).[26]

The Spalde

The territory of the *Spalde* ('dwellers by the drain') is conventionally identified with the region around the town of Spalding on the Lincolnshire silt fens. Although the name is Old English, the their polity formed the southern part of

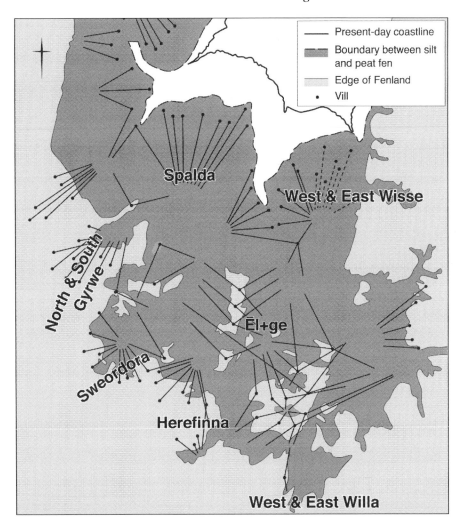

Present-day coastline
Boundary between silt and peat fen
Edge of Fenland
• Vill

Spalda

West & East Wisse

North & South Gyrwe

Ēl+ge

Sweordora

Herefinna

West & East Willa

FIGURE 4.3. A conjectural reconstruction of seventh-century folk territories across the fen region (© Susan Oosthuizen, after Neilson 1920).

a larger unit called Holland (**haiw-*, 'lake, swamp'), a late Brittonic territorial name that hints at ancient, at very least late Romano-British, origins and that also survives into the present.[27] Whether speakers of Brittonic or of Old English, the early medieval communities that made up the territory defined themselves in terms of their local geography – both names describe the fenny topography of the district; the 'drain' may refer to the rivers Welland and Glen at whose ancient confluence Spalding is located.[28] The territorial boundaries of the *Spalde* are believed to have followed those of the medieval Wapentake (hundred) of Elloe: they ran from salt marsh in the east, on the Wash's western shores, to a wide band of peat fen on the west that divided it from the Lincolnshire mainland. Their southern boundary was marked by drains that may have been maintained since the Roman period, establishing the southern limits of Great Postland and South Holland peat fens in which the men of south Holland held exclusive rights of common grazing (see Fig. 5.6).[29]

The Gyrwe

Darby, in a summary of the middle Anglo-Saxon evidence whose clarity has yet to be bettered, concluded that by about 600 the territory of the *Gyrwe* ('the fen') was located along the eastern Northamptonshire uplands to the north and south of Peterborough, extending just a short distance into the fen basin.[30] Bede provided helpful evidence for their location, recording in 731 that the monastery of *Medehamstede* (modern Peterborough, Northamptonshire) lay *in regione Gyruiorum*, 'in the independent, self-governing province of the *Gyrwe*' – solidly locating the territory along the western fen-edge.[31] His statement was confirmed by an entry for Crowland Abbey (Lincolnshire) in late ninth-century lists of saints' burial places which noted that it lay *in middan Girwan fænnen*, 'in the middle of the fen belonging to the *Gyrwe*', on the north-west edge of the fen basin.[32]

The mid-seventh-century grant of their territory to endow the royal Mercian monastic house implies that the zenith of the *Gyrwe* was already past by 653, and should perhaps be sought in the sixth century or before.[33] That decline is reflected in Bede's uncertainty in 731 about how to describe them. On the one hand, he noted that a churchman called Thomas, who was consecrated Bishop of East Anglia in 647–48, had come from the *kingdom* of the *Gyrwe* (*de provincia Gyruiorum*).[34] On the other hand, in recording the monastery's foundation in 653, just a few years later, Bede said that the abbey was established *in regione Gyruiorum*, 'the *province* of the *Gyrwe*'.[35] That impression of growing subordination to Mercia is strengthened by the absence of any reference to a king in the early sources. Bede, for instance, described Tondberht, who married the East Anglian princess Æthelthryth around 652, as *princeps* rather than *rex* (king) of the South *Gyrwe*, a title which contemporaries translated as 'ealdorman' (perhaps most similar to medieval conceptions of a duke).[36] By the mid-seventh century at the latest, it seems, the glory days of the *Gyrwe* already lay in the past.[37]

Like others in the region, the *Gyrwe* named themselves from the country that they lived in. In the twelfth century, the Peterborough chronicler Hugh *candidus* explained 'these men are called *Gyrwas* who dwell in the fen, or hard by the fen, since a deep bog [*palus profunda*] is called in the Saxon tongue *gyr*'.[38] That interpretation of their name appears to have been derived from Ælfric's grammar which, with satisfying coincidence, glosses Latin *palus*, 'marsh, swamp', as *gyrwefen*, a suggestion followed by modern scholars.[39] Although the polity had already been subdivided between the North and South *Gyrwe* by the time they were listed in the Tribal Hidage, the territories of each can be reconstructed.

The boundaries of the province of the North *Gyrwe* have been preserved in those of the two hundreds of Nassaburgh, coterminous with the Soke of Peterborough, and bounded by the rivers Nene in the south, the Welland in the north, and the canal called Catswater (*Must*) running along its eastern fen-edge.[40] Rights to intercommon in Borough Fen were exclusively held by men from these vills. Hart has argued that the boundaries of the South *Gyrwe* followed the Nene to the north, (perhaps) the Roman road called Ermine Street to the west, and to the south a stream called the '*seaxa broc*' (almost certainly the Holme Brook) that flowed eastward from Ermine Street towards the fen.[41] The fen-ward end of the brook was identified with the southern boundary of the *Gyrwe* in a charter of 957 which recorded that the northern boundary of an estate at Conington, Huntingdonshire, ran '*long broces on gyruwan fen*', along the brook to the *Gyrwan* fen.[42] There is, once more, a strong correlation between those boundaries and rights to a shallow area of wetland between the fen-edge and Whittlesey Mere listed in a charter for Stanground, Yaxley and Farcet in 956.[43]

The Sweord ora

A name that may place the territory of the *Sweord ora* on the south-western fen edge survives in Sword Point (*Swerord*), recorded in the foundation charter of Sawtry Abbey in 1146.[44] Like many of the other fenland polities discussed here, the most important identifier of their political identity was the landscape they occupied: their name is a precise description of Sword Point – *sweora*, 'neck', and *ord*, 'a point in the landscape' – which lies at the tip of a narrow strip of land driving into the south side of Whittlesey Mere, at the interface between fen and upland. [45] The possibility that their influence extended north of Whittlesey Mere is hinted at in the thirteenth-century name of Swerds (or Swords) Delf as an alternative for the King's Delph (972, *Cynges dælf*), an artificial course of the Nene running from west to east immediately south of Whittlesey.[46]

The landward extent of their territory can be inferred from that charter of 957 mentioned above, for a large estate at Conington.[47] Hart has argued that the Conington estate included Holme (in which Sword Point now lies), and Glatton; the rights of men from Woodwalton to intercommon in the same fens with Glatton and Conington suggests that that vill, too, should be included.[48] There is thus a solid coincidence between the area identified as the folk-country of the *Sweord ora* by Hart, and intercommons exclusively exploited by the same vills along the south-west fen-edge that were mapped by Neilson.[49]

The Herefinna/Hyrstingas

The identification of the *Herefinna* of the Tribal Hidage with the *Hyrstingas*, whose territory is preserved in the name of the Huntingdonshire double hundred of Hurstingstone, is long standing (Fig. 4.4).[50] Like the *Gyrwe* and the *Sweord ora*, the defining attribute of their political identity was not cultural but economic – they took their name from the wooded uplands that they occupied along the south-western fen-edge, many of whose vills have names describing a complex mosaic of wood- and grassland. They range from true woods (*hyrsts*) at Woodhurst (1209, *Wdeherst*), Warboys (1077, *Wærdebusc*), and Old Hurst (1227, *Waldhirst*), to wolds (*wald*), and wood pastures (*lēah*) like those at Pidley (1228, *Pydele*), Raveley (*c.*1060, *Ræflea*) and Stukeley (1086, *Stivecle*).[51] Although

FIGURE 4.4. The 'Abbot's Chair' or Hursting Stone marked the place where Hurstingstone hundred court met (© Norris Museum and St Ives Town Council, reproduced with permission). It stood on Hurstingstone Hill where the southern parish boundary of Old Hurst crossed the road to St Ives (now under Wyton airfield) (VCH Hunts. III, 149). The hundred court is believed to be a medieval reformulation of assemblies of the Herefinna/Hyrstingas. The stone is actually the base of a medieval cross.

predominantly focused on the uplands to the south of the fen-edge, the hundred boundaries extend into the fen as far north as the old course of the river Nene and as far east as the old course of the river Ouse, an area across which men from Ramsey in the west to those from the soke of Somersham in the east had exclusive rights of intercommon. [52] Here, once more, landscape and rights of common coincide in a definition of territory.

The West and East Willa

There are two groupings in the Tribal Hidage about whose location there is still controversy: the *Willa* and the *Wixna*. Ekwall placed the West and East *Willa* in upland Cambridgeshire south of the fen basin, on either side of the river Granta/Cam.[53] He was supported almost half a century later by Hart who argued in addition that the name of the *Willa* is preserved in that of the Old Well Stream, called *Wellenhe* in 1249–50.[54] Ekwall and Hart's proposition has received some cautious support though it remains controversial, since others prefer to locate the *Willa* around Ely in the southern peat fens.[55]

In the early medieval period, as today, the Old Well Stream was the principal natural watercourse flowing through the fens to the east of the Isle of Ely (Fig. 4.5). Today its modern outfall is at King's Lynn; until the high middle ages, though, it reached the sea at Wisbech. At that time it carried the waters of the river Granta/Cam catchment as well as of the rivers Lark, Little Ouse and Wissey, although there is some doubt about whether it then received any water from the Great Ouse along a course to the south of the Isle of Ely now called the West Water.[56] (At that time, the Ouse ran in a generally more north-westerly direction from its entrance into the fen basin to join the Nene at Benwick; the

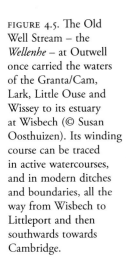

FIGURE 4.5. The Old Well Stream – the *Wellenhe* – at Outwell once carried the waters of the Granta/Cam, Lark, Little Ouse and Wissey to its estuary at Wisbech (© Susan Oosthuizen). Its winding course can be traced in active watercourses, and in modern ditches and boundaries, all the way from Wisbech to Littleport and then southwards towards Cambridge.

conjoined stream then flowed northwards to Wisbech to the west of Doddington and March).[57] The Granta and *Wellenhe* may simply have been different names for the same watercourse, one Brittonic and the other Old English in origin, and may have been applied to different sections of the same river. If that is the case, then it is just possible that the territory of the *Willa* might be identified with that of a late Romano-British polity called the *Grantasæte* (1086) who controlled the upland catchment of the river Granta/Cam, in the same way that the territory of Romano-British Holland in Lincolnshire was renamed as Old English *Spalde*.[58] That remains speculation, however, and there is little evidence to support any identification for the location of the *Willa*.

The Wigesta

Hart identified the *Wigesta* in the Tribal Hidage with the area now occupied by the four Wiggenhalls (St Germans, St Peter, St Mary Magdalene, St Mary the Virgin) but there is no evidence one way or another to support his suggestion.[59] *Wigrehala* (personal name, and *halh*, 'dry ground in marsh' or 'a piece of land projecting from, or detached from, its administrative centre') was first documented in 1086.[60] The archaeological evidence for early settlement is weak, being dominated by medieval and post-medieval material. There was a scatter of Ipswich ware along a watercourse in Wiggenhall St Mary the Virgin and another in St Germans; but even late Anglo-Saxon settlement is only apparent in St Germans.[61] More significantly, despite their proximity to fen grazing governed by the leet of Marshland (discussed below), the Wiggenhalls were not included within the leet and were excluded from intercommoning on its extensive pastures.[62] It is possible that this may have been because they had settled on land that had previously been subject to rights of common. If that were the case the law of assart would apply: no rights of common would be available to them because the land on which they had settled was already subject to common rights which could only be claimed from ancient arable holdings, among which their own could not be included.[63] (The same argument applies to Clenchwarton.) The relatively late appearance of the Wiggenhalls in the archaeological material, and their exclusion from rights of common in the fen, make it difficult to be sure that the *Wigesta* were located here.

The East and West Wixna/Wisse

We turn now to the East and West *Wixna,* who were listed in the late seventh-century Tribal Hidage, and the *Wisse,* an folk group recorded by St Felix in the early eighth-century, who were not and about whose identity place-name scholars are most divided. The problem hinges on whether the *Wixna* are the same as the *Wisse* within whose kingdom (*provincia*) Æthelbald, later one of the greatest kings of Mercia, found safe exile between about 709 and 716 (see Fig. 3.1).[64] They appear to have lived near enough to Crowland for Æthelbald's journey to visit Guthlac to be a relatively easy one. Since the *Spalde* and *Gyrwe* occupied the areas to the north and south of Crowland, and other polities controlled areas to the west, Ekwall suggested that the *Wixna/Wisse* may have occupied the region between Wisbech and the river Wissey.[65] Once more, Hart agreed that 'there is no etymological difficulty in identifying Felix's *Wisse* with the *Wixna* of the Tribal Hidage'.[66] Both he and Reaney were sure that Wisbech and the river Wissey in west Norfolk both took their name from the *Wisse.* Reaney added the river Ouse (which then flowed out into the Wash through Wisbech) to the weight of evidence, emphatically concluding that 'Ouse and Wissey are etymologically identical'.[67] That is, he not only felt that there was more evidence for the location of the *Wisse* on the north-eastern silt fens than had previously been considered, but that their territory stretched from Wisbech to the Wissey, and along at least part of the northern stretches of the river Ouse, at that time running northwards along the western side of March. There remains some controversy about his conclusion. Davies and Vierck, for example, have suggested that the *Wixna* were located beyond East Anglia and proposed instead that the isolated 'tribal area' of the West and East *Willa* might be identified with the Isle of Ely.[68]

On the other hand, a more recent review by Roffe has returned to and extended Hart's position, not only locating the *Wisse* between Wisbech and the Wissey, but also suggesting that they constituted a sub-kingdom of the *Wixna*.[69] Penn concurred, proposing that the *Wisse* should be located between Wisbech and the west Norfolk fen edge.[70] The current position is thus that the *provincia* of the *Wisse* extended eastward along the silt fen from the mouth of the Ouse/

Nene at Wisbech to the uplands along the river Wissey in the east. The region is called Marshland today. One of its distinctive features, explored below, is the pattern of common rights held by vills along the west Norfolk silts in an enormous area of fen grazing to the south.

The 'letam integram de marisco' *of Marshland: a sub-region of the* Wixna/ Wisse?

A significant archaic survival from the early Anglo-Saxon period was recorded by thirteenth-century jurors on the Bishop of Ely's estates to the east of Wisbech, who described their administrative structure of their region as a 'leet'.[71] They called it the *letam integram de marisco*, the 'whole leet of the marsh', and it is of particular interest here since leets are administrative units, smaller than a hundred, whose origins are believed to lie in folk territories that had emerged before the seventh century.[72] Both Hart and Roffe have suggested that it may have been a sub-region within the kingdom of the *Wisse/Wixna*.[73] The leet included the silt-land vills and their fields, and a huge 12,144 ha (30,000 acre) fen pasture called Marshland, in which the men of those vills intercommoned and over which its court had rights of fiscal and judicial governance. It had been sub-divided by the thirteenth century into a larger area called West Fen, and a smaller area called the Smeeth (Fig. 4.6).[74] Decisions taken by the leet court still took precedence over the manorial courts of the Bishop of Ely and the Abbey of Ramsey in the mid-thirteenth century.[75] Of the three vills that dominated the leet – Walsoken, West Walton and Walpole (later divided between St Peter and St Andrew) – the place-name of Walsoken has a particular significance. The *-sōcn* element, first recorded in 974, is a rare, archaic survival that refers to governance of a political unit that might vary in size from a large estate to a district; a definition that looks very similar to that of a leet.[76]

The inequitable distribution among the vills of the leet of rights of common in Marshland may reveal something of the evolution of that early territory. Men in Walsoken, West Walton and the Walpoles held by far the largest proportion of common rights in the leet; those in Terrington St Clement had a much smaller share, both in numbers and in percentages, while its (later) daughter settlement, Terrington St John, had virtually none. The Tilneys together had fewer rights than Walpole St Peter, and Clenchwarton had practically none; as noted above, the Wiggenhalls were excluded altogether.[77] The proportion of grazing rights in Marshland allocated to each vill may, then, record the chronology of settlement across the eastern silt land. The dominance of Walsoken, West Walton and the Walpoles might mean that most common rights in Marshland had already been allocated by the time that the settlements at Terrington St Clement and, later, at Walpole St Andrew, had emerged in the mid-seventh century – those settlements had noticeably fewer rights of common. By the time the Tilneys, the Wiggenhalls and Clenchwarton were established, access to common rights may have been almost completely restricted. Perhaps significantly, the four vills that dominated

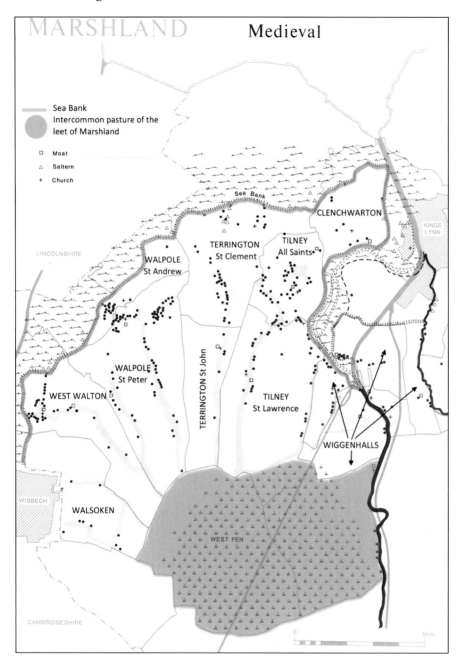

FIGURE 4.6. Marchland in the medieval period, showing finds and sites as well as the course of the Sea Bank (© Norfolk Archaeological Unit/ NPS Archaeology, with additions, reproduced with permission). Long droves (stippled) led from middle Anglo-Saxon settlements near the sites of later churches to their fen intercommons now subdivided between West Fen and the Smeeth.

collective exploitation and governance of Marshland were also those in which there is the earliest evidence of large-scale, permanent post-Roman settlement.[78] There were two large middle Anglo-Saxon settlements at Walpole St Peter, and a further two at West Walton; another at Terrington St Clement extended over more than 7 ha (17.2 acres) and was one of the largest in the region.[79] The vills that were almost completely excluded from commoning on Marshland are those in which there is relatively little evidence of occupation until the tenth or eleventh centuries – the Tilneys, the Wiggenhalls and Clenchwarton.[80]

It was argued in the previous chapter that the shared first element in the place-names of Walstoken, West Walton and the Walpoles may have been *wealh*, 'an individual or a group with a Romano-British background'. That reference to Romano-British culture, the antiquity of the *-sōcn*, the contiguity of its four principal vills, and their monopolisation of common rights in Marshland may indicate that the leet was a late survival of an ancient folk territory, perhaps Romano-British in origin, that extended from the higher ground of the eastern silts over an extensive area of rich pasture still capable of supporting more than 30,000 sheep in the sixteenth century.[81]

And more…

In among the larger units that controlled the fringes of the fen basin or the extensive pastures at its heart were others about whom nothing would be known were it not that their names have been preserved in some of the place- or field names discussed in the previous chapter. It is impossible to know if their modern modesty is because they were always small, subordinate to the large polities of the kind that might be noticed in the Tribal Hidage; or because they were relatively ephemeral groups temporarily under strong leadership that flashed briefly into the limelight.

The origin of some of these names is so early that their interpretation remains enigmatic; it is not even possible to be certain which languages were used in their formation. Of these names Mepal (twelfth-century *Meahala*, 'tribal name') is one of the most significant and is generally accepted to refer to an exceptionally early political unit.[82] Another is Elm (*c*.1121, *Ælm*; thirteenth century, *Eolum*), the location of an extensive early Anglo-Saxon cemetery.[83] Reaney considered that it may have been derived from *Eolum*, 'the name of one of the Germanic peoples visited by Widsith' in the sixth century, but modern interpretations of the place-name prefer simply 'elm trees'.[84] Rights of common in Grunty Fen (1221, *Gruntifen, gruntho*, 'muddy shallow', *-ing*) by all the vills in the southern part of the island of Ely may also indicate a small folk group, but there is no other evidence to support the suggestion. This large area of fenland is almost entirely enclosed by the island of Ely, connected only by a narrow channel to the wider peat fen. The name is not believed to include the *-ingas* element, although it is possible that its first element might be derived from the river Granta.[85]

Other, more certain, folk groups in the peat fens include those discussed in the previous chapter whose names may include the *-ingas* element: the *Bilsingge* and the *Beorningas*; folk groups on the silt fens included those from which Islington, Terrington, Leverington and Quadring are derived. The place-name of Clenchwarton embodies the same concept of public land. While the form of these place-names suggests the existence of a number of small polities in the fenland between about 400 and 700, it is impossible to say whether they were contemporaries or, more likely, represent instead the emergence and disappearance of local groupings at different times in different places over several centuries. Some appear only by inference: Clark has argued, for example that the charter by which Guthlac gained his estate at Crowland alienated the territory of a small, but otherwise un-named, British polity.[86] All that can be said about it, and those others whose names we do know, is that they existed once, contributing some detail, however slight, to our knowledge of long-standing political organisation in fenland.

Conclusion

Almost all the early medieval groups that collectively exploited its wetland resources shared two striking characteristics: the names of many of their polities are drawn from the landscapes they inhabited, rather than based on their cultural or historical backgrounds. A number describe the fen wetlands along which they lived, or the names of the rivers whose regions they controlled. Locality appears to have been more important than any other consideration in describing who they were. This may be because their commonality was focused on the fen pastures that they grazed and the other resources they exploited under rights of common. If kings ruled the people rather than the land, then the people were those with rights of common in territorial resources, rights that included the collective governance of the territories to which they belonged.[87] Those rights defined both membership and boundaries of territories and were, in many cases, implicit in the names of their polities – the *Gyrwe*, the *Spalde*, the *Sweord ora* and the *Wisse* named themselves from one or another of the principal features of the marshy landscapes on which they commoned.

Their second shared characteristic was geographic: that almost all were based on the fen-edge surrounding the basin, and their rights of common extended only limited distances into the fen. Neilson's map demonstrates the same *lacuna*: if rights of intercommon in fenland indicate the extent of early medieval territories, the governance of the larger part of the central peat wetlands remains unaccounted for. More recent historians have ignored the problem by taking the opposing position: they assumed that the Tribal Hidage described a coherent political geography; that is, that there were no gaps in the list and there were thus no 'empty spaces' between the early kingdoms and principalities that it recorded.[88] The next chapter attempts to resolve this contradiction by focusing on the large area of peat-based wetlands that lay across the centre of the region. Could this have been Darby's country of brigands and bandits, or was it as carefully governed as the fen-edge territories who intercommoned around the verges of the basin?

Notes

1. Darby 1934: 185.
2. Darby 1974, 9; see also Darby 1934, 192.
3. Neilson 1920, li; see also Hallam 1963.

4. Neilson 1920, xxxiv–xxxvi.

5. Neilson 1920, v–lviii.

6. Neilson 1920, v–lviii.

7. Neilson 1920, xlix. See Oosthuizen 2013b for a lengthier discussion of the historiography.

8. Neilson 1920, li. See also Homans 1953, 39; Hoskins and Stamp 1963, 6; Miller 1951, 13.

9. Oosthuizen 2016b; 2006, 52–56.

10. Davies and Vierck 1974, 223.

11. Faith 1997, 145.

12. Lewis *et al.* 1997, 184.

13. Fowler 2002, 224; Roberts 2008, 166, my addition; see also Oosthuizen 2013b.

14. Lewis *et al.* 1997, 55.

15. *BL* Harley 3271, f.6v.

16. *Bede* IV, 19.

17. *Guthlac*, LIII.

18. Hart 1971, 134, 137; Davies and Vierck 1974; Yorke 2000, 82–85.

19. Dumville 1989, 129.

20. *Bede* III, 21; Yorke 2000, 82–85.

21. Dumville 1989, 134.

22. Bassett 1989, 4.

23. Faith 1997, 2.

24. Roffe 2005, 3–4; for identification of locations, see *e.g.* Hart 1971; Davies and Vierck 1974; Roffe 2005.

25. *E.g.* Hart 1971; Davies and Vierck 1974; Bassett 1989; Yorke 2000, 82–85; Roffe 2005.

26. See also Neilson 1920, xlix–lviii; Roffe 1993, 2005.

27. Hallam 1954, 4; Hart 1971, 144–45; 1992, 181; Green 2012, 173, 178, 182.

28. Hayes and Lane 1993; Hallam 1954, 4; *KEPN*.

29. Owen 1982; Hayes and Lane 1992, 257; 1993, 68–69.

30. Darby 1934.

31. *Bede* IV: 6; Davies and Vierck 1974, 231; Hart 1992, 143.

32. Rollason 1978, 89; Roffe 1993; Green 2012, 154.

33. *Bede* IV, 6.

34. *Bede* III, 20.

35. *Bede* IV, 6.

36. *Bede* IV, 17; Dumville 1989, 131.

37. Featherstone 2001; Kelly 2009, 3; Green 2012, 155.

38. *Pet. Chron.*, 2.

39. Insley 1999, 230–32; Schram 1950, 437.

40. Bede IV: 6; Hart 1971; 1992, 154; Kelly 2009, 97–98, and 175–77.

41. Hart 1966, 23–24.

42. e-Sawyer S649.

43. e-Sawyer S595; Neilson 1920, xxxvii–xxxviii, and end paper.

44. Mawer and Stenton 1926, 190–91; Hart 1971, 145.

45. Mawer and Stenton 1926, 190–91; Hart 1971, 145.

46. *ECB*, f. 33r(2); Mawer and Stenton 1926, 185, 190–91; also Camden 1610, 'Huntingdonshire', 6. Mawer and Stenton identified King's Delph with what is now called Oakley Dike (1926, 185). Hall, however, has suggested that it should rather be identified with the artificial course of the river Nene still called King's Delph that runs from Stanground, past the southern shores of Whittlesey, to Benwick, and that

interpretation is followed here (Hall 1987, 56). Hart and Sawyer both suggest that the date of the charter should be 972, updating Mawer and Stenton's suggested date of 963 (Hart 1966, 25; e-Sawyer S787).

47. e-Sawyer S649.
48. Hart 1966, 23–24; VCH Hunts. III, 184, 203–12.
49. Neilson 1920, xxxvii–xxxviii; Hart 1971.
50. Mawer and Stenton 1926, 203–204; VCH Hunts. III, 149; Schram 1950, 436; Hart 1971, 145.
51. Mawer and Stenton 1926, 203–30.
52. Neilson 1920, xxxviii–xxxix.
53. Ekwall 1928, 465–67.
54. Hart 1971, 153.
55. *E.g.* Davies and Vierck 1974, 234; Roffe 2005, 29, 284–85.
56. Hall 1996, 158, 160.
57. Hall 1992, 9.
58. Smith 1980, 36–37; Reaney 1943, 6.
59. *KEPN*; National Archives http://discovery.nationalarchives.gov.uk/details/r/D7299291, accessed March 2017.
60. Hart 1971, 145.
61. Silvester 1988, 100, 105, 111–12; Norfolk HER, PAS, accessed March 2017.
62. Silvester 1988, 4, 32.
63. Neilson 1920, liv.
64. *Guthlac*, LIII.
65. Ekwall 1928, 465–67; see Hayes and Lane 1993 for early Anglo-Saxon polities living west of the *Spalde*.
66. Hart 1971, 144.
67. Reaney 1943, 13–14.
68. Davies and Vierck 1974, 273, 281–84.
69. Roffe 2005, 284–85.
70. Penn 2005, 298.
71. Douglas 1927, 195ff.
72. For example, Warner 1988, 26–31; see Campbell 2005 for a dissenting view.
73. Hart 1971; Roffe 2005, 285–86.
74. Silvester 1988, 32.
75. Douglas 1927, 195.
76. Hart 1966, 79, 241; *KEPN*. Hart (1966, 241) suggests a date of 969 x 983 for Ealdorman Æthelwine's (d. 992) bequest of 5 hides at Walsoken to Ramsey Abbey.
77. Darby 1974, 67–70; Silvester 1988, 34, 157.
78. Silvester 1988, 33–34, 157; Hall and Coles 1994, 126–28.
79. Silvester 1988, 37, 76, 90.
80. Silvester 1988, 17, 49, 60, 105, 111, 157, 159.
81. Camden 1610, 'Norfolk' 15.
82. Reaney 1943, xviii, 237.
83. Cambridgeshire HER, PAS, accessed March 2017.
84. *Widsith*, line 88; Reaney 1943, 266–67; *KEPN*.
85. Reaney 1943, 231.
86. Clark 2011.
87. Faith 1997, 2.
88. *E.g.* Hart 1971; Davies and Vierck 1974; Dumville 1989; Yorke 2000; Roffe 2005.

CHAPTER 5

Ely and the Central Peat Lands

FIGURE 5.1. Thirteenth-century wall-painting in Willingham church of Æthelthryth, the East Anglian princess born at the royal vill at Exning who founded the abbey of Ely in 673 (© Susan Oosthuizen).

There is a contradiction in the evidence described so far for the early Anglo-Saxon fenland: the entire basin was well-populated, yet documentary evidence for small seventh-century kingdoms, principalities and *regiones* appears to locate them around the upland verges of the fen, and the evidence of medieval common rights suggests that their territories extended only a relatively short distance into the basin. What then of the governance of the main body of the peat wetlands that were formed the late tenth-century endowment of the Abbey of Ely? Was it also structured within a stable political unit, or was this after all an area of untamed anarchy?

The chapter begins by exploring and explaining the absence of Ely from the Tribal Hidage, concluding that there is good evidence for that it was a substantial political unit in the early seventh century, and that it had almost certainly been included in the Hidage under the overlordship of the larger kingdom of East Anglia. It moves on to attempt to identify the seventh-century boundaries of that province: from patterns of commoning, from anomalies in the tenth-century reconstruction of the estate of the newly re-founded Abbey, and through the chronological relationship between that estate and the hundreds into which it had been subdivided by the late eleventh century. It concludes that the boundaries of the early medieval province of Ely seem likely to have been followed to a large degree by those of its tenth-century estate. Together with the groupings discussed in the previous chapter, that evidence may suggest that the entirety of the early Anglo-Saxon basin was controlled through one group or another, within stable, evolving political territories.

Ely and the Tribal Hidage

There is no evidence in the Tribal Hidage to answer the question of Ely's origins. On the other hand, in 731 – just a few decades after it was drawn up – Bede confidently described the *regione quae vocatur Elge*, 'the province that is called Ely', explaining that it had formed the endowment with which Æthelthryth, the daughter of King Anna of East Anglia, had founded her monastic house in about 673 (Fig. 5.1).[1]

That is, Bede's evidence indicates that at least part of the central peat fenland lay within a sizeable political unit assessed at 600 hides, at least as large as others that were listed in the Tribal Hidage. Since the Isle was already a *regio* when it was granted to Æthelthryth in the mid-seventh century, its origins cannot be later than the first decades of that century and were probably earlier. It certainly formed an early Anglo-Saxon folk-territory at one stage: the ninth-century Old English version of Bede's *History* translated his original Latin, quoted above, as *tham theodlande the is geceged Elige*, 'among the *nation* who call their territory Ely'.[2]

Ely's place-name is a monument to those beginnings. It refers both to a place, Ely, and to the wider administrative area of the Isle of Ely, which extends over the larger part of the peat fenland. The *-gē* suffix of the place-name is, as we have already seen, not only rare but went out of use exceptionally early in the Anglo-Saxon period.[3] As significantly, it may be related to the modern German '*gau*': a region rather like one of the English shires, locally controlled, but part of a larger federation.[4] By 673 the central fen basin formed the geographical basis for a large territorial unit whose history is likely to have extended back into the sixth century, and perhaps much earlier. Why, then, was it not included in the Tribal Hidage?

There are at least four possible answers to that question. First, it should have been included in the list but was simply left out for reasons we cannot discover. Or, it was omitted because it did not exist at the time the Tribal Hidage was compiled, and Bede simply assumed that conditions in the fenland were the same in 673 as they were when he wrote his *Ecclesiastical History* in 731. This is unlikely. He is generally regarded as a reliable historian and, writing only five or six decades after Æthelthryth's death, the detailed evidence he recorded appears to have been gathered from early documents or from people who had either known her personally or at only one remove. Others have adopted a third explanation: that Ely was included in the Tribal Hidage, but under a different name. So, for example, some have argued that, because Bede had noted that the *regio* was assessed at 600 hides, and because the territory of the East *Wixna* was assessed at 600 hides in the Tribal Hidage, the two names referred to the same group.[5] That might be so, but may as easily not be the case. Alternatively, it has been suggested that the central fenland lay in the territory of the West *Willa*, dominated by the Old Well Stream running north along the eastern side of the Isle.[6]

The fourth explanation is most commonly adopted: that Ely was invisible in the Tribal Hidage because it was included within the assessment of another territory to which it was subordinate. That polity is often asserted to be the principality of the South *Gyrwe* on the grounds that the twelfth-century *LE* stated that Æthelthryth had received the estate at Ely as her marriage-portion from her first husband Tondberht, *princeps* of the *Gyrwe*.[7] However, as Miller pointed out in 1951, that view has its roots in a modern misinterpretation of the medieval text.[8] A careful reading of the *LE* distinguishes between what the monastic chronicler did and did not say. What he actually wrote was: 'The *Gyrwe* are all the South Angles who live in the great fen in which the Isle of Ely is situated'.[9] That is, he did not say that Ely lay within the principality of the *Gyrwe*. What he did say was that the territories of the South *Gyrwe* and of the Isle of Ely both lay in the fen basin. His preceding sentence makes it clear that the boundaries of the two groups marched together, neither overlapping nor including one within the other: the boundaries of the Isle, he wrote, extend 'as far as the river near Peterborough which is called the Nene in the region of the *Gyrwe*'.[10] That is, the principality of the *Gyrwe* and the Isle of Ely were neighbouring territories.

Bede had the most convincing explanation for the omission of Ely from the Tribal Hidage. He judiciously explained that Ely was granted to Æthelthryth because the *regio* 'lies in the province of the East Angles' and because 'her forbears came from the province of the East Angles'.[11] That is, he took it for granted that Æthelthryth's religious house was established within an existing political territory whose origins and East Anglian fealty long predated the monastery's foundation.

Ely and the East Anglian kingdom

The close political allegiance that the *regio* of Ely owed to the early kingdom of East Anglia is mirrored in its proximity to the royal estate (*villa regia*) of Exning (Suffolk) where Æthelthryth was probably born, perhaps in the years following 630.[12] Like many other early Anglo-Saxon royal vills, Exning lies near a substantial Roman villa and close to an early Anglo-Saxon cemetery; its early church is dedicated to St Martin, favoured by the Merovingian kings from whose kingdom the first bishop arrived in East Anglia about 631.[13] Exning is only 20 km from Ely, and Bede's statement suggests that the gift to Æthelthryth of an established polity with close links to East Anglia mirrored her own place at the heart of the East Anglian royal family.[14]

There is a range of evidence to suggest that the boundaries of the medieval hundred of Staploe may have preserved those of the *villa regia* (Fig. 5.2). There were, for instance, ancient links between Soham and the East Anglian royal house. The early minster at Soham, believed to have been established by St Felix in 631 was royal, whose endowment came from Sigebeht, king of East Anglia from *c*.629 to *c*.634.[15] William of Malmesbury recorded in the twelfth century that 'there are still traces of a church there, wrecked and then burned by the Danes'.[16] If the connection between Soham and St Felix is accurate, then its location is typical: like other early royal minsters, it was sited at some distance – about 10 km – from the royal vill 'amidst its own lands and housed within its own enclosure'.[17] *DB* similarly records long-standing royal connections at Soham, Fordham and Isleham. They were the first three listed in only seven Cambridgeshire manors belonging to the king in 1086, and each was described as anciently royal. Forming a cohesive geographic unit, they accounted for

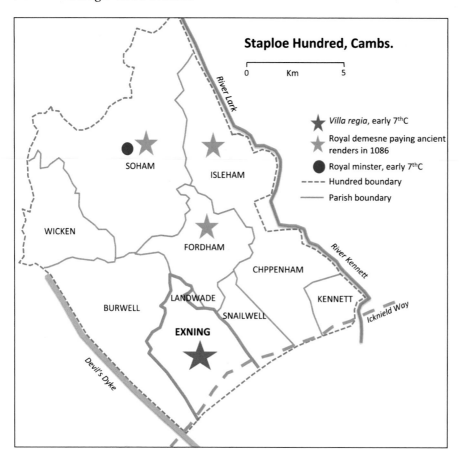

FIGURE 5.2. Staploe Hundred may preserve the boundaries of the extensive early Anglo-Saxon royal estate at Exning (now in Suffolk) where Æthelthryth is said to have been born (© Susan Oosthuizen).

around a quarter of the hundred's hidage and, significantly, each still rendered the ancient food rents (*feorm*) of corn, malt, and (especially) honey that indicate early Anglo-Saxon public renders to kings and lords.[18]

The boundaries that outline the neatly rectangular hundred have a similar appearance of antiquity, following either natural or very early man-made features. They run along the rivers Lark and Kennett on the north-east (the modern boundary between Cambridgeshire and Suffolk), and along the river Granta/Cam on the north-west (the boundary with the Isle). The Cam was still regarded as a territorial boundary between the Isle of Ely and the mainland in the tenth century when Upware, on the eastern bank of the river, was regarded not just as beyond the Isle, but located among the people of another, quite different, region.[19] The river's characterisation as a frontier can be found, too, in Little Thetford, whose place-name means the ford of the *thēod*, 'the nation'; the modern village lies on the western banks of the Cam, on the south-eastern shore of the island of Ely, where an ancient route from Ely to Exning crossed the river.[20] The south-eastern boundary of the hundred follows one of the routes of the Icknield Way. Deconstructive analysis of the meeting points between the boundaries of medieval parishes within the hundred also suggest its origins in a cohesive unit. The earliest boundaries appear to be those around Exning and Kennet, since only they intersect with the border of the hundred. While some of the other internal boundaries do indeed meet the outer hundred boundary, each also has at least one boundary that is subtended from that of one of the other sub-units, a characteristic that indicates subdivision of an earlier, larger, estate or territory.[21]

As significantly, the south-western boundary runs along the Devil's Dyke, the most magnificent of the four fifth- or sixth-century linear earthworks that transect the Icknield Way in north-east Cambridgeshire, at least two of which – the Bran Ditch and the Fleam Dyke – followed prehistoric alignments (Fig. 5.3). The Devil's Dyke was throughout the middle ages and is still the boundary of the Diocese of East Anglia, founded by St Felix in 630 to serve the eponymous kingdom. It is almost certain that it also formed part of the boundary of the early Anglo-Saxon kingdom of East Anglia.[22] That antiquity may be reflected more locally, too, in Exning's place-name – *Gyxen*, 'personal name', -*ingas*, 'folk territory'; if the creation of the royal estate perpetuated the area of an earlier folk territory, the origins of the hundred may be very early.[23]

The early seventh-century structure of the south-western corner of the kingdom of East Anglia, at that time extending over Norfolk, at least the northern part of Suffolk and possibly the eastern Cambridgeshire fen edge, thus comes dimly into view. The fenland province (*regio*) of Ely, subordinate to the East Anglian kings, lay alongside a contemporary upland polity centred on Exning, almost certainly by then held as an extensive royal estate. Just

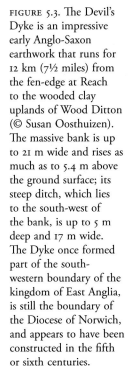

FIGURE 5.3. The Devil's Dyke is an impressive early Anglo-Saxon earthwork that runs for 12 km (7½ miles) from the fen-edge at Reach to the wooded clay uplands of Wood Ditton (© Susan Oosthuizen). The massive bank is up to 21 m wide and rises as much as to 5.4 m above the ground surface; its steep ditch, which lies to the south-west of the bank, is up to 5 m deep and 17 m wide. The Dyke once formed part of the south-western boundary of the kingdom of East Anglia, is still the boundary of the Diocese of Norwich, and appears to have been constructed in the fifth or sixth centuries.

a few kilometres of fen and river thus separated it from Æthelthryth's royal minster at *Cratendune* in Ely, and her house lay only 6 km from the other royal minster at Soham. The endowment of the new abbey at Ely with the territory of an established polity closely tied to East Anglia could also, then, be read as a management of risk: on the one hand, the grant to her new minster of an estate based on an ancient sub-kingdom of East Anglia offered the queen-abbess a degree of independence consonant with her royal status; on the other, the proximity of Ely to both Soham and Exning provided her with as good a guarantee of physical safety among, and protection by, her royal kin as was possible in the period.

Reconstructing the *regio* of the Ēlge

Although there is utility in the conclusion that at least part of the central fenland lay within the boundaries of an early medieval territory, it only offers a small part of the answer to the question with which this chapter began. There is after all no contemporary account of the bounds of the earlier *regio* with which Æthelthryth endowed her Abbey, and the current scholarly consensus is that they were more or less coincident with the large island on which the Abbey was founded. After its refoundation by Æthelwold in the late tenth century, however, its boundaries ran 'from the middle of Tydd Bridge as far as Upware, and from *Biscopesdelf* in the east as far as the river near Peterborough which is called the Nene'.[24] How old were those boundaries? Pugh's neat summary of the problem cannot be bettered: 'Whether the king [in 973] merely restored a state of affairs prevailing in earlier Saxon times', that is, whether he re-created the late seventh-century abbey estate, or whether the late tenth century endowment formed an entirely new, much more extensive, geography for the Abbey.[25] Underlying those questions is another: if the original folk territory of the Ēlge was indeed restricted to the island of Ely, what, then, was the form of governance – if any – over the remainder of the early wetlands?

This chapter argues that the re-foundation of the Abbey after 973 was indeed focused on the reconstruction of the seventh-century endowment, and that the early medieval *regio* extended over the entirety of the fen's peat wetlands (except, of course, for those pastures along the fen-edge that were included in other territories). The discussion focuses on four broad sets of evidence: patterns of commoning in the medieval peat fen; anomalies in the tenth-century reconstruction of the Abbey's estates; the origins of the hundreds that formed the administrative whole, commonly called the Isle of Ely, that mirrored the abbey's extensive estate focused on Ely; and the external boundaries of the Isle.

Patterns of commoning

Figure 4.1, above, shows the addition of information from the *ECB* about medieval commoning in the central peat fens to Neilson's original map of common rights across the fen basin.[26] The map and the documentary evidence show two distinctive differences in the organisation of medieval common rights in the Isle compared with that around the fen-edge. The first, as already noted, is that the common rights of upland vills along the edges of the fen were geographically limited, compared with those of vills within the Isle of Ely. The maximum depth of fen available to herds from Glatton or Ramsey, for instance, was often no greater than around 8–10 km (5 or 6 miles), and usually very much less. The men of the Isle, like those from Wisbech or Doddington, for example, could range for up to 24 km (15 miles) across the wetlands.

The second significant difference between rights of common held by upland vills and those in the Isle concerns the exclusivity of those rights. As Neilson explained, each cluster of vills around the edges of the fen basin commoned in its own discrete area of fen, thus preserving the shadowy outlines of early Anglo-Saxon folk territories.[27] Those in Hurstingstone Hundred had sole rights between the Huntingdonshire fen edge and the old courses of the rivers Nene and Ouse, while rights in Marshland were restricted to the vills of the *letam integram de marisco* to the east of Wisbech. That exclusivity was absent among the vills of the Isle. Here, overlapping clusters of vills intercommoned across the peat fens. Men from communities on the western slopes took their cattle into the extensive pastures to the south between the island and upland Cambridgeshire where they intercommoned with upland vills from the south Cambridge fen-edge; they also ranged westward into deep fens where they intercommoned with men from Chatteris and the soke of Doddington. Common rights across the peat fens were thus an intricate mesh of rights of common held by overlapping clusters of vills in pastures to which, by and large, no single group of vills had exclusive access.

What can be inferred from this of the ancient territorial history of the Isle? If the province of the *Ēlge* had originated through the amalgamation of a number of folk-groups, one might expect to find that the Isle was made up of discrete, neighbouring areas of common, each the exclusive preserve of a single cluster of vills. On the other hand, if the *regio* had anciently been a single polity, identified by its exclusive rights to the peat fens as a whole, that might explain the more complex framework of commoning there. Although the fundamental rule continued to be observed that each cluster of vills intercommoned in those fens to which they had most immediate access, the scattered geography of the fen islands meant that different commons were generally shared by different groups of vills. So the usual rule, observable among the fen-edge vills, that each set of vills had exclusive access to a specific common, no longer pertained. The vills of the Soke of Doddington, for instance, intercommoned in the deep fen to their east both with men from the western slopes of the island of Ely, and with those from Wisbech Hundred; and to their west, they and men from Wisbech

FIGURE 5.4. Looking west along the Old South Eau near Tydd St Giles, still the county boundary between Cambridgeshire and Lincolnshire, and also the northern boundary to Hey Fen in which the men of Wisbech Hundred intercommoned (© Susan Oosthuizen).

Hundred commoned as far as the Northamptonshire and Lincolnshire county boundaries (Fig. 5.4).[28] Patterns of medieval common rights, then, suggest that the province of the *Ēlge* had, perhaps from earliest times, extended over the whole of the area later included in the Isle.

Anomalies in the tenth-century reconstruction of the Abbey's estates

Did Bishop Æthelwold set out deliberately, then, to restore Æthelthryth's original estate? His re-endowment of the Abbey of Ely in the later tenth century clearly demonstrates his intention to create a solid landholding around the Abbey: by the early 1000s the Abbey's estates included almost all of the Isle. Against that should be set evidence from the *LE* that most of the eleventh-century Ely estate was either bought by Æthelwold on its behalf, or had come to the Abbey by gifts and bequests in much the same period. That is, the multiplicity of estates that made up the new endowment demonstrates the significant degree to which the seventh-century estate had been fragmented and expropriated by secular owners over the intervening centuries. The Viking raids of 870 are an obvious cause, but it is quite possible that the process of alienation had begun before then and been continuous over the centuries.

How, then, might traditions recording the extent of the landholdings of the original estate have been preserved if the original endowment had become so fractured over the intervening three centuries? The preservation of records or oral traditions *might* be inferred on the basis of the claim in the *LE* that the abbey at Ely continued to function, albeit in a reduced form, after the Danish raids of the late ninth century.[29] The suggestion is certainly feasible – the royal minster at nearby Horningsea was adopted by Danish patrons – but it is entirely unsubstantiated.[30] More useful is evidence of obligations owed to the Abbey from fenland manors beyond its estate. That evidence can be found in two of only three manors in the Isle that were not held by Ely by the early eleventh century. The two cases concern a manor held by Ramsey Abbey in part of Chatteris, and a manor held by Thorney Abbey in part of Whittlesey. Each was acquired through a late tenth-century sale or bequest from secular owners who made no mention of the Abbey of Ely in the transaction. Their significance is that, a century later Ely still retained the soke – rights of local jurisdiction – over both those manors and, in Chatteris at least, also claimed the early medieval public service of bridgework from the Ramsey tenants there.[31] The reservation of the soke of both manors to Ely in 1086 suggests that the abbey already had the soke in about 970 when they were respectively received by Ramsey and Thorney, since it is unlikely that those ancient rights of jurisdiction would have been a new addition to those holdings at the time that both new Abbeys were founded, or that they were attached to those manors afterwards.

To this extent the charters that recorded those particular transactions, the many lay gifts and bequests to Ely, and Æthelwold's purchases of apparently private estates across the fenland may say less than their authors knew. None mentions the soke held by the Abbey of Ely. Perhaps this is because the Abbey *already* owned and exercised those rights across all or most of the Isle, and those existing rights could not be sold or bequeathed because they did not belong to the laymen and women selling or granting their estates. The cases of these two manors suggest that, throughout the period intervening between Æthelthryth's death in 679 and the refoundation in 973, the Abbey continued to exercise some ancient rights of jurisdiction over land that had been alienated to secular owners – that is, the latter continued to render to the Abbey at least some of the ancient public obligations that were associated with folkland. If that was indeed the case, then the extent of the ancient *regio* may have been preserved into the tenth century through everyday knowledge of the practical details of public obligations owed to the Abbey and its geographically wide rights of jurisdiction.

The third exception to the cohesiveness of Ely's early eleventh-century fenland holding across the Isle was the site of Thorney Abbey itself, in the north-western peat fens in 972–3. Unlike Ely, Thorney Abbey was an entirely new foundation; if there ever was a seventh-century hermitage there, it had long since disappeared.[32] The Abbey of Ely's close involvement with Thorney Abbey, both at the time of its foundation and later, support the case that, even in the late tenth century, Ely still retained an overlord's interest in estates that had once formed part of its seventh-century *regio*. Hart, for example, noted that many of the signatories to King Edgar's charter confirming Thorney's new estates and privileges in 973 were men who 'figured prominently' in the late tenth-century affairs of the longer-established abbey at Ely.[33] Ely was actively involved in the foundation of the newer house, agreeing to trade its existing estate at Broughton (Huntingdonshire) for another so that Æthelwold could give Broughton to Thorney (although in the end the estate went to Ramsey instead).[34] That support continued into the eleventh century, when the Abbey was (still?) providing Thorney with extensive practical help, including a ship and nets, three harrows, 12 wagons with horses, 43 sows, 84 hogs, two herds, 40 oxen, 43 flitches [sides] of bacon, 54 spits or skewers, and a considerable sum of money in gold and silver.[35] Finally, the new Abbey lay on a small, previously uninhabited, gravel island in the north-east corner of the fen basin; it cannot have been larger, and was probably considerably smaller than the 97 ha (240 acres) of upland, including medieval assarts, set in 6474 ha (16,000 acres) of fen that it accounted for in 1574.[36] Bitter medieval disputes about access by Thorney to rights of common grazing in Hey Fen, the wide fen pastures of Wisbech Hundred, suggest that it was endowed with land that had once been part of that common.[37] On the one hand, Thorney's claim to common in Hey Fen makes sense if the island on which it stood had originally been part of that vast shared pasture. The men of Thorney might then argue that, in commoning across Hey Fen, they were simply doing what they had always done. On the other hand, the rejection of that claim by the vills of Wisbech Hundred makes sense too, since the charter that endowed Thorney with its new demesne was effectively an assart: it converted land previously governed under shared property rights into privately-held bookland, under which all rights of property were reserved to the new Abbey. The refusal of rights of common to property created from assart was most clearly described by Henry Bracton, the thirteenth-century jurist, who explained 'that to tenements in assart no rights of common could pertain, since the assart itself was originally subject to the common rights of the vill' or vills.[38]

The jurisdiction retained by Ely over non-Ely manors in fenland, the close support offered by Ely to Thorney, and the disputes about grazing in Hey Fen, all suggest that the territory of the seventh-century *regio* may indeed have extended across almost the entirety of the peat fen. There is, however, considerable debate about whether the four hundreds into which the Isle had been divided by 1086 represent the original extent of Æthelthryth's seventh-century endowment – and thus preserve older political structures – or whether they were the later, piecemeal, union of separate administrative areas into a single entity as the Abbey's estates were consolidated and extended after 970. Miller, in particular, contended that only the two hundreds on the island itself, Ely and South Witchford Hundreds, formed Æthelthryth's original endowment, and that North Witchford and Wisbech Hundreds were added after the Abbey's refoundation in 973; his view has not generally been challenged.[39]

The chronological relationship between the Isle as a whole and its constituent hundreds

By 1086, the Isle of Ely was sub-divided into four administrative units called hundreds: Ely Hundred, North and South Witchford Hundreds, and Wisbech Hundred. Vills elsewhere in Cambridgeshire were frequently divided between hundreds: Little and Great Gransden, for instance, respectively lie in Cambridgeshire and Huntingdonshire; Hatley St George lies in Longstowe Hundred, Cambridgeshire, East Hatley lies in Armingford Hundred in the same county, and Cockayne Hatley is in Bedfordshire; while Chesterton Hundred is made up of three geographically-separate groups of vills. That is not the case in fenland where there is no subdivision of vills between the hundreds in the Isle which have a coherent geography. Might the Ely hundreds, whatever the history of their union, preserve more ancient subdivisions of the Isle or were they created in the tenth century at the same time as those in the Cambridgeshire uplands?[40]

While the external boundaries of the hundreds coincide with the outer boundaries of the patterns of medieval commoning across the Isle, and with the county boundary, the arrangements of their internal boundaries within the Isle are more complicated. This is most evident around Manea Fen, an extensive extra-parochial intercommon that reached from Mepal to Upwell, and from Little Downham to Doddington (Fig. 5.5). The fen was included within South Witchford Hundred, but bounded to west, east and north by the boundaries of the other three hundreds. The men from all four hundreds nonetheless commoned within it. While that might suggest that the internal boundaries of the hundreds into which the Isle was subdivided cut across much more ancient landscapes, it seems most likely that this is simply the consequence of the extensive nineteenth-century rationalisation, extension and/or creation of the parish units that bordered on those fens that was discussed in Chapter 2. That the Isle was subdivided in some way at an early date is hinted at in the shared names of North and South Witchford hundreds, and in other evidence discussed below; whether the alignments of the hundred boundaries followed the pattern mapped in the nineteenth century seems less likely.

Two aspects of the organisational geography of the Isle may support that conclusion – the treatment of the Isle in *DB*, and aspects of its external boundary. The *DB* commissioners evidently considered the whole of the Isle of Ely as a single administrative entity. That perspective is clearly visible in their treatment of the Ely hundreds, which was quite different from that of the fourteen in south Cambridgeshire. First, they counted the four hundreds in pairs. For example, in the Isle of Ely *DB* listed 'the two Hundreds of Ely which meet at Witchford' (that is, North and South Witchford Hundreds) as a single unit; and then they combined in 'the other hundred' the two other hundreds (Wisbech and Ely Hundreds) whose eponymous centres they listed first (see Fig. 2.3).[41] This was quite different from their treatment of south Cambridgeshire, where each hundred was treated in its own right. Second, none of the Ely hundreds was named in *DB*. Each was simply called a 'hundred of Ely', even though the distinctive name of every south Cambridgeshire hundred was recorded: Wetherley, Longstowe, Flendish, Chesterton, and so on. For the *DB* commissioners, the dominant administrative unit for the peat fens was the Isle; its hundreds were a subordinate detail.[42]

Rights of lordship discussed above indicate that the extent of the seventh-

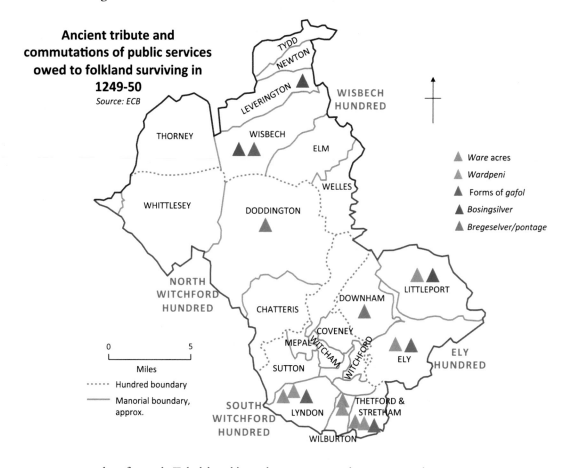

Ancient tribute and commutations of public services owed to folkland surviving in 1249-50

Source: ECB

TYDD
NEWTON
LEVERINGTON
WISBECH HUNDRED
THORNEY
WISBECH
ELM
WELLES
WHITTLESEY
DODDINGTON
NORTH WITCHFORD HUNDRED
CHATTERIS
DOWNHAM
LITTLEPORT
COVENEY
MEPAL
WITCHAM
WITCHFORD
ELY
ELY HUNDRED
SUTTON
SOUTH WITCHFORD HUNDRED
LYNDON
THETFORD & STRETHAM
WILBURTON

▲ *Ware* acres
▲ *Wardpeni*
▲ Forms of *gafol*
▲ *Bosingsilver*
▲ *Bregeselver/pontage*

0 — 5
Miles
····· Hundred boundary
——— Manorial boundary, approx.

century *regio* that formed Æthelthryth's endowment may have survived into the late tenth century, perhaps in the rights of lordship discussed above. That conclusion is based on two aspects of the external boundary of Æthelwold's reconstructed estate: its status as a county boundary along most of its length, and its relationship with patterns of commoning. Almost all the external boundaries of the Abbey's fenland estate are followed by county boundaries: by Lincolnshire in the north-west, by Northamptonshire on the west, by Huntingdonshire to south-west and south, and by Suffolk and Norfolk in the east. The only interruption to that pattern lies along the boundary with Cambridgeshire, with which the Isle was included in 1086, where it ran for about 16 km (10 miles) between Haddenham and Little Thetford along precursors of the West Water. The significance of this characteristic is problematic. On the one hand, county boundaries are believed to have been formalized in the tenth century – perhaps as early as 917 in Cambridgeshire, but possibly in the decades that followed; that might indicate that the boundary predates the re-endowment of the Abbey in the 970s. On the other hand, the coincidence might simply reflect the adjustments to the county boundaries once the Abbey's late Anglo-Saxon estate had been constructed by Æthelwold.[43] It was

FIGURE 5.5.
Ancient tribute and commutations of public services owed to folkland that were still being paid in vills across the Isle of Ely in 1249–50 (© Susan Oosthuizen).

not unusual for county boundaries to be adjusted to allow major lords to bring outlying manors into the same county as most of their other holdings. Great and Little Gransden, now respectively in Huntingdonshire and Cambridgeshire, were a single Huntingdonshire manor *c.*960; it was divided soon after between Earl Alfgar of Mercia, who held the larger manor of Great Gransden, and the newly re-founded Abbey of Ely, which held Little Gransden. It seems that the Abbey then arranged for the county boundary to be adjusted to bring Little Gransden into Cambridgeshire.[44] Could the same have happened on the Isle? Could negotiations have been held to adjust the boundaries of five counties to bring the multiplicity of small fenland estates that Bishop Æthelwold collated for his re-endowment of the Abbey into a single county? The proposition has an attractive simplicity.

The difficulty that it does not address, however, is that the external boundary of the Isle also runs along the divisions between much earlier Anglo-Saxon fen intercommons whose boundaries, as we have seen, quite often bore no relation to those of manorial holdings. There was no necessary overlap between them. It was therefore not inevitable that the final collection of manors with which Ely was re-endowed would coincide with patterns of commoning; it was, indeed, unlikely. This makes it more difficult to sustain the argument that considerable sections of five county boundaries were adjusted to bring the Abbey's fenland estate into Cambridgeshire.

A simpler solution is to suggest that the external boundaries of Æthelthryth's Ely estate were still known in the later tenth century because aspects of its jurisdiction, rights of commons, and their courts had survived. Owen has demonstrated that the section of the boundary of the Isle followed/was followed by the county boundary between Cambridgeshire and Lincolnshire was adjudicated in the thirteenth century on evidence for the boundary between rights of common held by men from the men of Holland in Lincolnshire, and those of the men of Ely.[45] Both the boundary of the Isle and of the counties thus followed early Anglo-Saxon alignments. If that was indeed the case, the coincidence suggests that Æthelwold was particularly intent on reconstructing the seventh-century estate based on the *regio* of the original endowment – a difficult task that, as the *LE* records, involved a great many small transactions. He did, however, have a particularly personal motive in his special veneration of Æthelthryth: she is prominent in his *Benedictional*, a book of benedictions and prayers made for his personal use; he even seems to have written the blessing for her feast himself; and it is the only benediction in the volume whose Amens are written in gold – all others are in red.[46] The importance of the re-endowment of Ely for Æthelwold may have been religious as much as strategic, a personal mission aimed not only at the re-establishment of the monastic house she had founded, but also honouring the saint herself through the reconstruction of her original endowment.

There is, however, a formidable stumbling block before that conclusion can be adopted: it lies in the arguments of other scholars that neither Wisbech nor North Witchford Hundreds, or their predecessors, were part of the early Anglo-

Saxon province. The history of those hundreds is thus critical to reconstructing its early political geography.

(a) North Witchford Hundred

Miller emphatically excluded both North Witchford and Wisbech Hundreds from the early territory of Ely. His rejection of North Witchford Hundred was drawn from Darby's suggestion in 1934 based on the derivation of March's place-name from *mearc*, 'boundary'.[47] Darby assumed that this meant a political boundary, and in that case the obvious boundary was that between the two Anglo-Saxon kingdoms that dominated the region, East Anglia and Mercia. He suggested that it ran from Wisbech in the north at least as far as Benwick in the south along the old course of the river Nene, just west of the Doddington archipelago. There is, however, simply no evidence to support that contention. For example, had the boundary existed, men from the Soke of Doddington would have commoned only up to the eastern banks of the river Nene which, at that time, ran close by the western shores of their archipelago; instead, their cattle ranged far to the west of the river, only stopping at a canal called the Catswater that followed the Northamptonshire fen-edge from Peterborough to Crowland.

There is, however, another boundary that might offer a better explanation for March's place-name: the 'well-defined boundary of exploitation' running from west to east along the interface between the silt and the peat fens, and between salt and sweet water, each offering quite different agricultural opportunities.[48] Sheep tended to be run on the silts, and cattle in the peat wetlands; there was extensive medieval reclamation for arable on the silts and relatively little in the peats; while coastal vills along the north boundary of the silt fens continued to extract salt throughout the early and later middle ages, this was an activity for which those in the peat fens had little opportunity.

There are, instead, two reasons to suggest that North Witchford Hundred had always been an integral part of the Isle of Ely. The first can be found in the extensive common rights held by men from Doddington and those from Ely. The men from each of those groups of vills ranged both west and east across the peat fens: to the west, they intercommoned with the men of Wisbech Hundred; to the east, they intercommoned with the men of one or another of all three of the other Ely hundreds in the deep fens bounded by the Old Well Stream in the north-east and by the island of Ely in the east. Neither group would have had such extensive, overlapping rights if North Witchford Hundred was only included in the Isle after the tenth century (see Fig. 4.1). The second reason has already been touched on: the shared names of North and South Witchford Hundreds.[49] They would be more to have been given different names if they originated independently as sub-units of quite different administrative areas; instead they share a common name.

Darby's and Miller's shared, flawed assumption about the interpretation of March's place-name formed the basis of the latter's rejection of North Witchford hundred as an early subdivision of the Isle. If, instead, the boundary was that between silt and peat fens, the objection falls away – a solution that makes better sense, too, of the shared name of the two Witchford hundreds. It is possible that they and their single predecessor were early administrative subdivisions of the Isle, the successors in turn to folk territories whose public rights and obligations had passed to them.[50]

(b) Wisbech Hundred

The relationship between the other three hundreds and Wisbech Hundred, however, remains contentious. Miller considered that Wisbech Hundred 'was probably a late addition to the Isle, rather awkwardly tacked on to the rest'.[51] He had two arguments for that exclusion from Æthelthryth's original endowment. He suggested, first, that the relatively unmanorialised economy of the Hundred – in which most revenues came from rents rather than services – set it apart from the remainder of the Isle. The evidence from the *ECB* discussed in Chapter 2, however, has demonstrated that a large proportion of the mid-thirteenth-century population across the Isle was similarly unmanorialised. Although the nomenclature of their payments and status varied from one vill to another, the underlying structures were the same; and although the proportions of such holdings were higher in Wisbech Hundred, across the Isle all had their origins in the same archaic forms of landholding that predated the gradual emergence of the manor as an institution from the middle Anglo-Saxon period onwards.

To that evidence can be added the relics of archaic services and dues that had their origins in early Anglo-Saxon folk-lands and that also persisted across the Isle as late as 1249–50 (Fig. 5.5).[52] One of the most ancient was the *gafol*, tribute paid in cash, which survived in the mid-thirteenth century fenland in services known as *govelacre*, *garserthe* or *filstingerthe* at Wisbech, Ely, Stretham and Lyndon (now called Haddenham).[53] Commutations of the three common burdens – ancient public obligations to contribute to the militia of a folk territory, to maintain roads and bridges, and to build and maintain fortifications – also survived across all four hundreds into the same period. W*ardpeni* was paid in commutation of obligations to build and maintain fortifications and to perform guard duties; *bregesilver*, or pontage, was paid in lieu of the maintenance of roads and bridges. Payments of *wardpeni* from Wilburton, for instance, amounted to 6s 5d each year; the total of *bregesilver* collected in Downham varied from 18d to 6s 4d each year, depending on the number of services that were commuted.[54]

Miller's second argument was that the 'social organisation' of Wisbech Hundred was quite different from the rest of the Isle of Ely and instead 'strongly suggests an early connection with the Norfolk Marshland'.[55] It seems likely that he was referring to the synergies between the history of the *ferthyng* in Wisbech Hundred – a relic of early Anglo-Saxon public obligations to provide money renders to their kings – and the similarly early origins of the *letam integram de marisco* to its east. That argument is based on two premises: first, that the early medieval organisation of the silt lands was unique; and second, that so, too, was its survival into the thirteenth century. The previous chapters have made it clear that neither of those premises holds. There is good evidence around the fen basin for similarly early territorial organisation in patterns of common rights, in place-names, and documentary evidence, all discussed in previous chapters.

The social organisation of the Isle was, in this sense at least – and in contradiction of Miller – similar across the Isle, since evidence of archaic forms of landholding, and public services and renders, both derived from early Anglo-Saxon folk territories, could still be found across all four hundreds in the mid-thirteenth century.

On the other hand, while that similarity makes it possible that Wisbech Hundred may have formed part of Æthelthryth's original endowment, it does not make it certain. Thirteenth-century payments from holdings in Wisbech Hundred of an archaic rent called *ferthyng* may, however, provide a relatively secure step towards that certainty. *Ferthyng* means a fourth, a quarter, and the payment represented a quarter of that received for an entire *region*, province or kingdom. The question thus is: of which territory was the unit that was later called Wisbech Hundred, then, a quarter? There are three options: that Wisbech was a quarter part of a territory that now lies either in Lincolnshire, or in Norfolk, or in the Isle of Ely (Fig. 5.6).

The first possibility can be dismissed quite quickly: there has never been a suggestion that Wisbech Hundred originally lay in Lincolnshire, from which it was divided by natural streams and deep fens. Indeed, late twelfth-century documentary evidence suggests that an ancient watercourse called the Old Eau had been recognised as the northern boundary to Hey Fen since time immemorial even if medieval Lincolnshire men claimed some rights on its borders.[56] The second option is most favoured: both Miller and Roffe suggested that Wisbech Hundred was originally a part of Freebridge Half-Hundred in Norfolk, which is made up of the vills on the silt lands along the north-eastern coast of the fen basin.[57] There are two sets of evidence to reject that view: the first concerns the character of the boundary between Wisbech Hundred and Freebridge Half-Hundred (also the boundary between Cambridgeshire and Norfolk), and the second are the arrangements for commoning in Wisbech Hundred. The boundary runs northwards along the winding course of the Old Croft River (also called the Old Well Stream) from the boundary between Upwell and Littleport in the south to Wisbech, where the river – by now augmented with the waters of the Nene and the Ouse (then flowing west of March) – once fell into the sea. Further north it follows the eastern coastline of the Wash, receding northwards as the river estuary gradually silted.[58] The eastern boundary of Wisbech Hundred thus has every aspect of antiquity. It follows the same natural feature continuously along its entire length, and the entirety of the Hundred – including Wisbech – lies to its west. Although its character as a county boundary is not definitive, it is significant that there are no detached portions of parishes, nor ecclesiastical dependencies, nor intra-parochial rights to each other's resources, to link vills in Wisbech Hundred with those in the Norfolk Half-Hundred of Freebridge (Fig. 5.6). The geography of the common rights of each of the hundreds tell the same story. The vills of the two hundreds had quite separate areas of common grazing – there was no intercommoning between them. The men of Wisbech Hundred grazed their beasts in Hey Fen to the west of the Old Well Stream, and those of the *letam integram* commoned in Marshland to the east of the river. Taken together, the totality of this evidence strongly suggests that Wisbech Hundred was never included in Norfolk.

If the early medieval predecessor of Wisbech Hundred lay neither in Lincolnshire nor in Norfolk, could it then have been part of the old, fifth- or sixth-century, *regio* of Ely? The earliest documentary reference to Wisbech 'with its appendages' – that is, Wisbech together with the silt land vills that made up the hundred to which it gave its name – was recorded in around 1000 when Oswy and Leoflede, the parents of a boy called Ælfwine, gave some scattered estates to the Abbey at Ely on the day that their son entered the religious community there.[59] Their gift came in three parts: a group of manors in Suffolk,

FIGURE 5.6.
Intercommoning vills and their commons on the Lincolnshire, Cambridgeshire and Norfolk silt fens (© David Roffe, reproduced with permission).

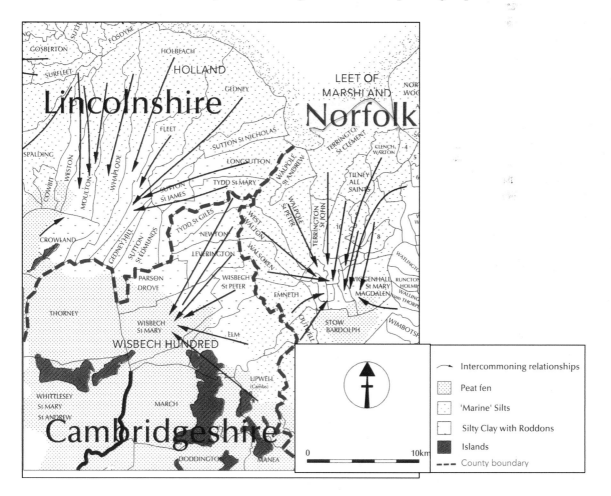

Walpole in Norfolk – and Wisbech. Roffe argued that the fact that Wisbech and Walpole were both included in the gift, and that they are neighbouring vills, indicated that they formed a single estate; therefore, he suggested, Wisbech was once part of Freebridge hundred.[60] The charter itself is now lost and so it is impossible to check its original wording. However, the twelfth-century record of the gift treated Walpole and Wisbech as quite separate estates, and even glossed the latter by explaining that it was 'a quarter of a hundred of the Isle'.[61] That is, as far as one can tell, there is no hint in the medieval evidence that Oswy and Leoflede's estates at Wisbech and Walpole were linked in any way.

If there are a number of reasons to reject the arguments for placing the origins of Wisbech Hundred in Norfolk, there are other reasons to suggest that it had always formed a fourth part of the Isle. The first lies in the location of the lost site of *Modich*, one of four places where assemblies of the Ely hundreds were held (the others being Wisbech, Ely and Witchford). It lay deep in the vast fen between March, Manea and Littleport at the intersection of the boundaries of all four of the Ely hundreds – and, significantly, in Manea, the *gemæne ēa*, 'common fen', in which they all intercommoned (see Fig. 5.6).[62] The twelfth-century author of the *LE* described *Modich* as 'a *ferthyng* of the hundreds' – perhaps intending to say that it was one of four meeting places where assemblies of the Isle might meet.[63]

The second, already discussed above, is that the payments of *ferthyng* from holdings in Wisbech Hundred make sense if the precursor of Wisbech Hundred was indeed one of four sub-units of the territory of the Isle. Third is the observation, also discussed above, of the extent of common rights in the peat fens held by holdings in Wisbech Hundred. They ranged across a vast area of peat wetland: the entirety of the western fenland as far south as Whittlesey, as far west as the Thorney boundary and as far east as the Old Well Stream, where they intercommoned with the men from the other three hundreds of the Isle. That is, the persistent iteration of the four fractions into which the Isle was subdivided and the four places at which assemblies were held, the commonality in the character of public services, renders and payments across the four hundreds, and their patterns of intercommoning offer stronger support for the origins of Wisbech Hundred within the Isle than for its exclusion from it.

A considerable range of evidence, none sufficiently strong on its own but together tending in the same direction, suggests that the Isle had inherited the general area, and the ancient rights and obligations of the geographically-cohesive *regio* with which the seventh-century Abbey was endowed. It includes the ancient jurisdiction over the Isle still held by the Abbey in the tenth century and later, and indications that the *regio* had been subdivided into four units whose rights to renders and responsibilities for governance, jurisdiction and taxation had passed the four hundreds of the Isle by the late eleventh century.

Conclusions

To return to the question with which this chapter began, it seems, then, that the omission of the Isle of Ely from the Tribal Hidage might be explained in the subordination of the *regio* to Anglo-Saxon kingdom of East Anglia by the beginning of the seventh century at the latest. The political organisation of the territory in the period is clear – Bede described it as a province, and the ancient *gē* element in Ely's place-name supports his definition. The pattern of common rights exercised by its medieval vills suggest its territory extended across almost the entirety of the peat fens. Ancient services, renders and money payments across its four subdivisions appear to corroborate that view.

Patterns of common rights, and the characteristics of the external boundary of the Isle indicate that Æthelwold more or less achieved his personal objective of reconstituting Æthelthryth's original mid-seventh-century endowment. There is, however, no incontrovertible evidence for that proposition. Following the principle of Occam's razor, the suggestion that that early folk territory can be identified in the boundaries of the late eleventh-century Isle simply offers the most straightforward solution to the problem of the Isle's origins – partly because the weight of evidence, although each element on its own is slight, tends in that direction, and because it requires the fewest assumptions. It is not conclusive, but the steps taken to reaching it are the least contorted.

The evidence of the Tribal Hidage explored in the previous chapter, and that concerning the origins of Ely in this, demonstrate consistent territorial organisation, within well-established polities, across the early Anglo-Saxon fen basin. It is difficult to recognise Darby's brigands and bandits in them. That many of the fen-edge polities took their names from their localities is a remarkable demonstration of the importance of place in forming early medieval folk identities across the fen basin. Such commonalities and the persistence of common rights across the *longue durée* suggest that it is as likely that some of those territories had Romano-British or post-Roman origins, later evolving into sub-kingdoms; other emergent territories were as likely to be new. These were well-ordered early and middle Anglo-Saxon communities with a long history of governance, as stable and coherent as those anywhere in England. The landscapes they exploited, while varied, were dominated by fertile natural water meadows principally used for pasture. Those rich grasslands were central to conceptions across fenland of territory, status, and cultural identity that were expressed in access to, governance of, and exercise of rights of common across them. The next chapters discuss the management of those resources.

Notes

1. *Bede* IV, 17; Campbell 1979.
2. *Bede* IV, 17 (my italics in the translation); see also *Bede* IV, 20; Skeat 1901, 52; Darby 1934, 196; Yorke 2000, 71.
3. Reaney 1943, xviii; see also Smith 1956, I, 196; Skeat 1901, 52.
4. Reaney 1943, 213–14; Dr Alex Woolf, pers. comm.
5. Hart 1971, 144.
6. Davies and Vierck 1974, 231, 234, 256.
7. *LE* I, Preface.
8. Miller 1951, 10–13
9. *LE* I, Preface.
10. *LE* I, Preface.
11. Bede IV, 19.
12. *LE* I, 3; Webster 1987; Oosthuizen 1998, 91–95. Although Exning is now in Suffolk, it lay in Cambridgeshire until the twelfth century (VCH Cambs. X, 332).
13. Morris 1989, 15; Oosthuizen 2001, 59–60.
14. Cf. Warner 1988, 17–21.
15. *LE* I, 6; *GP* II, 74, 2.
16. *GP* II, 74, 2.
17. Blair 1992, 246; see also 1988, 2.
18. *DB* Cambs. 1, 1–3; Faith 1997, 48, 104
19. *LE* II, 11.
20. Reaney 1943, 242; Yorke 2000, 71.
21. Flinders Petrie 1878, 172–73.
22. *Bede* III, 21; Kirby 1965–66, 2.
23. VCH Cambs. IV, 2, 4, 6, 10, 332; Mills 2011.
24. *LE* I, Preface.
25. VCH Cambs. IV, 4.
26. Neilson 1920, v–lviii; Oosthuizen 2011b; 2016a.
27. Neilson 1920, xlix.
28. *ECB*, f.25d(1)-f.25d(2).
29. *LE* I, 39–49.
30. Blair 2005, 294.
31. VCH Cambs. IV, 104.
32. VCH Cambs. IV, 221; Raban 1977, 6.
33. Hart 1966, 174.
34. Raban 1977, 8.
35. *BL* Add Ms 61735; Skeat 1902, 12–16; Hart 1966, 32; Naismith 2016.
36. Hall 1987, 52.
37. Neilson 1920, xxxv–xxxvii; VCH Cambs. IV, 238, 246; Owen 1982.
38. Neilson 1920, liv.
39. Miller 1951, 13–15.
40. Hart 1974, 12; Haslam 1982, 13; VCH Cambs. V, 87–99; see also Oosthuizen 2006, 26.
41. *DB* Cambs, preceding 5,44, and preceding 5,55.
42. That subdivision in 1086 explains the monastic chronicler's account that the 'the Isle is reckoned to consist … of two hundreds' even though the area he described included the whole of the Isle: they ran 'from the middle of Tydd Bridge all the way to Upware, and from the Bishop's Ditch as far as the river near Peterborough which is called the

Nene' (*LE* I, Preface; see also II, 54). His description of the bounds of those hundreds makes it clear that he was following the Domesday method of pairing them into two larger units.

43. Hart 1974, 12; Haslam 1982, 13; VCH Cambs. V, 87–99.
44. VCH Cambs.V, 87.
45. Owen 1982.
46. *BL* Add. Ms. 49598, http://www.bl.uk/manuscripts/FullDisplay.aspx?ref=add_ms_49598, accessed March 2017.
47. Darby 1934; Miller 1951, 14.
48. Roffe 2005, 283.
49. Hart 1974.
50. Faith 1997, 118.
51. Miller 1951, 14, see also 32–33.
52. *LE* I, Preface; *ECB*, f.33r(2); Neilson 1920, xlvii–xlix; Miller 1951, 32; Reaney 1943, 235–36.
53. *ECB*, f.38r(1), f.5r(2), f.15r(2), f.22r(1); Faith 1997, 105–106.
54. *ECB*, f.19d(2), f.10r(2); Faith 1997, 96–105.
55. Miller 1951, 14.
56. Owen 1982, 41–44.
57. Miller 1951, 14; Roffe 2005.
58. Owen 1982; Roffe 2005, 276–77.
59. *LE* II, 75; also Hart 1966, 214; VCH Cambs. IV, 243.
60. Roffe 2005, 17.
61. *LE* II, 75.
62. *LE* I, Preface; *ECB*, f.33r(2); Neilson 1920, xlvii–xlix; Miller 1951, 32; Reaney 1943, 235–36.
63. *LE* II, 54.

CHAPTER 6

Rich Hay and Commons

The early and middle Anglo-Saxon fen basin was, it seems, well-populated by stable communities some of whose histories may have reached back into the Roman or even prehistoric periods. This chapter seeks to answer three consequent questions: Was it an ecological wilderness or an exploited landscape? What was it about the match between the wider economy of the period and opportunities available in the fens that drew so many people to make a living here between about 400 and 1100? And if wetland resources contributed to the local economy, to what extent did successful livelihoods depend on their active management?

The chapter begins by discussing the evidence for ecological stability across the Anglo-Saxon fenland, and the impact of a climatic deterioration between about 600 and 800. It suggests that there is little evidence in pollen evidence, in palaeobotanical evidence, or in place- and field-names that the basin was abandoned at any time in the Anglo-Saxon period. Instead, the wetlands in particular appear to have supported a productive economy in which cattle, and especially dairying, was dominant, but in which other fen products were also important. The evidence of common rights in those resources, the chapter argues, appears to indicate that those resources, and thus the wider landscape, were carefully managed under cropping regimes that allowed individuals a sufficient volume of fen products each year to satisfy their needs, and that provided security of a sustainable future for them. Far from being an open resource, the early medieval fenlands were as carefully managed as they were in subsequent centuries.

Ecological stability in the Anglo-Saxon fenland

Wet meadows and grassland pasture, with sedge and some fen carr, were as characteristic of all periods of the prehistoric and Roman fen landscape as they were of the early medieval and later.[1] The cattle of Neolithic communities who met seasonally at Etton, north of Peterborough, grazed on fen grasses typical of wetland conditions.[2] Iron Age communities at Wardy Hill, in Coveney, and in Haddenham had lived in a landscape of 'much grassland against a background of fen'.[3] Pollen evidence consistently shows that 'an open terrain dominated by herb-rich grassland and wetland' fringed by small areas of alder and willow carr had already dominated the fen basin for at least 3000 years before the end of the Roman period – and continued to do so for the next 1500.[4] What was the impact on this landscape of the slow rise of about 1.5 m in water levels across the fen basin between about 600 and 800?

It is difficult to see the rising water levels of the seventh and eighth centuries in terms of ecological disaster for early medieval communities in the peat fens. Anyone exploiting its resources in any period had always had to adapt to water levels that rose and fell from time to time each year by up to 3.6 m (12 ft), often over short periods. The longer-term rise in the level of the flood line between about 600 and 800, while substantial, was after all quite gradual, spread over about two hundred years or around seven generations. It is true that there were changes. The lowest parts of the inland basin became wetter; already low-lying marshy stands of reed and sedge were transformed into shallow lakes, larger in winter than in the drier conditions of summer; existing meres simply became bigger. Dry pastures that had previously lain above the winter flood line were now susceptible to seasonal inundation.[5] Where the slope was relatively gentle and was thus most prone to flooding, the zone that supported fen meadows shifted higher – perhaps by as much as 1.5 m; seasonal flooding of the lower regions began a little sooner and ended a little later each year. Where the slope between the lowest and highest land was steeper, the effects may have been less pronounced. These were principally changes in the relative proportions and locations of water, wetland and drier pasture rather than in the local ecology. It is difficult to argue that the increase in the volume of water in the fen from about 600 created an environment alien to those making a living from it, or was necessarily catastrophic to their livelihoods.

Had the wetlands fallen into dereliction, the consequences would soon have been visible: 'The wet fen, if left to itself, soon develops a thick cover. To the grasses and peat, reeds, sedge and flags, it adds shrubs and trees' as it gradually becomes drier and more wooded.[6] Waterlogged sedge and reed beds, and fen pastures subject to seasonal inundation 'rapidly become rank and impenetrable and may change over time into dense scrub or woodland' if they are no longer exploited by men.[7] The grassy stems of the plants die back each autumn, and their uncleared leaves imperceptibly raise the ground surface by about 1 mm a year. The repetition of this process, year on year, eventually creates a sufficiently dry environment to allow the colonisation of water-tolerant shrubs and trees, especially alder and willow.[8] The results of post-medieval neglect of surviving areas of fen wetland are still visible today in relatively dense stands of nineteenth- and twentieth-century birch-dominated woodland at Woodwalton and Holme Fens in Huntingdonshire (Fig. 6.1). Yet there is little evidence to show that this happened anywhere on any scale in the early medieval fenland.

The fen basin is typical of much of England is offering remarkably little evidence in documents, pollen analyses or place-names for regenerated woodland on land abandoned at any time in the Anglo-Saxon period; its landscape seems, instead, to have been continuously occupied and exploited.[9] Roughly speaking, of every 75 named places along the boundaries of pre-Conquest fenland estates

FIGURE 6.1. Birch woodland at Holme Fen: Nineteenth- and twentieth-century neglect allowed the natural succession from fen to woodland to occur, and the reserve now holds one of the largest areas of birch woodland in Britain (© Susan Oosthuizen).

recorded in charters, only one was a tree – and trees made up less than 1.5% of all those boundary features.[10] This could be because there were so many trees that it was difficult to find a particular one remarkable enough to be noted; but it could also be that there were so few trees that any tree was unusual. The species of trees most commonly found in fenland charters – willow, aspen and alder – are, moreover, those that were 'evidently the general trees of farmland, hedges and watercourses', not those that were characteristic of an overgrown landscape.[11] By the thirteenth century the only stands of managed wood below the flood line were those of wetland species, especially aspen: Apes Holt (1249–50, *apesholt*) was a grove of aspens (*populus tremula*) in the higher fen just outside Littleport; the trees in the contemporary fens at Thorney, 'whose smooth height stretches towards the stars', may also have been aspens, which can grow to a height of 25 m.[12]

Early medieval evidence from pollen in soil samples and charred plant remains found during archaeological excavation tell the same story despite their scarcity, caused by widespread damage from agriculture to the upper layers of fen soils in which post-Roman pollens were deposited.[13] Palaeobotanical remains from early Anglo-Saxon sites on the Lincolnshire silt fens at Dowsby and Gosberton, in Lincolnshire, show that they stood in open, generally tree-less grassland interrupted by 'occasional stands of birch'.[14] Coastal salt marshes and, further inland, open grasslands studded with small trees continued to be exploited for summer grazing on the Norfolk silt lands throughout the period.[15] The general character of the peat wetlands to the south showed as little alteration.[16] Charred plant remains from settlements on the fen-edge near

Ely record a middle Anglo-Saxon landscape of rich, damp, open grassland whose principal change since the Romano-British period was – as might be expected – an increase in plants of standing water, especially the great fen sedges (*cladium mariscus*).[17] Pollen evidence and the remains of charred plants around the nearby contemporary settlement at Brandon (Suffolk) indicated a similarly treeless landscape of 'open grassland and marsh habitats', unchanged since the Roman period. [18] There, environmental continuity was so striking that specialists considered it was deliberately managed for pasture, perhaps also for meadow, across the first millennium.

Local names for different parts of the fen overwhelmingly support that evidence. Most early medieval and medieval woodland it seems, perhaps unexpectedly, stood on the fen islands, well above the winter flood line. Brittonic place-names referring to wood and wood-pasture at Chatteris, Chittering and Chettisham (each preserving British Celtic *cēt*, 'wood') have already been mentioned; Old English parish names often record specific species – lime trees (perhaps) at Linden End in Haddenham, wych elms at Witcham and Witchford, and scrubby hawthorns dominating two small islands, each named Thorney – one north-east of Ely and the other north of Whittlesey. Local names tell the same story.[19] One of the most common is *wald*: not dense woodland, but 'sheep pasture characterised by stands of wood'.[20] That open, tree-studded landscape seems to have extended over much of the higher land of the Isle: from the *Weld'* (1221) at Ely, leading west to *Brodwold* (1986) at Little Downham, past *Bryn(n)eswold* (thirteenth century) in Witcham and on to *weales* (1589) at Mepal.[21] Further south, the wolds extended to *Walde* (1170) at Witchford, *Waldune* (thirteenth century, now Woolden Lane) at Haddenham and across Sutton where there was *Waldelowe* (1320–21, a mound in the pasture), *Waldehethe* (1294, heathy wood pasture), *Waldweye* and *Waldewere* (both thirteenth century), as well as *Heghwolde* (1399); *Waldelowe* must have been near the boundary with Wentworth where Waddelows Hills preserves the name.[22] Traditions at Ramsey Abbey held that the island was covered by an ash-wood at the time that the monastery was founded there in the later tenth century.[23] The general restriction of such stands of trees to the uplands and their persistence long enough for their names to be recorded in documents not only suggests their value as sources of wood in a largely wetland landscape, but also how limited opportunities in the basin were for growing wood-producing trees like oak, elm, and ash.

Minor names – those not of vills and later parishes, but of streams, local fens and other landscape features – can show remarkable persistence over time in contrast to the higher mutability of parish names (Fig. 6.2). There are, nonetheless, relatively few that predate the widespread emergence in the eleventh century of literate administrators who were responsible for the sudden proliferation of medieval records. Of the 615 minor names from 1249–50 or earlier collected for this study, only 70 were recorded before 1066.[24] They frequently describe water-courses, plants, animals, markers like posts or fords, and local conditions in specific places at the time the name was created; where their meanings refer to soil, drainage,

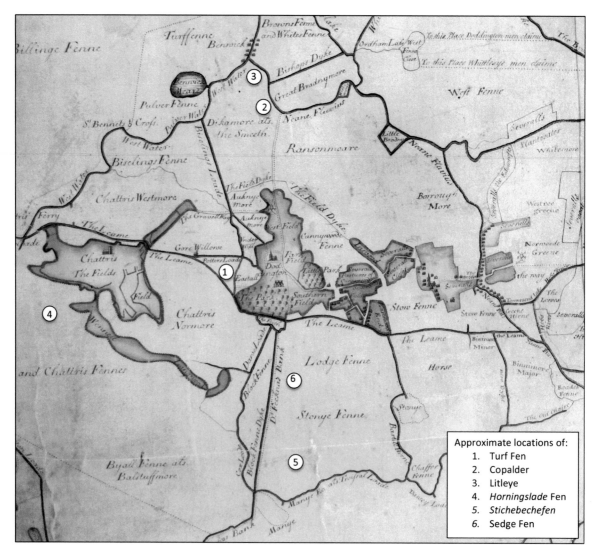

Approximate locations of:
1. Turf Fen
2. Copalder
3. Litleye
4. *Horningslade* Fen
5. *Stichebechefen*
6. Sedge Fen

Binnimore	enclosed, poss 13th C
Biselings Fenne	*-ingas* 'folk group' 13th C
Block Fenne	black, 1549
Borrough More	fishing weir by the burh, *c.*1175
Bradneymore	broad river [Nene]
Byallfenne	by the river, *ECB*
Canneywode Fenne	poss. royal wood, *ECB*
Chaffer Fenne	poss. grass-eating beetle
Copalder	alder pollards, 1244
Darcey Lode	wild animals' stream, *ECB*
Dawe Lode	poss. muddy, 1221
Dikamore	by the dyke (bank)
Frith	rough, fodder fen, *ECB*
Gore Willowe	triangular piece of ground
Horningslade	lode with a bend, 1240
Horse [Fen]	horse, 1636
Leam	artificial water-course
Litleye	little island, *ECB*
Lodge Fenne	weir on sluggish water, *ECB*
Normore	north, *ECB*
Old Chaire river	winding
Plantewater	river filled with plants, 1320
Ransonmore	by the raven's ridge, 1227
Reades Fenne	reeds, 1669
Sedge Fen	sedge, 1426
Smeeth	smooth (improved)
Stichebechefen	piece by a stream, *ECB*
Stonye Fenne	gravelly fen, 1170
Stow Fenne	a place, 1227
Turf Fenne	for cutting peat, poss. 12th C
West Water	old course of R. Ouse, 1589
Westmore	west, 1221
Whitemore	white, *ECB*

location or vegetation, they are likely to have remained continuously fresh and might reasonably be expected to describe the pre-Conquest landscape.[25] Those in the soke of Doddington were typical: *Ravenesho* (1227) 'marsh by the raven's ridge'; *Dudingtonfrith* (1249–50), the rough pasture of the estate, *Wellenhes more* (1249–50), the rough fen along the Old Well Stream, *Stichebechefen* (1249–50), fen by 'a stitch' – a stretch of river bank, *Hoo* (1221), fen marked by a spur of higher ground, *Bradenhee* (1221), the broad river – in this case, the Nene, and *Whitemore* (1325), named from the colour of the plants on the fen.[26] If parts of that wetland had been underexploited for any length of time, then at least some contemporary local names might be expected to describe an overgrown landscape in the same way that the 'stocking', 'breach' or 'wood' furlongs of medieval arable reminded ploughmen of the woods that they had assarted to make their fields. But, like the dog that did not bark, the class of local name that is significant by its absence is that which describes fen invaded by scrub or woodland. Only two of those 615 minor names refer to such landscapes:

- *bramewere* (1086, Ely), perhaps a meadow abandoned long enough to be overgrown with brambles;[27]
- *le stocking* (*c.*1250, Chatteris), a group of stumps – frequently used of an area of cleared woodland.[28]

A local name frequently cited as evidence for abandonment of the fens is *carr*, 'overgrown with rushes, shrubs, reeds and small trees'.[29] There is, however, no evidence for this name anywhere in the early medieval fenland. The sole instance might be thought to be the Romano-British canal now called Car Dyke that runs across Waterbeach, Landbeach and Cottenham; however, its medieval name appears to have been *Tillinge* (1235, perhaps 'to load, unload') and its current name appears to be modern.[30] Indeed, the most detailed investigation of the surviving wetlands at Wicken Fen has concluded that most of the carr fen there was of nineteenth- or twentieth-century origin.[31]

Rough pastures are sometimes claimed as evidence of lack of exploitation, places like *Rumere* in Wisbech (1226), 'rough mere or marsh', *Roweye* in Somersham (1249–50), 'rough marshy ground', or *Rouwepollingsheved* in Doddington (1249–50), 'rough headland for shearing sheep').[32] Yet it is far from certain that this was a barely used and/or unvalued resource. Located in the damper parts of the fen, these were the fenland equivalents of what were called 'wood pastures' on the uplands. They supported a varied range of grasses and browsing plants, were studded with small trees or shrubs where they were drier, offered sources of winter fodder, firing (including sedges and reeds) where they were wetter, and provided opportunities for the extraction of peat.[33] Their value was recognised until drainage.[34] Found in almost every fenland community, such fens were commonly called 'frith' (*fryde*) and by the early seventeenth century were 'used for digging the necessary firinge of the Inhabitants there as flaggs hassocks and turffes and a great part whereof there growth reed and sedge'.[35] The 'logs and stubble for kindling, … thatch for the roofing of their houses' described by the mid-twelfth century Peterborough chronicler were

FIGURE 6.2 *(opposite).* Extract from William Hayward's map of 1604 shows local names for fens in the area around Doddington, and some additions from the *ECB*. Few describe overgrown, wooded or otherwise neglected wetlands, suggesting long-term management of the fen landscape (CA R59/31/40/1, © Cambridge Archives, reproduced with permission).

products of the frith fen.[36] Wood, brushwood and withies were cropped at the *strodes,* 'brushwood fens', in Doddington (1227) and in Fenton (1228).[37] Brushwood was commonly used for firing, especially for baking and brewing that needed the residual heat of a very hot short-lived fire; it also provided an economic way of bulking up and in-filling the spaces in timber structures; and could be used in its own right, for example in fencing or making fish weirs.[38]

There is, in short, no evidence in documents, pollen records or in local names for any widespread neglect or underuse of the fen basin across the centuries between the withdrawal of Roman administration from Britain and the re-foundation of the monasteries in the later tenth century. There was instead considerable stability in the open grassland character of the fen landscape not only across the two millennia before the Norman conquest, but also into the medieval period and beyond.

The early and middle Anglo-Saxon economies, and opportunities in fenland

The continued exploitation of the fen basin by a sizeable population throughout the Anglo-Saxon period suggests some synergy between developments in the wider economy of Britain and opportunities available in the fens. There was a considerable change in the agricultural economy following the withdrawal of Roman administration from Britain in about 400. Cultivators who had specialised in the production of particular crops or animal products for sale in urban markets, buying in or bartering for the other foods and goods they needed, became post-Roman farmers practising mixed arable and pastoral husbandry, intensely focused on subsistence from one year to the next. These were changes that farmers across the fen basin were well-placed to take advantage of. The collapse in the market for surplus grain would have been no inhibition to men whose primary interests had always been in their animals rather than their crops, and for whom there were in any case only limited opportunities for arable cultivation. Across England, husbandmen generally maintained control of the entirety of their holdings simply by increasing the sizes of their flocks and herds. The natural water meadows of the fen basin and the fenmen who had the understanding necessary for their successful exploitation were perfectly matched to meet such changing agricultural objectives.

The stock that dominated the fenland landscape were an indication of the enthusiasm with which pastoralism was regarded in the early medieval fenland (and long before).[39] There were significantly more cattle on the early medieval south-east Lincolnshire fens, for instance, than there had been in the Roman period, even though fewer people were living there.[40] Cattle made up around 63% of the larger animals raised at early Anglo-Saxon Quarrington, Lincolnshire, and 59% in the middle Anglo-Saxon period.[41] Sheep just had the edge at middle Anglo-Saxon Walpole St Andrew and Terrington St Clement on the Norfolk silt fens, where about 45% of the larger animals were cattle, but around half were sheep.[42] In the peat fens around the Isle of Ely, where most excavation

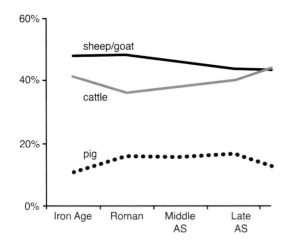

FIGURE 6.3. Cattle formed a large – and growing – proportion of the animals on early and middle Anglo-Saxon fen farms; this example is from Ely (© Susan Oosthuizen, after Appleby *et al.* 2009, 53).

has been concentrated, the post-Roman period saw an increasing emphasis on cattle-based pastoralism, and the proportion among the larger animals of cattle there followed national trends, rising from around 35% in the early Anglo-Saxon centuries to above 40% in the later seventh and eighth (Fig. 6.3).[43] Forty-one per cent and 43% of the larger animals respectively on the Middle Anglo-Saxon sites at the Downham Road and Walsingham Way sites on the Isle of Ely were cattle, for example, while 36% and 34% respectively were sheep.[44]

The herds on the silt fens appear to have been raised for meat, leather and (in the case of sheep) for wool.[45] On the peat fens, by contrast, the emphasis appears to have been on dairying. There, the cattle that survived for four or five years before slaughter were cows who appear to have been deliberately brought into milk by the birth of a calf each spring. The high number of calves that were butchered within the first 18 months of their lives suggests that the point of their birth was the dairy produce of their mothers, rather than an extension to the herd.[46] Although the size of early medieval fen herds is unknown, such large numbers of cattle fed on the medieval wetlands that they were customarily and vividly recorded as simply grazing 'horn under horn'.[47] That grassland continued to dominate over 4000 square km of the early medieval fenland after 400, and a concomitant lack of regenerated woodland, suggests that it may have been possible to describe early medieval herds in the same way.

The products of the fen, especially those from dairying, were key to the underlying prosperity of fen communities from prehistory into the early seventeenth century. Continuities in the grassland environment of the fen basin and the dominant place of cattle suggests that the local economy of early Anglo-Saxon settlements at Brandon and Ely was as focused on pastoral husbandry as that of nineteenth-century commoners at Cottenham a millennium and a half later. Those continuities may mean that medieval documents may illuminate, at least darkly, what archaeology cannot, of the importance of the wetlands in the early medieval economy. That is, that it may have been as true in the Anglo-Saxon period as it was in the thirteenth century that men with little or no arable land but who held rights of common in fen grazing and other products, could live very well, often better than an upland peasant with a standard arable holding.[48] Typical early medieval herds that held between four and eight cattle will have been familiar to late thirteenth-century peasants at Ramsey, most of whom owned between four and five.[49] Three and four centuries later, that pattern was unchanged: in the late sixteenth century, when 'the keeping of cattle was almost universal among the peasantry', there were between eight and ten cattle in the average fenland herd – numbers still comparable with early medieval herds which rarely exceeded twelve head except on the demesnes.[50]

Early medieval pastoral husbandry appear to have been focused on dairy production.[51] When levels of production were first recorded in fenland, they show that the demesne herds of the abbeys of Ely and Crowland could produce between 317 kg and 363 kg (700–800 lb) of cheese each year in the twelfth and thirteenth centuries.[52] The productivity of the smaller herds of the independent peasantry may have had more in common with Henry Wythington of Tydd St Mary (Lincolnshire), one of the poorer farmers in his community, who left 63.5 kg (140 lb) of cheese in his store when he died in 1537.[53] Cheese was still being produced in Cottenham in the late nineteenth century when 'in summer this fen or common was covered with the finest milch cows, and produced a cheese similar to but richer than Stilton, and in autumn a specialist, "Single Cottenham", with the flavour and consistency of Camembert' (Fig. 6.4).[54] Long-term synergies in sizes of peasant herds focused on dairying may indicate that the broad outlines of an Anglo-Saxon pastoral economy could be discerned in those later documents.[55]

However, cattle-raising offered more just the possibility of wealth to Anglo-Saxon freemen; they had a symbolic value too. The iconic status of cattle in early medieval society was derived from their 'striking' importance in the prehistoric and Romano-British periods, expressed in their use as currency, in feasting and in gift-exchange (Fig. 6.5).[56] That cultural significance remained

FIGURE 6.4 *(top)*. Two colourful bulls face each other over the lintel of the front door of a nineteenth-century cottage in Reach (© Susan Oosthuizen). Although their origin and precise meaning is obscure, they speak to a fascination with cattle that has been part of British culture since prehistory.

FIGURE 6.5 *(bottom)*. Early seventh-century silver-gilt fittings mounted on a modern horn, from the early Anglo-Saxon burial at Sutton Hoo, and now in the British Museum (© Susan Oosthuizen).

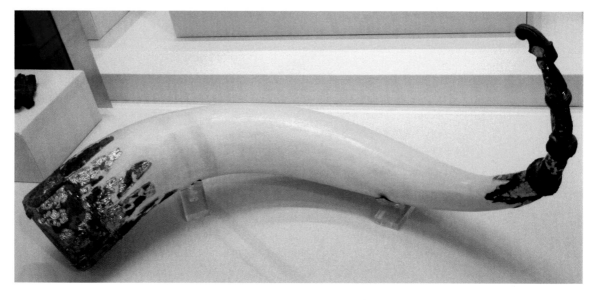

emphatic across the early medieval period, to the point that the Anglo-Saxon word for 'inheritance', *orfe*, has its origin in its earlier meaning, 'cattle'.[57] Cuts of beef were the focal point of high status feasting, elaborately-decorated drinking horns (which could hardly be less suited to the purpose) took central place in banqueting assemblages and, as late as the tenth century, English law codes were still primarily focused on penalties for cattle-raiding, even though farmers across southern and central England were by then increasingly turning to arable husbandry.[58] Cattle continued for centuries to be treated as 'moveable wealth' in places where pastoral husbandry remained the principal focus of household economies.[59] The importance of cattle in early medieval England extended far beyond the needs of a subsistence economy.

Yet fenmen in all periods were better off than their upland counterparts not simply because of their dairy herds, but also because their household economies were supported, extended and enriched by a wide range of other wetland products. Archaeological evidence for prehistoric, Romano-British and Anglo-Saxon fen farms (illuminated by medieval documents) shows the significant collective contribution made to livelihoods by other fenland products, including fish, fowl, reeds, sedge, osiers and turf.[60] It was the totality of those fen products that supported their solid, if modest, standards of living, even if cattle had the dominant role. The fenland thus had the potential to offer an excellent match for the agricultural and social ambitions of early and middle Anglo-Saxon husbandmen. How then, were those opportunities managed?

A managed landscape

The consistent archaeological, palynological and documentary evidence for the ecological stability of the wetland from prehistory until drainage in the mid-seventeenth century suggests that the landscape was carefully managed across the millennia to assure the volume and quality of its different products. O'Connor has argued that such stability can only have been the result of the 'quite deliberate management of the landscape to maintain that landscape as it ought to be'.[61] The landscape of the fen basin 'ought' in every period to have included large areas of natural watermeadows and other pastures, as well as stands of wetland grasses, accessible volumes of turf, large numbers of fish and fowl. It appears to have been carefully managed in all periods to achieve those ends. There were extensive Iron Age osier beds at Wardy Hill, for example, requiring cutting every 5–9 years; while the practice of cropping sedge every 3–4 years for animal litter, thatching and fuel was already common in the Roman fenland near Ely, and continued to be a staple of household economies throughout the Anglo-Saxon period (both dealt with in more detail below).[62] Management of production from dryland woods, osiers, and the frith fens can be seen in the standardised timbers and hurdles, made from withies and poles of uniform diameter, used to construct Bronze Age causeways across the shallower reaches of the fen at Flag Fen (Northamptonshire), and across the river Cam between Little Thetford and Fordey.[63] Similar prehistoric and later causeways have been found across the wetlands of the Somerset Levels, using timber, hurdles, poles and brushwood from managed resources in various combinations.[64] The construction of Aldreth Causeway, believed to have been undertaken by William I towards the end of the eleventh century, simply followed that ancient tradition (Fig. 6.6). Without the time to construct a more solid foundation for his causeway, he is said to have sunk boats instead, laying wicker hurdles, either pegging them with poles or laying rows of poles in a corduroy pattern above them, to provide the footway for his soldiers who, when they had crossed, 'scarcely made it, in the end, to solid ground through pitfalls and eddies of mud'.[65]

The management of fen resources is evident, too, in the restrictions on access to the early Anglo-Saxon fens implicit in its subdivision between territorial groups, each of which held exclusive rights to a particular part of the fen; and in the allocation of rights of common only to those individuals within those territories who fulfilled criteria of membership and status.[66] Both suggest that two risks had by then become apparent (if not long before): that the current needs of all households might not be satisfied if open access were allowed; and that the long-term sustainability of the volume of grazing and other products taken from the fen by each household each year could not be assured under the same conditions. If a resource were so plentiful as not to require management, then its exploitation would be not need to be restricted and there would be no necessity for resource allocation through rights of common. Instead, there appears to have been a degree of competition for resources not only between territorial groups but also between the households within them. That competition can most easily be inferred from rights of common – property rights, defensible in law, that provide a framework for managing competition for natural resources by restricting access to a resource to an exclusive group. Collective governance of those resources through exclusive access to them mediates those risks: it assures all right holders of a sufficient volume of the resource to meet their current needs, it demonstrates the transparent, equitable, predictable distribution of the resource between them, and at the same time safeguards its long-term sustainability by limiting the possibility of its over-exploitation. That is, if common rights over a natural resource can be shown – as they demonstrably can in fenland – the legal regulation and management of that resource is implied. It is particularly telling in this context that the most valuable common rights were those that provided access to fen grazing for cattle. Perhaps counter-intuitively, the wetland part of the fen basin was not an early medieval Arcadia from which households could take as much as they wished, from as many resources as they wished, whenever they wished.

How could there have been so much competition for the apparently almost limitless natural resources of the basin that it was necessary to manage them under the legal provisions of common property rights from 400 (if not before)? The answer lies in the fen ecology: this was not a uniform landscape, but a mosaic of varied ecological opportunities whose accessibility and products were dependent on quite small changes in water-levels that rose and fell both predictably and unpredictably across the year (see Fig. 1.3). The variety of local names for those grasslands is expressive of that range: *smithyfen* (1343, Cottenham, *smeeth*, 'marsh in smooth low-lying land'), *frith* (1326, Landbeach, 'winter fodder' on rough pasture, perhaps studded with brushwood), *stacks* (1249–50, Willingham), *hasse* (1404, Soham, *hassuc*, 'coarse grass'), *foderfen* (1325, Soham), *kalfeycnol* (1200, Downham), the island knoll where calves were pastured; *horsecroft* (1343, Soham) and *snyt(e)fen* (1350) for the snipe which nest under tussocks of grass.[67]

That diversity depended on the successful, sustainable management of fen resources through a range of cropping regimes, each tailored to a particular micro-ecology that supported a specific resource. Management was based on a careful assessment of the balance between the degree of waterlogging, relatively subtle changes in height above sea level, the underlying geology – *and* the physical needs and management regime of the plant species most likely to be successful in that particular combination of conditions. Different kinds of pasture, reed, rush, sedge, osiers, wood, and peat were restricted to specialist habitats, and each depended for its sustainability on a regular cycle of cropping since 'control of the intervals between mowing determines which crop develops at the expense of others, reeds, sedge, flags or grass'.[68] Because intervals between cropping reeds, rush, sedge and osiers might extend over several years, an annual supply of each could only be achieved by dividing their beds into sections, such that at least one section could be cropped each year while the remainder could be left to grow. Seasonality was also an important aspect of cropping. Reedbeds (*phragmites australis*) tend to develop where the water table is at about ground level for most of the year, and – like those *at redmer* and *thakfen* in Littleport (1249–50) – were cut annually, but only after midsummer.[69] Sedge (*cladium mariscus*) used for thatching and kindling usually grows in damp areas where the water level varies between 40 cm above and –15 cm below modern sea levels (see Fig. 1.4).[70] It needs careful management to assure a predictable supply and should be cut at intervals of about 5 years. If it is cut more often, the plants will eventually weaken and die; if it is not cut often enough, decaying leaves will raise the ground level too high above the water for the plant to flourish, and it will be replaced by dry land species. Vast quantities were grown in the fen, sometimes in specialist beds like *le lesschfen* (1381, Whittlesey) or *leccwerefen* (*c*.1320, Wimblington). Withies are most commonly cut from the shoots of heavily-managed willow, grown in osier beds and cropped every 5–9 years on a cycle designed to produce rods of a standard diameter for weaving into hurdles and other uses, for walling buildings, and so on.[71] Eels – which are amphibious – could only be trapped with a gleave on flooded meadows in Spalding and Pinchbeck on four days in the week between the end of September and early February, and two days in the week between February and the end of March; the breeding season for fish, between early February and the end of March, and that for fowl, had to be respected, and so on (Fig. 6.7).[72]

Regulation was undertaken collectively by regular assemblies of commoners like the court of the *letam integram de marisco* that managed grazing in Marshland, or that at Modich in the *gemæne ēa* where the four hundreds of the Isle met, collectively formulated, agreed and amended by-laws that they collectively agreed in order to optimise the sustainability and productivity of fen grazing, taking the requirements of the land, the beasts and their own production objectives into account.[73] They are evidence that, as Hallam remarked, communities 'tended [their fen commons] as lovingly as their fields' in order to balance sustainability with subsistence, each fen product to its own timetable, and each within the framework of common rights.[74]

Managing pasture for grazing

Areas of grazing required as careful management. The pastoral husbandry that dominated the wetland economy depended for its success on more than simply keeping areas of grazing free of trees and scrub. It required a deep knowledge of the complex characteristics of land and of stock across the seasons so that access to different areas of pasture could be timetabled in a way that met the needs of the animals while also maintaining the quality of the land. The richness and variety of the mix of grasses on which the animals fed would otherwise decline to the point where it could no longer support stock of any kind. With these

FIGURE 6.7. Fenland dominates the map of fisheries and the numbers of eels rendered to manorial lords across England in 1086 (© Dr Willem Dekker, reproduced with permission).

objectives in mind, commoners agreed, set up and enforced complex timetables that juggled competing seasonal needs of different types of land and different kinds of stock – heifers and bullocks, oxen, bulls, horses, sheep, and their young – in different seasons, in order to establish an equilibrium between production and the long-term sustainability of their livelihoods.[75]

Knowledge of the soft soils and grassland plants of the wetland landscape was key. It included detailed expertise in the minute variations of underlying geology, ground cover and carrying capacity between different parts of pastures and meadows in the intermediate and deeper fen. The wet soils of the basin are susceptible to trampling by cattle that, if let onto the fen too early in the year, can be so damaging to grass that its ability to regenerate may permanently be inhibited.[76] Pastures cannot be grazed without a break; they need periods of rest at discrete intervals to allow the grass to recover its nutritional value. The mineral content of pasture depends not only on the variety and mix of grass species in each area, but also on the underlying soils, the season, and the history of management of each section of grazing.[77] Commoners needed to be aware of the stocking capacity of different kinds of pasture, too, since 'the perfection of grazing is reckoned to consist not only in the choice of stock, but in nicely proportioning it to the breadth of land'.[78] Grass on understocked pastures grows too long for cattle to be able to feed properly; overgrazing offers a self-evident risk.[79] Even today, the fenland needs 'just the right level of grazing (neither too heavy nor too light). Light early summer grazing by traditional breeds of cattle is usually ideal'.[80] That understanding of stocking capacity requires an awareness of the demands made on pasture by different species of animals and, within each group, those of different levels of maturity. In the mid-twentieth century, for example, one cow was considered to need the same area of grazing as two 1-year-old heifers or bullocks, one horse, between five and eight sheep, or between 10 and 16 lambs.[81]

Expertise in the physical characteristics of the fen had to be complemented with a knowledge of the browsing habits and dietary needs of different groups of beasts, and the purposes for which each group was being kept, whether for dairying, meat production, traction, sale at market and so on. Timetabling their access to pasture across the seasons of the pastoral year had to match the character of different types of grassland – their degree of waterlogging, mineral content, richness of species, speed of regrowth – against those requirements. The potassium deficiencies that tend to increase in late summer on low-lying grassland, for example, may affect the fertility of cattle; they can, on the other hand, be controlled by limiting the period that the animals spend on each area of pasture to between four and six weeks.[82] Dairy cattle need a continuous supply of new, rich grazing in their milk-producing months as well as ready access to water, a condition not always as straightforwardly met as might be expected in a flat, fenny environment where watercourses required regular clearing and other maintenance, and overgrown drains might become stagnant.[83] And they need grass of an appropriate length: unlike sheep, they need longer grass that they can tear, whereas sheep bite the plants; horses by contrast can feed much closer to the ground surface.[84] Management regimes therefore generally allow cattle first onto previously-closed grassland between spring and autumn. Animals like sheep, horses or the bull, kept on poorer pasture during most of the year, might be put on better quality grass in autumn to support their health during the dearth of winter; pregnant stock was generally fed well in autumn to strengthen it for the coming period in stall; young beasts destined for slaughter at between 12 and 18 months needed feeding up for about 6 weeks before they went to the butcher; and so on.[85]

By-laws provide a detailed illustration of the coherent, complex, and holistic character of regulations within which shared resources in the fen were managed. Timetabling was focused on sub-dividing the fens to allow their rotation for different uses in different months, whose objectives were to maintain the quality of the grazing, to sustain the health of the herd, to ensure equitable exploitation among right holders, to maximise production, and to assure the long-term sustainability of fen pastures. The same management regimes are also recognisable not only in judgements of early modern Commissions of Sewers, but also in modern conservation advice for floodplain meadows: to include an annual hay cut, use to livestock from August to keep the grass from re-growing, to keep hedgerows and other boundaries in good repair, to control weeds, and to maintain ditches and other watercourses.[86] Surviving by-laws for fen commons speak to that detailed knowledge of the needs of their stock, the condition and potential of every inch of their pastures, and the requirements for maximizing both their exploitation and their long-term sustainability.[87] In 1665, for instance, the commoners of Willingham, Cambridgeshire, stipulated that hay grown on their deepest fen, the Hempsall, 'bee mowen every year before ye first day of August'; it was then closed for six weeks to produce a new grass crop before the cattle were let in 'from Michaelmas Day until ye feast of St Luke' (that is, between 29 September and 18 October).[88] By-laws for part of Hempsall Fen belonging to the neighbouring village of Rampton in 1754 stipulated its closure for growing grass from Candlemas (2 February) until 21 September, limited grazing on the new grass solely to cattle between 21 September and 21 December, and allowed only by horses and mares to feed there until it was closed again on the next 2 February.[89] The commons in March (Cambridgeshire) were similarly treated in 1669: they were closed for growing grass between Lady Day (25 March) and May Day (1 May); the new grass was so restricted to dairy cattle between May Day and Michaelmas (29 September) that calves were only allowed in in the same period if they were with their mothers, and even then only until they were six weeks old; the commons were then opened to all animals over the winter, until Lady Day when they were once more closed for the grass to grow.[90] The point of these records was not the construction of new by-laws, but the periodic adjustment of usage and timetabling in order to adapt to small-scale changes in local climatic and other conditions. As Ravensdale explained in 1974, commoners 'not only looked to the allocation of the commons between alternative uses, and allotted the time and place for each kind of stock, they also saw to the maintenance and improvement of the quality of the ground, and of the common flocks and herds', but also ensured the long-term sustainability of the pastures by preventing overgrazing and overstocking.[91]

Figure 6.8 offers a diagrammatic example of that sophisticated timetabling. It draws on by-laws made between 1681 and 1754 by the commoners at Rampton, a fen-edge community in Cambridgeshire, for the management of the four areas of common pasture in the vill.[92] The Old Meadow was the highest, occupying drier, gravel hards standing at about 5 m above sea level; Nether and Hither Iram occupied the intermediate fen around 3 m, while the Hempsall included the lowest, dampest and most frequently-flooded pasture along the Old West river, lying at between 1 m and 2 m above sea level.

The principles underlying the timetable are:

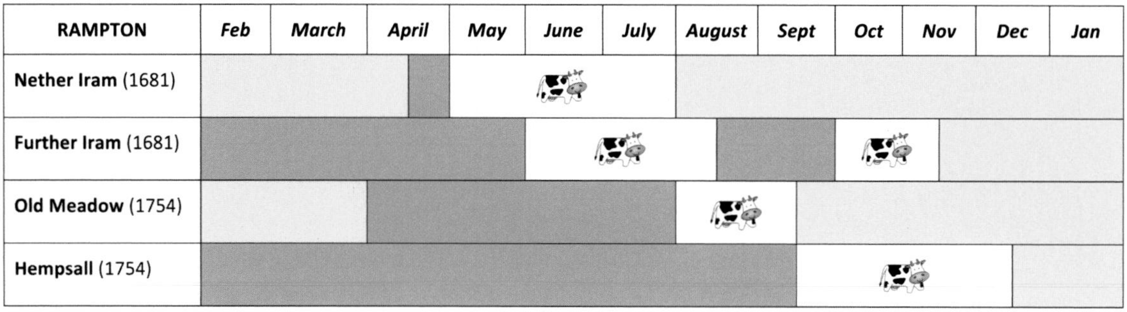

RAMPTON	Feb	March	April	May	June	July	August	Sept	Oct	Nov	Dec	Jan
Nether Iram (1681)					🐄							
Further Iram (1681)						🐄			🐄			
Old Meadow (1754)							🐄					
Hempsall (1754)									🐄			

Key: green = closed for growing grass; yellow = grazed by all stock; cow = grazing limited to dairy herd. The by-laws for the Old Meadow and Hempsall were not amended in 1681; the earliest record of their amendment is 1754. (Souces: CA 606/M3, L2/1)

1. to prioritise the claim of the dairy herd, who get the 'first bite' of each pasture when it is opened to grazing;
2. to balance the needs of the dairy herd against the months in which each pasture reaches peak condition;
3. to provide the dairy herd with a continuous supply of new grass by moving it every 4–8 weeks;
4. to assure an adequate supply of hay for feeding stalled beasts in winter and in early spring during calving, foaling or lambing;
5. to enable all stock to be fattened in the autumn months for overwintering, sale, or culling, on pastures that 'in six weeks will fatten a bullock though put into it bone lean'.[93]

FIGURE 6.8. Timetabling the use of the commons in Rampton between 1681 and 1754 (© Susan Oosthuizen).

The existence of extensive rights of commons in the early medieval fenland, together with pollen and place-name evidence for their long-term management for grazing, suggests that successful husbandry in that period depended as much on this complex body of knowledge as it did in the sixteenth and seventeenth centuries, and does today. Generally referred to as 'the custom of the marsh', the *consuetudo marisco*, the totality of regulations for access to, management and regulation of, fen commons – was already recognised as ancient by the time it was first recorded in documents from the twelfth century onwards.[94] Godric of Coningsby, the earliest recorded reeve of a fenland common, had already been managing Wildmore fen in Lincolnshire for 40 years on behalf of the communities that commoned there when he was named in a document in 1139.[95] By 1189, it was taken for granted that Crowland fen should be 'put into defence' (closed to grazing) for growing hay towards the end of May each year.[96] The volume of peat allowed to those with rights of turbary (peat) in Cottenham Fen was as precisely stipulated in 1344 as it might have been three hundred years later: each commoner might cut as many turves as would make a stack 36 ft (10.7 m) long, four turves in width and 21 turves high.[97]

The existence of early medieval by-laws is beyond doubt: if management of fen resources was not required, there would be no necessity for their regulation under systems of shared rights of property. Whether they were as, more, or less complex than those of the twelfth century is unknowable. At a minimum, however, they could be expected to limit access to the common by articulating entitlement to rights of common in it, to regulate and enforce its equitable exploitation, and to stipulate and enforce a management regime that kept grasslands, beasts and other resources in good health, assured a sufficient volume of fen resources to each commoner, and safeguarded the sustainability of those resources in the longer term.

Conclusion

Evidence from palynological research, palaeobotanical and faunal remains recovered during archaeological excavation, and place- and field-names, demonstrate the long-term stability of the mosaic of species that made up the varied specialised environments of the fen basin, and a long history of early medieval dairying. Documentary evidence of early rights of common indicate the deliberate, careful management of the fen landscape throughout the early medieval period, focused on maintaining the ecological mosaics that sustained rich grazing for cattle and a wide range of other fen products. The social mechanism adopted to achieve those aims was the sub-division of the wetlands between territories; entitlement within each territory to exploit the resources of the basin was restricted to individuals, qualified by kinship and status. Shared access to fen resources through systems of common rights provided the framework for collective governance, regulation and careful management that assured a minimum level of prosperity to those who held them, and at the same time balanced the immediate allocation of a resource against its long-term sustainability. Common rights also signaled a minimum level of prosperity, free status, offered opportunities to interact on equal terms with others of different rank and wealth, and brought with them treasured concomitant responsibilities for participation in the active governance of a territory as a whole. There were good reasons that 'nowhere in England were common rights more important', that such rights in fenland were so ancient, and that the cultural identity of early medieval territories was structured around them.[98]

The wetlands, especially the peat fen, were, however, a particularly specialised environment. Managed and timed closure of meadows for hay, and managed and timed access to specific areas of the fen not only by dairy herds but also by other beasts, were essential to peasant livelihoods. The thousands of square kilometres of fen pastures of all kinds and qualities on which that income depended could be put at risk by seasonal – and unseasonal – flooding in which water levels could rise by several metres. The risk was especially severe across the fen basin because water could spread so rapidly across its relatively flat floor. The next chapter considers whether and how Anglo-Saxon fen men managed the benefits and the risks associated with the predictable floods that came each winter and the unpredictable waters that followed unseasonable rains.

Notes

1. Pryor 2001, 368–73; French 2001, 403; Evans and Hodder 2006, 5; Malim 2010, 72; Evans 2003a, 212–13.
2. Pryor 1998, 284–92; Godwin 1940, 299.
3. Evans 2003b, 121; see also Evans and Serjeantson 1988, 365–68.
4. Evans 2003b, 83; see also Ballantyne 2004, 189; Gibson and Knight 2006, 129; Oosthuizen 2016a.
5. Hall 1996, 8.
6. Ravensdale 1974, 45.
7. English Nature 2004, 10; see also Rackham 1987, 97.
8. Rowell 1986, 142; Waller 1994, 40.
9. Murphy 1994, 37; Dark 2000, ch. 5; Foard 2001.
10. Rackham 1987, 214.
11. Rackham 1987, 212.
12. *GP* IV, 186, trans. Darby 1974, 54; see also Gelling 1984, 196; Rackham 1987, 87, 141, 210; MacKenzie 2010, 21.
13. *E.g.* Shennan 1986, 163; Waller 1994, 23, 88, 124.
14. Crowson *et al.* 2005, 60, see also 96, 260–61.
15. Silvester 1988, 158.
16. *E.g.* Appleby *et al.* 2009, 50; Hutton 2010, 9; Slater 2011, 48.
17. Mortimer *et al.* 2005, 99, 101, 112–13.
18. Tester *et al.* 2014, 320–21, 331–33.
19. Reaney 1943, 247, 217, 185–87, 234–35, 237, 235, 221, 280.
20. Hooke 1978, 333–34.
21. Reaney 1943, 246.
22. Reaney 1943, 240, 246.
23. *RABB*, 5–6.
24. *E.g.* Baines 1996, 172; Oosthuizen 2008, 323–24; Hall 2012, 111.
25. Oosthuizen 2008.
26. Reaney 1943, 252, 253, 254, 258, 265.
27. Reaney 1943, 217.
28. Reaney 1943, 251.
29. Ravensdale 1974, 23.
30. Fox 1923, 180; Ravensdale 1974, 26.
31. Friday *et al.* 1997, 82; Reaney 1943, 33.
32. *ECB*, f.34d(1), f.49d(1), f.25d(2).
33. Denman *et al.* 1967, 87; Banham and Faith 2014, 144.
34. Ravensdale 1974, 45–46.
35. Cited in Reaney 1943, 179,
36. *Pet. Chron.*, 2.
37. *ECB*, f.26r(2); Reaney 1943, 346; Mawer and Stenton 1926, 212.
38. *E.g. ECB*, f.9r(1)-f.9d(1), f.30d(1), f.49d(1), f.50d(2).
39. Pastoralism dominated the fen economy from the Neolithic onwards, generally – but not always – based on a preponderance of cattle. See, for example, Evans and Serjeantson 1988, 366; Pryor 1998, 283; Evans 2003b, 127; Evans and Hodder 2006, vol. ii, 5; Appleby *et al.* 2009, 52–53; Evans and vander Linden 2009, 116; Tabor 2010a, 35; 2010b, 3; 2011, 20; Evans 2013, 61.
40. Hayes and Lane 1992, 213, 253.
41. Crabtree 2010, 124.

42. Crabtree 2010, 124; see also Crowson *et al.* 2005, 140, 216–28.
43. Mortimer *et al.* 2005, 91, Figure 5.1; see also Crabtree 2010, 127.
44. Appleby *et al.* 2009, 53; Slater 2011, 43; see also Masser 2000.
45. Crowson *et al.* 2005, 140, 216–18.
46. Crabtree 1990, 69–74; Mortimer *et al.* 2005, 92.
47. Neilson 1920, xxxviii, xliii, xlix; Darby 1974, 68.
48. Darby 1974, 22–38; Spufford 1974, 131–34; VCH Cambs. IX, 250; see also Thirsk 1953a, 29.
49. Hamerow 2002, 130; Postan 1973, 230, 245.
50. Ravensdale 1974, 61; Hamerow 2002, 139; see also Moore 1685, 59; Thirsk 1953a, 29; Spufford 1974, 130–33.
51. Hamerow 2002, 128.
52. Ravensdale 1974, 59–60.
53. Thirsk 1953a, 29.
54. Cited in Ravensdale 1974, 59.
55. Crabtree 1990, 69–74; Mortimer *et al.* 2005, 92.
56. Crabtree 2010, 126; also Oosthuizen 2011b.
57. Charles-Edwards 1979, 98.
58. Whitelock 1979; Oosthuizen 2013b, 20–23.
59. Davies and Dixon 2007, 43; O'Connor 2011, 367.
60. *E.g.* Mortimer *et al.* 2001; Crowson *et al.* 2005; Tester *et al.* 2014.
61. O'Connor 2009, 11.
62. Evans 2003b, 83; Ballantyne 2004, 195.
63. Pryor 2001, 152, 171; Lethbridge 1934.
64. Coles and Coles 1986, pls x and xi.
65. *LE* II, 110.
66. *E.g.* Neilson 1920, xlix; Oosthuizen 2016a.
67. Reaney 1943, 150, 174–76, 180, 198; 2004, 344; see also OS 1:25 000, Sheets 225, 226.
68. Ravensdale 1974, 45; also Rackham 1987, 330.
69. Rowell 1986; Natural England 2008, 103, 54; English Nature 2004, 4; see also Brears 1929.
70. Rowell 1986, 142.
71. Rackham 1987, 87.
72. Hallam 1963.
73. Oosthuizen 2011b, 160–62; 2016b; see *Prologue* above.
74. Hallam 1963, 45, my addition.
75. *E.g.* Cunningham 1910; Brears 1929; Hallam 1963.
76. Ravensdale 1974, 67.
77. *E.g.* Denman *et al.* 1967; English Nature 2004; Rothero *et al.* 2016.
78. Gooch 1811, 189.
79. There is little evidence of stinting – limiting the number of cattle each right holder could pasture – beyond restricting numbers to those that could be overwintered, before the later middle ages (Ravensdale 1974, 78; Coleman 1996, 5, items 65 and 99; Darby 1974, 70; Brears 1929, 59–60).
80. English Nature 2004, 11.
81. Denman *et al.* 1967, 339.
82. Davies 2009, 8–9.
83. Owen 1965, 41.
84. Rothero *et al.* 2016, 59.

85. See Denman *et al.* 1967, 14–15 for similar advice.
86. *E.g.* Cunningham 1910; Brears 1929; Thirsk 1953b; Kirkus 1959; Hallam 1963; Owen 1977; Rothero *et al.* 2016, 57–60.
87. *E.g.* Cunningham 1910; Brears 1929; Hallam 1963.
88. CA R/59.14.5.9.(b).
89. CA L2/1.
90. CA 606/M2.
91. Ravensdale 1974, 68.
92. CA L2/1, 606/M3; CUL Add Ms 6971. Each set of by-laws.
93. Gooch 1811, 186; see also Page 1929, 605; Oschinsky 1971, 275, 285, 331, 337; Biddick 1989, 19–21, 92; Rothero *et al.* 2016.
94. Neilson 1920, xlix–lviii.
95. Neilson 1920, xviii–xix.
96. Page 1906, 107 ff. The bitter dispute that led to the documentation of the tradition was not against the closure itself, but against the unilateral action of the Abbot of Crowland in closing the common when the decision should have been taken by the commoners. He had treated common land as if it were part of the Abbey's demesne.
97. Page 1934, 25–26.
98. Darby 1974, 68.

CHAPTER 7

Managing Commons for a Livelihood

Across the last four millennia and more the richest economic resource in the peat wetland was, as we have seen, summer pasturage on its natural water meadows. The intermediate fen, drier in summer and flooded in winter, produced a species-rich whiteseed grass called fen hay, 'plenteous and ranke of a certain fatte grosse', that grew so abundantly that it could be mown twice or more each year.[1] Medieval chroniclers were euphoric about its 'delectable' meadows.[2] The twelfth-century Ramsey spring meadows were 'just as if painted with flowers which are looking at you merrily'.[3] 'Many fertile meads and pastures' encircled Peterborough in the mid-twelfth century.[4] William of Malmesbury fondly remembered between 1118 and 1125 how 'the Plain [at Thorney] is as level as the Sea, which with the flourishing of its grass allureth the Eye, and so smooth that there is nothing to hinder him that runs through it'.[5] Nearly 500 years later Camden was as entranced, describing the peat fens as 'a tract passing greene, fresh and gay by reason of most plenteous pasture'.[6] When the details of manorial income began to be recorded systematically in the mid-twelfth century, the rental value of an acre of fen meadow, or the dairy produce (lactage) from a single cow grazing upon it, could bring in three times or more income than an acre of arable land.[7] Even in the early nineteenth century, the fen hay could fatten 'the leanest bullock' in six weeks.[8] The richness of dairying in the fen could not, said Vancouver, 'be ascribed to any particular mode in the management of the dairies, but solely to the nature of the herbage on the commons'.[9]

This chapter explores the conditions for the successful production of fen grazing, in particular the vital – if risky – role played by water. It explains how the quality of grazing depended on seasonal levels of water, and how this was managed by linking canals and their subordinate feeder ditches with natural water courses (Fig. 7.1). Although post-medieval drainage destroyed most medieval evidence for day-to-day water management in the basin, the system can be inferred from surviving lodes because they disrupted the natural drainage. Such engineering is generally believed to have been introduced after the refoundation of the monasteries in the later tenth century. Evidence for extensive, sophisticated water engineering across the basin before 970 is discussed below, together with its implications for the complexity of land management to support pastoral husbandry in the early medieval fenland.

FIGURE 7.1. Wicken Lode leads from the fen-edge south-west of the medieval settlement of Wicken, to meet the river Granta/Cam near Upware. It is fed by two catchwater drains that run along the fen-edge to meet it at its northern end (© Susan Oosthuizen).

Conditions for the production of fen hay and other fen grasses

The range of grassland mosaics suitable for the varied purposes of fen stockmen – hay, rough pasture, meadow grazing, and litter – depended on the degree of waterlogging that each required in different seasons, and that was in turn a response to five interdependent factors.[10] First, it depended where each area of grazing lay along the 3.6 m (12 ft) difference in height between sea level and the maximum reach of the floods (see Fig. 1.3). Self-evidently, grasses on the lower slopes were flooded more regularly and for longer than those that lay higher up. Second, the complex underlying geology of the peat fens, in which different combinations and varying thicknesses of peat, alluvium, gravel and/or clay are interleaved from area to area, creates quite different drainage conditions even between pastures at the same height above sea level. Pastures whose underlying soils include gravel or alluvium, for example, are less prone to waterlogging than others at the same height that lie over heavier soils.[11] Third, the strong, healthy growth of grasses in fen meadows and pastures relies on the presence in the flood waters, in sufficient volumes and appropriate relative proportions, of the three essential nutrients for plant health: nitrogen, phosphorus and potassium.[12] Fourth, the percentage of oxygen in the flood waters depends on whether the water lies stagnant or is moved by currents or turbulence; movement in the water encourages the oxygenation that benefits even those plants in which growth is still dormant.[13] And, fifth, the alkalinity of the calcareous water coming into the fen basin was important in supporting the rich diversity of its wetland grasses. Had the water been acidic, there would have been fewer, weaker and slower-growing species of grasses.[14] The striking commonality between all five is that they are all about aspects of the water supply to grasses whose productivity outstripped upland meadows and pasture by a considerable margin. As Dugdale remarked in 1662, 'the richness of the soyl, being gained from the waters, doth … for the most part exceed the high grounds thereon bordering'.[15]

Water, its volume and quality, was the most important contributor to the wealth of peasants whose income depended on grazing their cattle in the pre-drainage wetlands. Because the basin floor was relatively flat, it could carry a large volume of flood water at generally shallow depths. When the river Ouse in the southern part of the basin was embanked in the early seventeenth century causing long episodes of severe flooding, local men described earlier conditions before the banks were built, when floods had been relatively shallow, wide-ranging and drained away relatively quickly: 'where the waters formerly in times of inundations and landflouds had their passage over the whole face of the soyle for four or five miles [c.6.5–8 km] space, by means whereof the floud speedily passed away with little hurt doing'.[16] Their dependency on water was evidently not without risk.

Winter floods were generally welcomed, since the water not only brought nutrients but protected underlying grasses from frost.[17] The species-rich intermediate meadows lying between modern sea-levels and the flood line, only inundated in winter and dry in summer, produced the fen hay. In 1618 they were neatly described: 'nearest to the Hilles & in the best parte, *soonest drowned, and soonest drayned*, & the best soyle receiving, refreshing, & as it were manured by the overfloweing Water'.[18] Even where flooding on meadows and pastures was prolonged, the water was rarely stagnant since it was continually entering and flowing across the basin towards its outlet at the Wash, even if its pace was often slow. That constant movement and the consequent currents, however slight, within it produced a sufficient level of oxygenation in flood water to protect the underlying grasses against anaerobic conditions.[19] Grasses can, moreover, sustain lengthy inundations provided that temperatures remain at or below 5 °C.[20] A rise in temperatures above that level, however, stimulates growth. If, in that case, the water is not let off within a few days, the quality of the grazing under the floods may be damaged, possibly permanently. That explains why lower rough pastures with fewer species lying closer to sea level, but not at or below it, and that remained waterlogged for longer, were described as 'the 'meere Fennes whose soil is commonly mare & being further from the head Rivers do yield Turf & Hasses which swimmith'.[21]

Unpredictable variations in the volume of water, the season of its arrival, and the length of inundation offered the greatest risk to fen livelihoods. The winter floods might not come, depriving pastures of the water, minerals and rich silts on which the fen hay depended; if they were prolonged into early spring the

production of early grass might be delayed just when the size of herds began to be increased by the arrival of calves, and supplies of the previous year's hay and fodder began to run out. Dry springs and summers respectively restricted the strength and richness of the first flush of grass and its re-growth on pastures already grazed. In winter, when the many species that made up the sward were largely dormant, floods might linger for weeks with no ill-effect provided the weather remained cold (Fig. 7.2) The 'key window of 21 days' within which the water must be removed was critical for James Winslade (whose pastures on the Somerset Levels were inundated during exceptionally heavy flooding in January 2014) because average temperatures were higher than usual and the grass was beginning to grow.[22] Summer floods were beneficial if they passed quickly, since the water and nutrients they brought gave the pastures and fen hay an extra burst of growth during a drier time of year. But prolonged flooding in warmer seasons when the grass was growing reduced the variety of grasses in the sward, restricted the area of grazing available to the dairy herd, and threatened the production of the hay on which the stock would feed over the coming winter.

The reasons are straightforward: 'Occasional inundation is probably essential in maintaining base status … prolonged inundation leading to stagnation, particularly in the spring or summer months, is likely to kill some species and lead to development of less diverse vegetation types'.[23] Commoners at Cottenham, Cambridgeshire vividly described in 1618 the balance that they sought:

'We say that in Cottenham there are divers grounds, some half several and some common, both which upon extraordinary floods are sometimes overflown and upon the fall of the river do forthwith drain again as the upland meadows do; but unless

FIGURE 7.2. Winter floods at Sutton Gault, within the wide catchwater constructed during the mid-seventeenth century (© Susan Oosthuizen). The water extends widely across the almost flat floor of the basin, with the result that the floods are rarely deep. The silt brought down in the floods is spread across a large area of natural water-meadow and, because the water is relatively shallow, it tends not to stay for long. Both conditions help to sustain the richness of the fen pastures.

the said floods do happen to overflow them in the summer season (which is very seldom) we do find that the said grounds receive more benefit than hurt thereby and are thereby much bettered and enriched: for those grounds which lie lowest, and are oftenest and longest overflown in the winter season are the most fertile grounds, and yield the best yearly value ... unless it be some dry year when they are not overflown, for then the white fodder decayeth, and the grounds turn to a small kind of hamer segge which the cattle like not so well, the stuff being much worse'.[24]

Farmers across the centuries have expressed the same anxieties about risks relating to the waters in their pastures. In 1742 men from Rampton and neighbouring parishes complained to the Commissioners of the Bedford Level Corporation that 'the old River Ouze ... is now grown up (which was the only River or Drain for carrying the Water of your Petitioners' Lands) and that whilst it remains in the present Condition your Petitioners' Lands must in a wet season remain drowned'.[25] The same grievance was expressed 400 years earlier when over 800 ha (2000 acres) of 'Meadow, Moor and Fen' as well as 'all the Meadows, Lands, Pastures, Fens and Turbaries' on the Abbey of Crowland's estates in the western fen basin were flooded in 1330 by damming the river Nene at Outwell, over 27 km (16 miles)

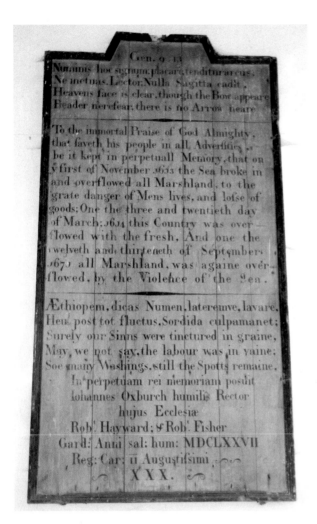

FIGURE 7.3. 'So many Washings, still the Spotts remain': a board erected in St Mary's church, West Walton, in 1671 recorded terrible sea floods in Marshland in 1613, 1614 and 1671 (© Susan Oosthuizen).

to the east, and there were widespread protests that pastures 'in floud times were overflowed and drowned'.[26] Mr Winslade (see above) in 2014 and the commoners of Rampton in 1742 were not complaining about flooding on their pastures, but about problems with their ability to manage the water off that land.[27] The emphasis of the petitioners from Rampton, for instance, was that the lands '*remain* drowned' – it was not the flooding itself that they objected to, but the persistence of the water after it could have been expected to have receded.[28] Precisely the same complaint was made in 1330: the problem was that the waters '*could not pass away as they had used to do*; so that the Lords of those fens and their Tenants, as also the Commoners in them, *did totally lose the benefit* which had belonged to them thereby'.[29]

Although the timing and volume of exceptional floods were beyond prediction or management (Fig. 7.3), under normal circumstances optimal conditions might be achieved in fen pastures and meadows if two contributory variables could be managed: the volume of water coming into the fen from upland streams and minor rivers; and the general degree of wetness required for the maintenance of the various parts of the fens across the year. By adding or subtracting water to different areas in different seasons, farmers could maintain particular ecologies at different points in their growing cycles. Ditches that helped to take excess water out of the grasslands in winter, for example, might become closed reservoirs maintaining necessary water levels in summer. As Gooch explained, water management in the intermediate fens was integral to the early growth of fen hay: 'the land is purposely inundated till the crops appears above the water, then (where it can be effected) the water *is let off*.'[30] When there were floods, the system helped to keep the length of the period of inundation within the limits appropriate to enrich and maintain the fen hay; in drier periods, water might be kept in the ditches in order to keep the wetlands moist rather than being sent into the rivers, in precisely the same way that water is sometimes pumped into Wicken Sedge Fen, one of the few pieces of undrained wetland in the fen basin, in order to maintain water levels there.

It should be emphasised that this was not a system aimed at drainage. It was a system engineered to manage the seasonal volume of water in each area of wetland in order to maximise the quality of grass of different kinds. How might such systems of water management work? And might they have been present in the early medieval landscape?

Water management in the fen landscape

It is generally accepted that the management of water was already being undertaken across the peat fens in the late Anglo-Saxon period. To take just one example, Hall's work on the Fenland Project demonstrated how the course of the river Nene across the southern fen basin was re-routed at least twice before the Norman Conquest – first, to the south, and then to the north, of Whittlesey Mere. Initially flowing south into the fen at Peterborough, it ran between Farcet and an island in Farcet Fen and was then directed into Whittlesey Mere along a canal called *Merelade* (now called Conquest Lode); it then flowed along a more or less natural course towards Ramsey Mere, and then north to Benwick and the Wash.[31] By the early eleventh century, it had been re-directed into a northerly course that took it to Benwick along a partially canalised course that hugged the southern contours of the island of Whittlesey. The engineers who ordered these works often incorporated existing watercourses, but were as capable of constructing completely artificial cuts. An active creek was deepened in places and straightened in others in formalising the eastern boundary of the Abbey of Ely's estates, the *Abbotesdelf*, between about 970 and 996.[32] On the other hand, the course of the West Water that carried the old course of the river Ouse from its entry into the fen basin at Earith to its confluence with the Nene at Benwick included several canalised sections; some – like Hollode – follow a natural feature or stream, while others – like Crollode – have the distinctive straightness of an artificial cut.[33] These works range from regional

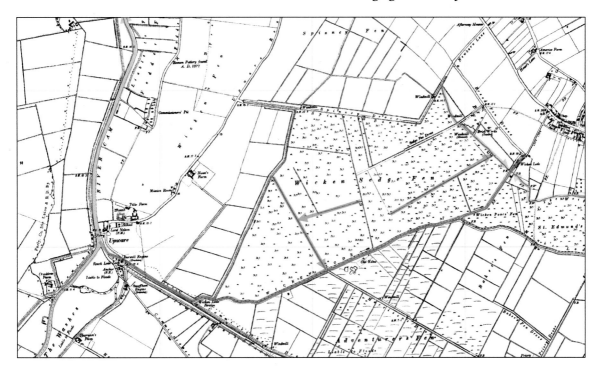

FIGURE 7.4. Wicken Lode (dark blue) led from the fen edge to the river Cam (mid-blue); it was fed by two catchwaters (orange). The history of Wicken Sedge Fen (light green) can be traced at least into the middle ages. Once the lode had been constructed, the ground and rain water that collected in the fen was managed by the construction of ditches (mid-green). Whether these are the original ditches is unknown; they were the first to be documented, between 1600 and 1700 (Rowell 1997, table xiv). (Ordnance Survey 6in:mile, 1900, my additions; © Crown Copyright and Landmark Information Group Limited (2017). All rights reserved (1900).

and supra-regional projects to the localised, every-day management of water. All were gravity-drained systems whose components included canals (locally called lodes), catchwater drains and a restricted number of intermediate ditches (*e.g.* Fig. 7.4).

Lodes and catchwaters

The word 'lode' embodies its objective: to manage water. It is derived from the Old English *(ge)lād*, 'to lead', just as water is still 'led' in channels today.[34] Lodes are canals into which water from upland streams and springs is diverted (led) away from the wetlands and taken straight into the nearest river instead. They usually follow the most direct route between the two points, taking changes in underlying geology and height above modern sea levels into account. By the mid-thirteenth century there were several lodes in the fens of most communities: the Doddington fens were transected by *Hymelode, Hyrdelode, Cokeslode*, and *Danelode*, for example, while *Edyvelode, Wertelode* and *Alderhelode* ran the relatively short distance from Wilburton, on the southern slopes of the island of Ely, towards an earlier watercourse now replaced by the river Ouse.[35]

The details of their construction are illustrated in a survey of five lodes in north-east Cambridgeshire: Bottisham Lode, Swaffham Lode, Reach Lode, Burwell Lode, and Wicken Lode.[36] They vary in length from around 3–5 km (1.8–3 miles), and in width from 6–12 m (19.6–39 ft). Most are embanked and were likely to have been from the outset, at least towards their landward ends.

FIGURE 7.5. The Weirs at Burwell – a catchwater drain running along the fen-edge towards Burwell Lode (© Susan Oosthuizen). The uplands lie to the right of the catchwater, while the substantial bank that runs along the left-hand side of the Weirs protects the fens to the left from upland flooding.

This is because most cut across the natural drainage pattern and engineering was thus required to ensure that the water they carried was retained within them. Wicken Lode, a parish boundary along almost its entire length, has a continuous, 3.6 m (12 ft) high, retaining bank along its southern side separating it from the deeper fens in Burwell; Monks Lode in Wicken has a similar, 3 m (10 ft) high bank along its south side; Bottisham Lode has 'high retaining banks on both sides'; the banks on either side of Reach Lode are up to 9 m (30 ft) wide.[37] Like the banks [*wallias*] along the canals [*watergagia*] of Romney Marsh in Kent in 1258, these were traditional constructional techniques, '*sicut antiquiter utebatur*', 'as it was done from the earliest times'.[38] The customs of Romney Marsh, the first to be recorded in detail, were accepted then and since as an exemplar of long-standing traditions of wetland management across medieval England, 'not creating new regulations but merely recording what had been going on time out of mind'.[39] That continuity persisted. A statute of 1427 governing the by-laws of sewers (canals and drains) in Lincolnshire remained in force, largely unchanged, until 1930.[40]

The lodes are fed by catchwater drains that collect water flowing from the uplands and divert it into the lode, to prevent it from running into the fen. The origins of the catchwaters are self-evidently artificial, since they run along the flood line rather than across it, from high to low ground. The banks that run along the fenward sides of the catchwaters are an essential part of the engineering that enables each drain to work successfully: they are bulwarks that shore the catchwater up and prevent the water within it from running into the fen. Those fenward banks are, however, almost always higher than they need to be, rising markedly above the level of the ground surface to the landward side of the drain (Fig. 7.5). The reason is revealed in the case of flooding: if heavy rainfall on the uplands so filled a catchwater that it burst its banks, the floods encroached on the properties of the houses that lined the landward banks long before they topped the retaining bank towards the fen. Fen men were, it seems, prepared to lose part or all of their homesteads before they sacrificed their pastures and meadows. A glance at Ordnance Survey maps reveals these systems in almost every fen-edge and island settlement, sometimes almost complete, at other times visible only in diminished ditches. There are virtually intact catchwaters, for example, at places like Burwell, Reach, Yaxley and Swavesey; in other places, like Witcham, Aldreth, Downham and Isleham, ditches and sometimes only footpaths preserve their original alignments.[41]

Lodes were constantly being constructed, refurbished or decommissioned. Hall argued that Cnut's Dyke, linking Ramsey with an ancient course of the river Nene, was dug in the later tenth century to bring building stone for the Abbey from the Northamptonshire uplands.[42] It has now all but disappeared: the modern road and roadside ditches between Ramsey and Pondersbridge preserve the alignment of its southern course; its northern channel is followed in part by the Oakley Dike. Many had medieval origins, like Beach Lode in Landbeach, constructed in 1235, or Salter's Lode, built in the same century to connect the eastern section of the river Nene with its new outfall at King's Lynn.[43] In 1487 Bishop Morton commissioned a new cut to carry the western section of the Nene for 18 km (11 miles) from Stanground near Peterborough to Wisbech; Burwell New Lode was built in the mid-seventeenth century as part of a programme of fen drainage; and both Swaffham and Reach Lodes have been re-cut in the post-medieval period along alignments parallel to their earlier courses.[44] Silting from upland waters, episodes of marine flooding, and deliberate raising of the beds of existing natural and artificial watercourses to make it easier for animals to cross them, all contributed to the impermanence of these works. By 1618, for example, Bishop Morton's Leam – by then only around 130 years old – was already 'much decayed as well in its own passage, by certain high gravells layd therein, as also by the decay of Wisbech outfall' through silting up from the sea.[45]

Between the lodes

The north-east Cambridgeshire fen edge is one of the few areas where the potentially catastrophic impact of the construction of lodes on the natural drainage has been mapped (Fig. 7.6).[46] Each lode cuts across the small winding creeks and streams that had previously carried water through the wetland to the river Cam. Although the upland waters now no longer flowed into the fen after the lode was built, those low-lying pastures continued to receive water from two other sources: rainfall, and groundwater. Heavy rainfall over the fen self-evidently adds water to the landscape. Ground water flows along the water table from higher to lower ground (the hydraulic gradient), under the banks and catchwaters that keep the water of rivers and streams out of the fen. The height of the water table fluctuates seasonally, rising closer to ground surface

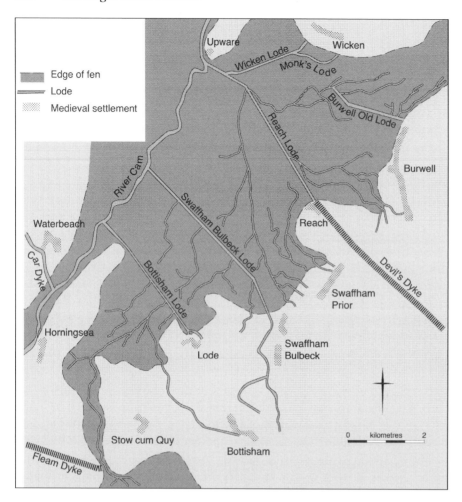

FIGURE 7.6. Lodes cut across natural drainage in the north-east Cambridgeshire fens (© Susan Oosthuizen, after RCHME 1972, fig. 7).

in winter and falling away in summer.[47] Volumes could be considerable in wet seasons. The consequence is that the small creeks and streams below the flood line were unable to discharge the water that collected in them since their courses were now blocked by the lode. They would eventually overflow, flooding the surrounding pasture, meadow or other grass crops and thus threatening the livelihoods of fen farmers.

The problem was dealt with by digging a restricted number of ditches – restricted because their aim was water management rather than drainage – within each area of fen now crossed by lodes, and allowing that water to flow, under the influence of gravity either into the sections of the lodes nearer the river or into the river itself. Thus the headwaters of the north-east Cambridgeshire system were taken into Bottisham Lode, water from the central section into Swaffham Lode, and that from the most northerly section into Reach Lode.[48] Within each area of fen, water flowed from the highest to the lowest ditch and was directed into the lode through wooden pipes (gotes and, if they were small, pisgotes, that were made by slotting hollowed tree-trunks together end-to-end) that were set in the banks of the lode (Figs 7.7 and 7.8). A thirteenth-century pipe was excavated under the Sea Bank near Newton, in Cambridgeshire. It was over 10 m (32 ft) long and 1 m (3.2 ft) in diameter, made by linking three hollowed-out elm trunks together. It lay on sleeper beams, stabilised with uprights and covered with planks, and provided an outfall into the Wash at low tide for fresh water that accumulated in the reclaimed fields of the silt fens behind the Bank during the preceding high tide.[49] The workings of these pipes was clearly explained in the mid-sixteenth century Lincolnshire fens when Thomas Irby was commanded to 'lay [one] holl' tree or pyshegote in the bank of the seyd Rusgate Ee of the south syde for the drayne of the water owte of the surres [sewers, *i.e.* drains] and other places'.[50] The use of hollowed trees as pipes has an ancient history: they were used for managing water in Dutch marshland as early as 175 BC, were widely used across Roman Britain from Lincolnshire to Hadrian's Wall, and were in everyday use in British towns into the eighteenth century.[51] Alternatively, where possible, a ditch might lead directly into a natural watercourse without the requirement for a pipe.

The outfall from pipes and drains was controlled by hinged one-way 'clapper' doors, called clows, that allowed water only to flow out of the fen. When water levels were higher in the rivers/lodes than in the fen, the pressure of water in the river/lode pressed against the door and kept it closed, protecting the fen from flooding; when levels were higher in the fen, then the water was able to flow out into the river/lode through the clow. The same principle worked on the coast, where the clows were closed by high tides, and pushed open at low tide by fresh water that had collected inland. The principle is clearly explained in Figure 7.7, which shows the Iron Age timber pipe with a clow at its sea-ward end that drained water collected in coastal marshes into the estuary of the river Rhine in Holland.[52] That excavated example is identical in structure to

FIGURE 7.7. Prehistoric and early Roman water management in marshland: A system for water management had been constructed by about 175 BC in the marshes along the northern shore of the Rhine estuary, and was rebuilt a number of times over the following 350 years (© Tim De Ridder, reproduced with permission). Banks were built along the shore to make dams in which water in the marshes collected during high tide (top right); at low tide the water flowed into the estuary along a timber pipe that led water from the dam through the bank, and whose entrance was protected by a clapper door that closed when the tide came in. An identical thirteenth-century example has been excavated under the Sea Bank, and sixteenth-century documents from Lincolnshire describe the same form of engineering.

the thirteenth-century example excavated under the Sea Bank, and to the four late medieval hollowed pipes and their clapper doors that controlled the flow of water into the Wash at Tydd St Giles (Fig. 7.8). A record from the fens of Pinchbeck and Spalding in 1553 explained the use of clows between drains and rivers where there was no requirement for a pipe. It specified the conditions under which the clow controlling water flowing into the river Welland from a drain called Sterfenngote could be closed by hand:

> 'the course of the waters in no place to be letted nor stopped and that the said clowgh ought to be open all times of year as well in wynter as in somer oonles the fresshe water shalbe so abundant and greate or the range of the see so vehement that the said sewer of Sterrfengote shall not be sufficient to resceyve and convey the same fresshe water to the (river Weylond afforsaid) and then it shall be lawful to the inhabytauntes of Spaldyng and Pynchbeck to latt down the said clowgh and to receive the fresshe water therby ... for the salvgard of the countre of Holland'.[53]

That is, the fen commoners could usually expect that Sterrfengote would continuously protect their pastures against flooding, and the sluice would to stay open throughout the year to achieve that. The only exception allowed was when/ if floods in the Welland were so great as to threaten fields and settlements on the silt uplands of south Holland. The sluice would then be closed deliberately and the fen commons between Pinchbeck and Spalding would temporarily store the flood waters until they could be diverted once more into the lode. It was possible, too, to reverse the flow when required: when 'William Goottes hath & kepeth one gutter or holl' tree in the bank at Wryghtbold and taketh water owte of the common sewer to the great noyans and hyndrans of the seyd sewer' in 1555, he was running the water out of the canal and into his pastures.[54]

Since it can reasonably be assumed that the construction of a lode would, in most cases, interfere with the natural drainage of the surrounding fen, the existence of Anglo-Saxon lodes implies the contemporary existence of a system of water management in the wetlands around them. What was the chronology of their introduction?

The beginnings of water management in the Anglo-Saxon fenland

The period in which lodes were first constructed continues to be disputed. Although canals – including a precursor of the Fen Causeway as well as the Cambridgeshire Car Dyke, and others around March – were constructed in the Roman fenland, some had already silted by the third century; Hall argued that most had gone out of use by the early fifth century.[55] The RCHME, on the other hand, considered in 1972 that, apart from the modern course of Burwell Lode, the north-east Cambridgeshire lodes were almost certainly Roman in date, pointing out that the construction of Reach Lode appeared to pre-date that of the Devil's Dyke, built between the fifth and seventh centuries, and that Roman finds had been made along the course of the Lode.[56] Continuity of this kind implies consistent maintenance of the watercourse over the intervening centuries:

FIGURE 7.8. The Four
Gotes at Tydd St Giles:
A late sixteenth-century
copy of a medieval map
shows four drains coming
in from the lower left
hand corner of the map
(© Wisbech and Fenland
Museum, reproduced
with permission). They
converged at Tydd St
Giles where they met the
Sea Bank, running from
bottom to top along the
centre of the map. There,
four circles represent the
Four Gotes (the timber
pipes) – and their clows
– through which water
was led out from the fen,
under the Bank and into
the Wash.

maintenance of the banks to keep the water within them and out of the fen,
clearance of weeds and silt to keep the course open, and other similar tasks.
A few examples indicate this possibility: Owen suggested that the canal called
Langreche, running along the southern fen-edge of Holland in Lincolnshire, might
just possibly be Roman given its straightness and its early use as the northern
boundary to Hey Fen in which the men of Wisbech Hundred intercommoned.[57]
Fosse Dyke may have been refurbished to supply the eighth- and ninth-century
trading centre at Torksey (Lincolnshire), and stretches of the Lincolnshire Car
Dyke may also have been renovated in the same period.[58]

Hall offered an alternative, late Anglo-Saxon, date for the first post-Roman construction of lodes in north-east Cambridgeshire, rejecting the possibility of the survival of Roman canals. He noted that other explanations might reasonably be found for the presence of Roman material along Reach Lode, and argued that the leadership and organisational infrastructure required for such large-scale engineering could only have been present in fenland after large estates, previously fragmented among many owners, were concentrated in the hands of the monasteries re-founded in the late tenth century.[59] He suggested on this basis that the century between about 970 and the Norman Conquest saw the introduction of extensive engineering across the fenland that involved 'a re-arrangement of the drainage of all the silt fen', large-scale engineering works including the construction of the Catswater along the Northamptonshire fen-edge, and the diversion of the Nene first between Whittlesey and Whittlesey Mere and then (or later) across the gravel hards to the north of March.[60]

The proposition of an Anglo-Saxon date for the initial construction of a number of lodes is supported by their adoption as administrative boundaries. *Abbotsdelf* was the eastern boundary of the estates of the Abbey of Ely from at least the 970s, and another *Abbotesdik*, now called Gold Dyke, was dug to mark the eastern boundary of the fenland estate of Thorney Abbey.[61] Lodes like Monks Lode in Wicken, the original course of Swaffham Lode, and *Cappelode* in Sutton were already being used as parish boundaries in 1086, and must therefore have been constructed well before the later eleventh century.[62]

Reach and Chear Lodes are conventionally regarded as the earliest Cambridgeshire canals for which there is documentary evidence. William the Conqueror stationed a garrison at the ditch (*fovea*) at Reach at the time of Hereward's rebellion around 1069–70, but whether *fovea* means the Lode or the ditch of the Devil's Dyke is unknown.[63] He also arranged a rendezvous for his forces at *Cotingelade*, the earlier name for what is now called Chear Lode, a canal taking water from the Cottenham fens into the Old West river, a watercourse running from west to east towards its junction with the river Cam/Granta between the south Cambridgeshire fen edge and the island of Ely.[64] The fens alongside the lode were still called Cottingham Fen in the fifteenth century. If the identifications can be relied upon, both must at the latest have been constructed by the early to mid-eleventh century. Even earlier is the name of *Ladwere* in Elm – a fishing weir in a lode – recorded in an early eleventh-century memorandum of the Abbey of Ely; the name survives today in Laddus Fen.[65]

The evidence summarised so far offers a reasonable case for the argument that the late tenth-century re-foundation of the monasteries provided the catalyst for the introduction of systems of water management across the peat wetlands (Fig. 7.9). There are, however, at least eight lodes and catchwaters that were constructed before 970 – that is, *before* the new monastic houses came into existence. They are discussed below, taking the most recently recorded example first.

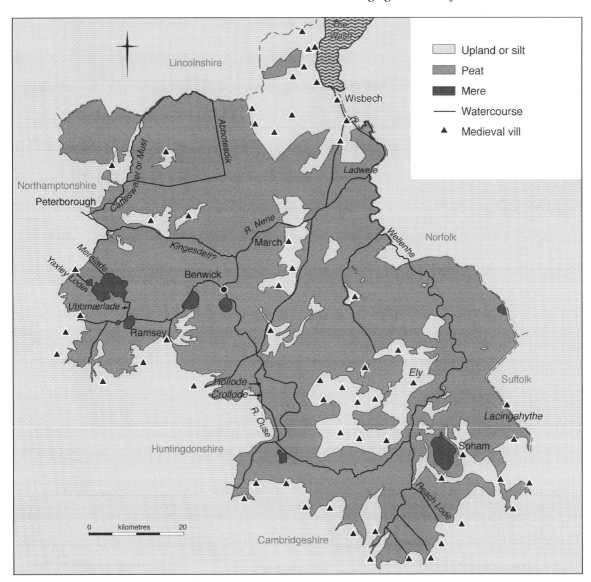

FIGURE 7.9. Anglo-Saxon lodes constructed before 970 could be found across the fen basin (© Susan Oosthuizen). The distribution is, however, a better reflection of the partial survival of Anglo-Saxon documents than it is of surviving early medieval engineering.

Two existing lodes/drains were recorded in the same charter of 972 with which King Edgar endowed Peterborough Abbey with extensive estates in the south-west fen basin:

1. *Kingesdelf* (also called *Cynges delf*) forms part of an artificial route along which the river Nene was re-routed between Stanground and Benwick.[66] It was reputedly dug (hence *delf*, 'to dig') by order of King Cnut but as it was clearly present by 972, at least a generation before 1016 when Cnut's reign began, the name must be as spurious as those supposedly connecting other landscape features with Oliver Cromwell.[67]

2. *Ubbemaerelade* connected (the now-vanished) Ugg and Whittlesey Meres.[68]

A charter of 956 for Yaxley and Farcet on the south-western fen edge provides evidence for the existence of lodes, catchwaters and clows in the mid-tenth century.[69]

3. Hart, who had a detailed knowledge of the landscape of both parishes, suggested that features listed in their boundaries could be identified with artificial watercourses and proposed the following locations for them (Fig. 7.10): *tham dicum*, 'the lode', now called Yaxley Lode whose earlier course is still discernible a little to the south-west of the modern lode; *dichythe,* 'the hythe along the ditch', lay on a fen-edge catchwater drain, now called the Pig Water, near its confluence with the old course of Yaxley Lode; *sudhythe*, 'the southern hythe', and *nordhythe*, 'the northern hythe', lay on either side of the Pig Water where the then boundary – now unknown – between the two communities intersected with the catchwater. The charter also recorded the presence of a hatch, *tham hæcce*, perhaps at the junction of the Pig Water in Farcet with the old, canalised course of the river Nene.[70] Then, as now, a hatch was a gate so hinged as only to open in one direction. Perhaps it was a clow constructed to controlled the flow of water between the two watercourses.

4. The Anglo-Saxon hythe at *Lacingahide* had already given its name to the large 5-hide Lakenheath estate by 945.[71] The existence of the hythe implies the presence of a lode, since the former lay on the fen edge, connected to the river Little Ouse 5 km away by Lakenheath Old Lode.

Three artificial watercourses form part of the Cambridgeshire county boundary, perhaps established in the second decade of the tenth century; each also formed the boundary between early Anglo-Saxon territorial intercommons.[72]

5. *Must,* also listed in Edgar's charter to Peterborough in 972, was another name for the Catswater, the catchwater drain running along the medieval fen-edge between Peterborough and Crowland that was used in the boundary between Cambridgeshire and Huntingdonshire.[73] It formed the western boundary of the vast intercommons of the Isle of Ely.

    To that should be added two canalised sections of the old course of the river Ouse between its entry into the fen basin to its confluence with the Nene at Benwick. They also formed a section of the boundary between intercommons shared by the vills of Hurstingstone hundred, to the south-west, and commoners from the Isle of Ely to the north-east. They are

6. Hollode, and
7. Crollode, both of which are followed by the county boundary between Cambridgeshire and Huntingdonshire.[74]

Finally,

8. *Merelade,* now called Conquest Lode, was also listed in Edgar's charter of 972 (Fig. 7.10).[75] Hall identified it with the earlier, southern, canalisation of the Nene linking the river with Whittlesey Mere. It was not only the county boundary between Cambridgeshire and Huntingdonshire, but also marked part of the southern boundary of intercommons shared by vills from the Isle of Ely.[76] It is especially interesting given its inclusion in a twelfth-century forgery of the charter, purported to have been written in 664, with which King Wulfhere of Mercia endowed the new abbey at *Medehamstead* (Peterborough).[77] While Morris, in a carefully-constructed

FIGURE 7.10 *(opposite).* Early lodes and catchwaters near Yaxley: Mid-tenth century or earlier water management was recorded in charters for Yaxley and Farcet in 956 that intersected with an early course of the river Nene (mid-blue): Yaxley Lode and Conquest Lode (dark blue), catchwaters flowing into Yaxley Lode (orange), and the possible location of a mid-tenth-century sluice preventing water from the Nene from entering the catchwater (Ordnance Survey 6 in:mile, 1900, my additions; © Crown Copyright and Landmark Information Group Limited (2017). All rights reserved (1900).

argument, agreed that most of the boundaries of *Medehamstead's* estate listed in the charter were twelfth-century fabrications, she also argued that the boundaries in the south-western part of the fen basin, in which *Merelade* was located, drew on much older oral traditions, and/or a much earlier – perhaps seventh-century – document.[78] If she is right, then the date of *Merelade*, while still unknown, might just be pushed back into the middle Anglo-Saxon period or before.

At its most conservative, the presence in different parts of the fen basin of these eight lodes takes the history of Anglo-Saxon engineering for water management into the first decade of the tenth century, and perhaps as far back as the middle or even the early Anglo-Saxon period (Fig. 7.10). Canals were being constructed as a matter of course in other parts of Britain and Europe in that period. Charlemagne, for instance, famously attempted to build a 1.6 km canal in Bavaria in 793 to link the Rhine with the Danube. The successful diversion of tributaries of the river Seine into canalised courses between 840 and 877 is equally well-known – the river Nonette at Senlis, the river Oise at Noyon, and

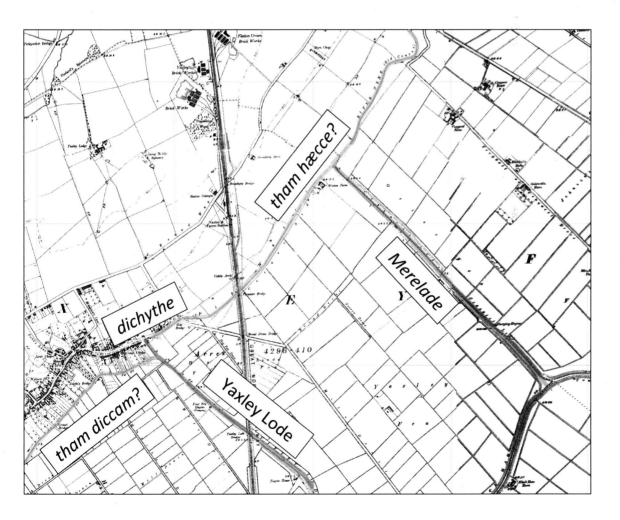

the river Eure at Chartres.[79] Closer to hand, radiocarbon dating of wooden stakes and timbers revetting the landward banks of a canal linking the abbey at Glastonbury with the river Brue produced two date ranges: one between 670 and 1030, and the other between 830 and 990. The excavators suggested a mid-tenth-century date for the canal in order to make a link with the re-foundation of Glastonbury Abbey by St Dunstan between 946 and 957. Since the connection with St Dunstan is an assumption, perhaps the best that can be said without documentary evidence is that the canal may have been constructed in the late ninth or early tenth centuries.[80] The eighth-century refurbishment of Fosse Dyke and Car Dyke in Lincolnshire has already been noted.[81] The complex water engineering associated with watermills provides another example of technological ability in the period: seventh- and eighth- century watermills have been found across England from Kent to Northumberland; extensive numbers have been found in contemporary Ireland and in Carolingian Europe where almost every valley is said to have had one.[82]

Who led the construction of artificial Anglo-Saxon water management systems in the fens?

The construction and maintenance of each lode, its catchwaters and subordinate ditches represented a considerable investment of time and labour. They were expensive undertakings. Scholarly opinion is divided on whether lords, either individually or in concert with others, were responsible for initiating and managing such large-scale changes in the landscape, or whether the work could also have been undertaken by peasant communities. Some have argued that only manorial lords had the authority to initiate, direct and co-ordinate strategic work on this scale, to enforce the participation of large numbers of labourers, or overcome the innate conservatism of farming communities.[83] Anglo-Saxon landowners certainly did initiate such works. Æthelwold, for example, is said to have constructed a canal at Abingdon between about 954 and 963 when he was abbot there, and other canals in Winchester in the following two decades after he was raised to the bishopric.[84] Abingdon Abbey was also responsible for the cutting of the Swift Ditch in Oxford between 1052 and 1065 as an aid to navigation.[85] *Abbotesdelf*, Cnut's Dyke and Bishop Morton's Leam are obvious fenland examples, as is the work undertaken in 1329 for managing water within the precinct of the Abbey of Crowland.[86]

By the late tenth century the later seventh-century estate of Æthelthryth's Abbey had been broken up and alienated – perhaps as a consequence of the Scandinavian settlement in 870, but possibly in a process that had begun long before. Bishop Æthelwold's strategic consolidation of landed endowments around 970 revealed a landscape of fragmented landholdings, relatively small estates held by a wide range of secular owners. The interval in which there was an absence of extensive lordship across the fen basin might conservatively be estimated at between 870 and around 1000 if there was an interval after

970 in which the monastic houses established systems for accounting for, and managing, their new large estates. Who might then have been responsible for the construction and maintenance of lodes and their subordinate systems in the ninth and tenth centuries? An answer might be found in Dyer's submission that large-scale landscape remodelling could as well be undertaken by local communities as by manorial lords, a proposition refined by Faith who has suggested that collective action was probably undertaken by the 'substantial farming families' in each vill, rather than by the entire population.[87]

That possibility is worth pursuing since, across the fen basin, men with rights of common in the fen were expected to contribute to the maintenance of the ditches and banks that protected their common pastures, and to help to maintain and protect the condition of the resources that they exploited. As Neilson explained, the 'ancient liability' for maintaining a common had time out of mind lain with the communities that grazed upon it.[88] The principle underlying that liability was that collective responsibilities attended individual benefits in shared resources held by an exclusive group of owners of common rights. It was neatly expressed at Sutton (Lincolnshire) in 1563 when it was explained that it was 'meyte and of old custome it owght that all owners farmers and all other that have anye profftyte off the commen wyth there cattell shall comme hollye to theyre mynwyrkes in Sutton as offten and manye tymes as it shalbe warned be the dyggrawes'.[89] That is, anyone who benefitted from a right of common had a responsibility, too, to contribute to the maintenance of the resource being exploited. The principle of balance between rights and responsibilities underpins the oldest English record of the responsibilities of shared ownership in a common resource, the well-known late seventh century law of King Ine of Wessex which reminded landholders that those with rights of common property in a natural resource should also share the costs and labour involved in maintaining it.[90] In 1249–50, men with common rights in Wisbech Hundred were expected to 'do ditching when required for half a day on *Rammesmeredik*', the southern boundary of the fens on which they intercommoned.[91] Similarly, in 1294–95 'all the tenants of the Lands of Pachefeld, and Kirkefeld, in the Towns of Utwelle and Upwelle, [were expected] to repair the Banks and Ditches in those Fields'.[92] The sixteenth-century commoners of Holland Fen (Lincolnshire) maintained a bank around the 20-mile (*c.*32 km) boundary of their fen.[93] In 1639 each common right holder in Cottenham was expected to do a 'common dayes work', that included maintaining the fen banks which should be 'four feete hie and five feete broade on the toppe'.[94]

The principle of collective responsibility for common resources was called 'mynwyrke' (sometimes shown as *menework*) (see above), a word that had evolved from an early Old English phrase *gemæne weorc*, 'work shared in common'.[95] It expressed the responsibility of those with rights of common to contribute collective labour for the good of their shared commons. The element *(ge)mæne* survives in modern Dutch as *gemeenschap*, and in modern German as *gemeinschaft*, 'community'; it survives, too, in the place-name of Manea

FIGURE 7.11. Willows planted along Delph Dike in Whittlesey to strengthen its bank had a dual purpose as their long history of pollarding shows (© Susan Oosthuizen).

(1177), the *gemæne ea*, the huge common fen intercommoned by all four of the Ely hundreds.[96] It was, by the thirteenth century, regarded as a custom of exceptional antiquity: something done *sicut antiquiter utebatur*, 'as it was done from the earliest times', since time immemorial – beyond memory.[97]

That belief seems to have been correct since the principle was, as we have seen, already accepted in the late seventh century. It was maintained as long as a common remained a shared resource – and it included the construction and maintenance of man-made watercourses. The commoners of the leet of Marshland, for example, constructed the Old Podyke in 1223–24 along the southern boundary of their common to exclude flood water that threatened their grazing from the deeper peat fens to the south.[98] The men of Landbeach still remembered in the sixteenth century that they had collectively 'made [Beach Lode] at their own liberty and will' in 1235 'to drain their common pasture from water'.[99] In 1381 all those who benefitted from the bank between Elm and Upwell that protected their fen pastures against floodwater were commanded to plant willows along it 'to hold up the waters in flood time, to maintain the dyke, and to provide stakes quickly when required' (Fig. 7.11).[100] Right holders in Wainfleet in 1422 were expected to 'repair le dame so that the waters of East Fen can get to the sea', while the communities that intercommoned in the fen between Kesteven and Holland had the 'duty of keeping the bridges and causeys in repair and of maintaining the ditches and dikes, whereby the waters of Kesteven got their access to the sea'.[101] In 1436–37 'the Townes Doddington, Merche, Witheford, and Wimblington ought and were wont and accustomed to ditch and cleanse one sewer called Idenhea [an ancient, much-reduced course of the river Nene], in breadth 32 foote [9.8 m], and from Idenhea Plante unto Redich Lake, soe that the water may have his course unto the greate river in Wisbech'.[102] Commoners were still constructing canals in the Lincolnshire fens in 1555 when a 'newe drayn & suer' was ordered to be 'made & dyked [embanked] for the conveyaunce of the water distendying into … Eight Hundreth Fen', a Lincolnshire intercommon so ancient that it was shared between the vills of eight hundreds.[103] And so on.

Like other aspects of the governance of fen commons, the direction, regulation and judicial oversight of *menework* relating to water management was undertaken collectively by the ancient courts in which all those with rights of common were expected to participate.[104] In Marshland, it was '*letam integram … in marisco*' of 1257, already encountered in Chapter 4; in Fleet (Lincolnshire) it was the court *de barra* (perhaps a bar allowing access to fen intercommons).[105] The court for Hey Fen was, as we have seen, that of Wisbech Hundred, the late Anglo-Saxon successor to an earlier folk territory.[106] The courts maintained 'the custom of the marsh': collectively they agreed by-laws for the management of their commons, adjudicated on disputes and infringements, and appointed as executive officers fen-reeves or dik-reeves (*custodes fossatum*), who maintained the custom of the commons.[107] Although Hulf, the late twelfth-century *dicgreive* at Long Sutton (Lincolnshire), was one of the first to be recorded, the role is generally agreed to have been considerably more ancient, 'from a time of which there is no memory'.[108] The reeves were empowered to impound animals belonging to men without rights of common found on the pastures, reporting other infringements to the court, implementing the court's decisions (including the collection of fines), and directing and managing the *menework* that maintained systems of water management in the fen.[109]

The significance of the phrase *gemæne weorc* in this context is that it was assumed to include collective responsibilities to construct and maintain systems of water management in the fen basin, it took for granted the recognition of those responsibilities as the 'customs of the marsh', and their governance by the same courts that governed the common pastures. It is difficult to see why lodes, catchwaters and ditches would have been collectively maintained within a set of communal tasks with the overall label of *gemæne weorc*, if those water management systems had not also been collectively planned and built. Had their construction been ordered and managed by lords, the owners of extensive estates, their maintenance would not have been by *menework* but by customary services. Water management seems to have been another aspect of the careful collective management of the fen environment that was outlined in the previous chapter.

Conclusions

The successful exploitation of fen grazing in the early medieval fenland depended not only on the management of beasts and the pastures they grazed, but also on the deliberate introduction of engineered management of seasonal water levels in those wetlands. Previously believed to have been introduced after the refoundation of the monasteries in the later tenth century, documentary evidence for the presence of canals and their subsidiary catchwaters across the fen basin before 970 indicates the presence of extensive, sophisticated systems of engineering for water management across the basin in the middle Anglo-Saxon period and perhaps earlier, supporting and complementing complex timetables for the cropping and management of the many ecologies that were exploited across the basin in the Anglo-Saxon period. The early origins of the phrase *menework* suggest that the management of water to maintain the productivity of fen pastures was being collectively undertaken across the basin from a very early date by substantial communities living within structured, ordered polities.[110] It provides yet another example of the extent to which early medieval society, economy and landscape across the fen basin were mutually sustained over the *longue durée* within systems of collective governance over shared rights of property – often across whole territories.

Notes

1. Camden 1610, 'Cambridgeshire', 12; see also Raftis 1957, 153, 157; English Nature 2006; Rothero *et al.* 2016, 45–56.
2. *MP* V, 570.
3. *RABB*, 6.
4. *Pet. Chron.*, 2; see also VCH Northants. II, 83; Kelly 2009, 4–5.
5. *GP* IV, 186, trans. Dugdale 1662, 360.
6. Camden 1610, 'Cambridgeshire', 2.
7. Campbell 2000, 146.
8. Gooch 1811, 179–80.
9. Vancouver 1794, 127.
10. Rothero *et al.* 2016, 38–44.
11. Hall 1987, 2–10; 1996, 3–8; BGS, Sheet 188.
12. Environment Agency 2010, 35–36; Rothero *et al.* 2016, 31–37.
13. Cutting and Cummings 2007.
14. JNCC 2012.
15. Dugdale 1662, Preface.
16. Wells 1828–30, ii, 88.
17. Cutting and Cummings 2007, 71–74.
18. Cited in Ravensdale 1974, 42, my emphasis; see Thirsk 1953b, 23–25.
19. Cook 2007, 105; Cummings and Cutting 2007.
20. Cutting and Cummings 2007, 74.
21. Ravensdale 1974, 42, my addition; see also Thirsk 1953b, 23–25.
22. BBC Radio 4, *Today*, 27 January 2014, 7.32–7.45 am; Met Office, January 2014 Weather Summary, http://www.metoffice.gov.uk/climate/uk/summaries/2014/january.

23. Environment Agency 2010, 36.
24. Cited in Ravensdale 1974, 64.
25. CA R59/14/5/9(c).
26. Dugdale 1662, 201 and 305 respectively.
27. CA R59/14/5/9(c).
28. Dugdale 1662, 201, my emphasis.
29. Dugdale 1662, 305, my emphasis.
30. Gooch 1811, 179–80, my emphasis.
31. Hall 1987, 56, 59.
32. Reaney 1943, 209; *LE* II, 54.
33. Hall 1992, 94.
34. Reaney 1943, 131, 335; Cole 2007, 77–78.
35. *ECB*, f.25d(1)–f.25d(2) and f.17d(1). While there is no doubt that the lodes were also used for transport, trade and communication, these appear to have been secondary in most cases to their water management function (see Oosthuizen 2012).
36. RCHME 1972, figs 6 and 7, and parish essays.
37. RCHME 1972, 81, see also 42–43.
38. *Charter of Romney Marsh*, 15.
39. Kirkus 1959, xiii; see also Owen 1981.
40. Owen 1981, 15.
41. Oosthuizen 2012.
42. Hall 1992, 42, fig. 25.
43. Ravensdale 1974, 26–27; VCH Hunts. III, 253–54.
44. VCH Hunts. III, 249–90; RCHME 1972, 42–43, 113, 129.
45. Wells 1828–30, ii, 76, also 80
46. RCHME 1972, liv–lv, figs 6 and 7.
47. Friday and Rowell 1997, 17.
48. RCHME 1972, figs 7 and 8.
49. Taylor 1977, 63–65; Hall 1977; see Hallam 1954 and 1965 for detail of reclamation on the Lincolnshire silt fens.
50. Kirkus 1959, 56.
51. De Ridder 1999; English Heritage 2012, 3; Schladweiler 2016.
52. De Ridder 1999.
53. Kirkus 1959, 39.
54. Kirkus 1959, 56.
55. Hall 1987, 41–42, fig. 23; 1996, 123–24, 159.
56. RCHME 1972, lv, 129, 144.
57. Owen 1982, 41–43.
58. Bond 2007, 175–76.
59. Hall 1996, 112.
60. Hall 1987, 46; see also pp. 36–37, 56.
61. *LE* I, Preface; Reaney 1943, 280.
62. RCHME 1972, 42–43, 113; Hall 1996, 60.
63. *LE* II, 106.
64. *LE* II, 107; Ravensdale 1974, 24–25. See Hallam 1988, 497, for similar late eleventh-century Lincolnshire examples.
65. *BL* Add. Ms. 61735; Reaney 1943, 268; Hart 1966, 32; Naismith 2016.
66. e-Sawyer S787; Hart 1966, 25. In 1926 Mawer and Stenton assigned the charter to 963, but both Hart and Sawyer suggest 972 is a more accurate date. See Kelly 2009, 278–79 for critical evaluations of this geography.

67. Mawer and Stenton 1926, 185; Hall 1987, 56, 59; Reaney 1943, 319.
68. e-Sawyer S787; Hart 1966, 25–26; Mawer and Stenton 1926, 216. The latter suggested a date of 1022 for this name, but both Hart and Sawyer (see also e-Sawyer S595) agree on 972.
69. e-Sawyer S595; Hart 1966, 159–65; see also Hall 1992, 19–25.
70. Hart 1966, 164; Old English Dictionary.
71. Dumville 1993, 38; Mills 2011; Cole 2007, 68.
72. Hart 1974, 12–13.
73. e-Sawyer S787; Hart 1966, 26; Hall 1987, 36–37; Reaney 1943, 3–4, 7–8.
74. Hall 1992, 94.
75. e-Sawyer S787.
76. Hall 1992, 19, 22.
77. e-Sawyer S68; Hart 1966, 21, 97–98.
78. Morris 2006, 173.
79. Bond 2007, 170–72.
80. Hollinrake and Hollinrake 2007, 237; see also VCH Som. II, 84; Bond 2007, 175–76.
81. Bond 2007, 175–76.
82. See Oosthuizen 2013b, 122–23 for examples.
83. See, for example, Harvey 1989, 36; Hooke 1998, 119–20.
84. Bond 2007, 179.
85. Bond 2004, 304.
86. Hallam 1988, 499.
87. Faith 1997, 146–47; see also Dyer 1996, 306.
88. Neilson 1920, lvii.
89. Kirkus 1959, 105. That is, it was 'proper and old custom that all owners farmers and anyone who profits from grazing their cattle on the common should fulfill all their collective labour duties in Sutton whenever and ask often as the managers of the fen commons required their presence'.
90. Whitelock 1979, 403.
91. *ECB*, f.35r(1).
92. Dugdale 1662, 247.
93. Thirsk 1953a, 25.
94. CA P50/28/3.
95. Kirkus 1959, xxx; Neilson 1920, xvi, xxvi, xlvii.
96. Reaney 1943, 235–36.
97. De Bathe 1286, 15; see also Kirkus 1959, xiii; Owen 1981.
98. Dugdale 1662, 245; Douglas 1927, 196–97; see also Darby 1974, 167.
99. Cited in Ravensdale 1974, 26, my addition.
100. Hallam 1988, 499.
101. Neilson 1920, xvii and xx, respectively.
102. Wells 1828–30, ii, 12, my addition.
103. Kirkus 1959, 26, my addition.
104. Douglas 1927, 198.
105. Douglas 1927, 195; Neilson 1920, xvi.
106. Neilson 1920, xlvii.
107. Neilson 1920, xxvi.
108. Hallam 1963, 41; see also Owen 1977, ix.
109. Neilson 1920, xlvi, xlviii–xlix.
110. See Kirkus 1959, xxx.

Epilogue

A new history of the Anglo-Saxon fenland emerges in the preceding chapters through the identification of inherited ideas and traditional institutions, of others that were genuinely new, and of yet others that represented evolution and adaptation to changing circumstance. That approach has been based on the proposition that it maybe easier to model how processes unfolded or institutions evolved, to consider the interplay and relative importance of external or internally-generated influences, if change is set against a background that identifies both old and new. The early medieval fenland offers a case study of what Holling has described as a panarchy: Complex social and ecological systems which operate at a range of scales from super-regional to micro-local, and which change at different paces – some demonstrating long-term stability, some changing rapidly and significantly, others simply evolving slightly but quickly, and yet others changing slowly but in important ways, and others adapting slowly in incremental steps. In this way, he argues, the system is able to sustain itself over the longer term, while also being sufficiently stable to experiment creatively with new ways of doing things and to incorporate them if they are useful – 'combining learning with continuity'.[1]

Traditions of collective pastoral husbandry in fenland across the *longue durée* provide that long-term context. In all weathers, in all social circumstances, in all political conditions, the day-to-day preoccupation of most men was focused on how to generate a sufficient volume of food and other goods to support their households from one day, one week, one month and one year to the next. A lack of attention to that objective could be disastrous in an economy in which a minimum level of subsistence had to be produced at home. The stability and long-term maintenance of the environment on which their livelihoods depended was a critical factor in underpinning the fenland economy, but also in sustaining their personal and territorial identities and social relationships. To that extent, the argument in the preceding pages has focused on continuities. The fenland appears to have been settled uninterruptedly from the Romano-British into the Anglo-Saxon periods by communities whose ancestry largely lay in the region's prehistoric past, and among whom incomers were soon assimilated. Early medieval fen men and women lived within a complicated, changing hierarchy of dominant and subordinate polities, principalities and kingdoms whose names frequently expressed collective identities drawn from the landscapes they occupied, and among whom continuity may have been as commonplace as transformation.

There is a little evidence from which to evaluate the balance in the fen basin between political security and instability across the Anglo-Saxon period. A battle was said in about 834 to have been fought north of Spalding *c*.500.[2] Violent disputes are evident in the wake of the appropriation by Guthlac of a territory (folkland) belonging to a Brittonic-speaking folk group, as folkland was transformed into extensive estates for monastic institutions across the 'long' eighth century.[3] Whether or not 'wild and untamable British people' really 'ravaged' around St Ives (Huntingdonshire) in the eleventh century is not known – but it was certainly believed to have been possible.[4] On the other hand, the remarkable continuity across the *longue durée* between the early fifth and the seventeenth centuries in the ecology of the basin, and in the geography of rights of common property that were exercised in the fen – themselves derived from territorial institutions – suggests that most political change was either very short-lived and/or adaptive and evolutionary, rather than characterised by any sudden revolutionary transformation.

Agricultural economies in the fens were intensely focused on common property rights in shared wetland resources that belonged to the territory as a whole. Those rights formed a nexus for economic success, social status and political identity. They were managed through cropping regimes that had two principal objectives: to extract a sufficient supply of each resource to provide a reasonable livelihood for each right holder across the agricultural year, and to assure the sustainability of each resource over the longer term. Each right holder needed to be sure that he would be able to cut sufficient reeds, catch enough eels, graze a large enough herd to keep his family over the coming year; and he also needed to be sure that he would be able to do the same thing next year, and the year after that, for the foreseeable future.

The most important rights of common were those in the collectively-managed extensive wetland pastures and meadows that supported large communal herds of dairy cattle. That activity required active management not only of the stock and the grasslands they grazed, but also of the volume of water in the fen. Water was central to fen men's prosperity, yet also posed their greatest risk and, exceptional events aside, it was usually possible to manage average volumes in each season through the collective construction of sophisticated hierarchies of lodes, catchwaters and ditches.

Although documentary evidence for the history of the fen landscape is dominated by medieval records concerning collective institutions and rights of common, good archaeological evidence for the existence – and intensification – of hierarchical social structures across the Anglo-Saxon period suggests that individuals were as likely to have played a part in supporting and initiating change. That powerful individuals capable of directing change were present in the early Anglo-Saxon fenland is plain in their high status burials, accompanied by exceptional pieces of gold and garnet jewelry, glass cups, reliquaries and other items, in cemeteries for which they often formed a central focus. Individual agency across the social scale is strikingly apparent, too, in the almost universal distribution across the basin of goods that, by the middle of the fifth century, had more in common with north-west Europe than with the late Roman Mediterranean. The combination of style, fabric and decoration of each 'Germanic' artifact represents deliberate choices by the person who ordered or made it; the widespread presence of these goods in houses or graves across the basin by the mid-fifth century suggests that large numbers of individuals were buying or otherwise acquiring things that they had chosen to like. The distribution of Brittonic and Old English elements in place-names across the basin may mean that the choice of a name among bi- or even multi-lingual communities may have been influenced by individual factors so idiosyncratic that they cannot now be descried. In the absence of more extensive documentary evidence, these small actions stand for others that may have been enacted on a larger scale. The actions of individuals are, for instance, hinted at in the *wealh worthigs* recorded at Horningsea and Ely, in the planned settlements laid out at regular intervals across the Norfolk silt fens, and in the small assarted fields that were gained from the coastal marsh. The construction of some lodes and their subordinate drains may have been directed by lords, the precursors of Bishop Morton (although no evidence survives to demonstrate it), just as those supported by *gemæne worc* appear to have been initiated by commoners.

The story of early-medieval fen men, their social relationships, cultural identities and their livelihoods has a wider relevance. It suggests that to contrast 'Romano-British' versus 'Anglo-Saxon' communities may be a false dichotomy. There is little evidence in the fenland of any early medieval social restructuring in which 'Anglo-Saxon' migrant elites reduced existing 'Romano-British' communities to servile status. Instead, continuity of exploitation of the fen environment, and an inability to differentiate between communities in terms of their political structure, the languages they spoke, or their material culture, suggests that local groups continued to occupy land their ancestors had held, and that incomers, whether small or large in number, were by and large assimilated. British-Celtic names indicate a level of administrative continuity from Romano-British political territories, sometimes re-named in Old English; others may have been entirely new in construction. Some were long-lived, others less permanent. There is, however, no evidence to suggest a political takeover by 'Anglo-Saxons' of existing communities, or their foundation of new, different 'Germanic' kingdoms. Nor does the vividly apparent change in the material culture of the region indicate demographic, cultural or social upheaval. Early medieval households across the fenland used the same goods, lived in the same kinds of houses, farmed the same kinds of fields, and drove their cattle to the same shared pastures. It is impossible to distinguish between them in terms of their cultural background. This is not to argue that there was never displacement or conquest of one population by another either in fenland or elsewhere – simply that continuity should be assumed unless there is clear evidence to the contrary. In the absence of other evidence, any alternative model demands the construction of such complicated explanations, based on so many assumptions, that their practical implications run counter to the principle of Occam's Razor: that the most straightforward argument, based on the fewest assumptions, is most likely to be accurate.

This was a society whose origins could be found in prehistoric Britain, which had developed through the period of Roman control and into the post-imperial decades and centuries that followed. The rich and complex history of the Anglo-Saxon fenland reveals, it is argued, an ancient society collectively evolving, adapting and innovating in response to individual actions, to events, sudden or expected, and to influences and processes, new or changing, rapid or slow, and in which the role of migration in stimulating or influencing the direction of those changes remains unknown.

Notes

1. Holling 2001, 390.
2. Green 2012, 182.
3. Clark 2011.
4. Clark 2011.

Glossary

Assart Common land taken into private ownership.

Bookland Land held by charter that could be disposed of at the will of the owner.

Bordarius (pl. *bodarii*) Individuals who performed specialized, higher status tasks on the home farms (inlands) of extensive estates, and who were granted smallholdings in return for their services.

Ceorl A free man with full rights of property over his landholding.

Clow A one-way hatch in a canal to control the flow of water such that water can only flow out of, but not into the canal.

Cottager Householder who held no land beyond the plot on which his/her cottage stood.

Demesne Medieval term for manorial land cultivated directly on behalf of the lord; similar to the inland of Anglo-Saxon estates.

Dyke Originally a drain or ditch; by the later Anglo-Saxon period it also came to be used to mean a bank.

Extensive estate Large estates, made up of a number of communities, granted by charter to middle Anglo-Saxon ecclesiastical institutions, and to members of royal and aristocratic families from the mid-seventh century onwards.

Feorm Public renders in kind owed from free landholdings to the king, and later transferred in charters to the lords of extensive estates.

Ferthyng A fourth part (a quarter) of, for example, a land unit or a penny; from Old English *feórþling*.

Filstingerthe Perhaps a form of *garserthe*, see below.

Folk-group An early Anglo-Saxon territorial grouping, whose members were (at least nominally) connected by kinship, in which all landholders shared the collective resources of the territory, owed distinctive public obligations and responsibilities, and held concomitant rights to participate in its collective governance.

Folk-land The territory belonging to a folk-group.

Freeman A landholding peasant with full property rights over his land, and with full rights to all its profits.

Gafol Tribute rendered in cash to the king or other overlord.

Garserthe Public obligation of ploughing service on king or other overlord's inland in return for pasture rights, perhaps one of the most ancient services.

Gleave A short tensile fork or spear for catching eels, usually with three or four wide, often serrated, tines relatively narrowly separated.

Gote A narrow drain or pipe leading to a sluice.

Govelacre A holding to which the public obligation to render *gafol* was attached.

Gutter A sluice.

Hassock/hasse Coarse vegetation especially grass or sedge on marshy land.

Hide An area of land sufficient to maintain the extended household of a *ceorl*.

Hundred By the later tenth century, hundreds were the administrative sub-divisions of counties. They oversaw the local administration of justice and military defence, the regional organisation of public duties, and the collection of taxes. Some were newly-created, others were adaptations of older territorial structures.

Hundredor A free peasant holding land from a hundred, not from a manor.

Inland That area of an extensive estate that was directly cultivated for its owner, as to opposed to land that was ceded or leased out to tenants in return for services and /or rents. It had evolved by the middle ages into demesne.

Intercommon Commons shared by two or more vills or townships.

Leet   A unit of governance over an area smaller than a hundred, that almost certainly originated as an administrative sub-division of an early Anglo-Saxon folk-group.

Lode   A man-made watercourse or canal, frequently embanked.

Menework   Public obligation on free landholdings to maintain the physical infrastructure of the commons in which they had common rights.

Minster   An Anglo-Saxon monastic institution charged, in the early and middle Anglo-Saxon periods, with the pastoral care of all the inhabitants of a kingdom, of one of its sub-regions, or of a royal extensive estate.

Pisgote   A pipe constructed from hollowed tree trunks, along which water was discharged from a drain into a larger watercourse.

Reeve   The principal official charged with carrying out the directions, and otherwise managing the affairs, of a group of commoners, of an institution (like a minster) or of a secular estate owner.

Regio   A province or sub-kingdom within a larger kingdom.

Roddon   A hard ridge in the peat fen, formed by the silting up of an earlier watercourse.

Servus (pl. *servi*)   An unfree peasant, tied to an estate.

Sewer   An embanked canal.

Sixtiethpeni   An early Anglo-Saxon public obligation of a money render from each hide.

Soke   An estate or landholding over which whose holder exercised full property rights, including jurisdiction, and to which were attached public obligations of services and renders. (A sokeman lived on such an estate, who owed renders and services to the administrative centre of the soke).

Tepidarium   The warm bath, heated by a hypocaust, in a complex of Roman baths.

Thegn   A landowner of some status who, by the later Anglo-Saxon period, was expected to hold his estate by charter.

Vill   An administrative unit based on a single community, sometimes called a township, whose boundaries are sometimes preserved in modern parish boundaries.

Villa regia   The central settlement of a royal early or middle Anglo-Saxon extensive estate.

Villein   An individual owing a range of labour services and other duties, as well as some payments in money or kind, to a manorial lord in return for an arable holding that included a dwelling.

Wardpeni   The commutation of the early Anglo-Saxon public obligation from each hide to contribute to the construction and maintenance of fortifications, and to perform guard duties.

Ware acre   An early Anglo-Saxon arable holding to which was attached public obligations, services and renders of money and food.

Primary Sources

British Library (BL)

Add Ms 61735 Farming Memoranda of Ely Abbey, *c.*1007–25. http://www.bl.uk/manuscripts/FullDisplay.aspx?ref=Add_MS_61735, accessed 30 June 2016.

Cotton Claudius C.xi Ely Coucher Book, thirteenth-century ms.

Cotton Tiberius B.ii 1222 Survey of Ely Episcopal Manors.

Harley 3271, f.6v The Tribal Hidage, early eleventh century. http://www.bl.uk/manuscripts/Viewer.aspx?ref=harley_ms_3271_f006v, accessed 30 June 2016.

Cambridgeshire Archives (CA)

126/M39, 40-48 Whittlesey, Courts Leet October 1694–95.

381/M/1 Doddington, Manorial court book 1686–91.

606/M1 Doddington, Manorial court book, 1686.

606/M2, M3, M9 March, Common by-laws, 1669–70, and Rampton, Common by-laws, 1678–81.

L2/1, 8 Rampton, Common by-laws 1754 and 1823.

P116/1/4 March, Tithes n.d. sixteenth century.

P116/28/19-20 March, late nineteenth-century transcription of copies of documents relating to March 1222 – sixteenth century.

P50/28/3-6 Cottenham, Orders for the Town Common, 1639–65.

Q/RDc71 Rampton, Parliamentary enclosure award.

R51/28/1A-C March, Tithe Map and Schedule 1840.

R52/24/31 Jonas Moore *c.*1706: *Mapp of ye Great Levell of ye Fenns extending into ye Covntyes of Northampton, Norfolk, Suffolke, Lyncolne, Cambridg[e] and Huntington and the Isle of Ely as it is now drained, described by, Sr. Jonas Moore. Svrveyr. Genl.*

R59/14/5/9(a)-(j) Willingham, Common by-laws 1602–1790.

R59/31/40/1 Hand-drawn and coloured copy of William Hayward's 1604 map of the fens, by R. Peylor Smyth, 1727.

R59/31/40/176 Printed copy of William Hayward's 1604 map of the fens, by T. Badeslade, 1727.

S/B/SP436 Petition of the inhabitants of Willingham and Rampton, 1742.

Cambridge University Library (CUL)

Add Ms 6971 Rampton, Parliamentary Enclosure notes, 1837.

G.3.27 Ely Diocesan Records Liber R, Ely Coucher Book 1249–50 (fourteenth-century copy).

Maps.bb.53(1).93.114- Map of Doddington, Wimblington and March *c.*1601–03. Photostat copy made in 1939 from an original, now mislaid, then in the ownership of March District Council.

National archives (NA)

MPC 1/45 Map of Bedford Level, Cambridgeshire, ?late fourteenth century.

MPC 1/54 Map of Bedford Level, Cambridgeshire, ?fifteenth century.

Spalding Gentleman's Society

Late medieval maps of the fenland collected by Maurice Johnson.

Wisbech and Fenland Museum (WFM)

Wisbech Hundred map, *c.*1540.

Descriptio illius partis comitate Norfolc – occidentale – ripa owse patria tota de Marshlade continens., etc. map *c.*1590.

The countrye of Marshland, map by William Hayward, 1591.

Published primary sources

Bede. *Ecclesiastical History of the English People,* ed. L. Sherley-Price (1990), Penguin, London [English translation].

Bede. *Historia Ecclesiasticam Gentis Anglorum,* The Latin Library, n.d. *http://www.thelatinlibrary.com/bede.html,* accessed 30 June 2016 [Latin text].

Camden, W. (1610). *Britain, or, a Chorographicall Description of the Most Flourishing Kingdomes, England, Scotland, and Ireland*, George Bishop and John Norton, London, ed. D. Sutton (2004). *http://www.philological.bham.ac.uk/cambrit/* accessed 30 June 2016.

Charter of Romney Marsh: Or the Laws and Customs of Romney Marsh: Framed and Contrived by the Venerable Justice, Henry de Bathe [1258] S. Keble, London (1686).

Domesday Book, Cambridgeshire, ed. A. Rumble (1981), Phillimore, Chichester.

Domesday Book, Norfolk, ed. J. Morris (1975), Phillimore, Chichester.

Dugdale, W. (1662) *The History of Imbanking and Drayning of Divers Fenns and Marshes*, A. Warren, London.

Electronic Sawyer, Online Catalogue of Anglo-Saxon Charters, http://www.esawyer.org.uk/about/index.html, accessed 30 June 2016.

Ely Coucher Book, 1249–50, The Bishop of Ely's Manors in the Cambridgeshire Fenland, eds F. Willmoth and S. Oosthuizen (2015), Cambridgeshire Records Society, Cambridge [English translation].

Felix's Life of Saint Guthlac. Texts, Translation and Notes, ed B. Colgrave (1985), Cambridge University Press, Cambridge [Latin text and English translation].

Geological Survey of England and Wales, New Series, 1:63,350/ 1:50,000 Solid and Drift Sheets: *144 Spalding* (1992), *158 Peterborough* (1984), *159 Wisbech* (1995), *172 Ramsey* (1994), *173 Ely* (1980), British Geological Survey, Nottingham.

Gildas. The Ruin of Britain and Other Works, ed. M. Winterbottom (1978), Phillimore, Chichester [English translation].

Inquisitio Comitatus Cantabrigiensis, ed. N. S. A. Hamilton (1876a), Murray, London [Latin text].

Inquisitio Eliensis, ed. N. S. A. Hamilton (1876b) Murray, London [Latin text].

Liber Eliensis, ed. E. O. Blake (1962), Camden Third Series 92, Royal Historical Society, London [Latin text].

Liber Eliensis, ed. J. Fairweather (2005), Boydell and Brewer, Woodbridge [English translation].

Matthæi Parisiensis Monachi Sancti Albani, Chronica Majora, Volume V, AD 1248 to AD 1269, ed H. R. Luard (1880), Longman, London [Latin text].

Ordnance Survey, First edition 6 in:mile maps. http://digimap.edina.ac.uk, accessed 30 June 2016.

Peterborough Chronicle of Hugh Candidus, ed. W. T. Mellows (1980 edition), Peterborough Museum Society, Peterborough [English translation].

Ramsey Abbey's Book of Benefactors, Part One: The Abbey's Foundation, ed. Susan Edgington (1998), M. K. Book Services, Huntingdon [English translation].

Widsith. In *Old English Minor Heroic Poems*, ed. Joyce Hill, (1983), Durham Medieval Texts 4, Durham [Old English text].

Widsith, ed Kemp Malone (1936), Methuen, London. Via http://www.phil-fak.uni-duesseldorf.de/fileadmin/Redaktion/Institute/Anglistik/Anglistik_I/Downloads/Archiv/SS_06/VL06_Widsith.pdf, accessed 30 June 2016. [Old English text and modern English translation]

William of Malmesbury, *Gesta Pontificum Anglorum, The History of the English Bishops. Volume I: Text and Translation*, ed M. Winterbottom (2007), Clarendon Press, Oxford [Latin text and English translation].

Bibliography

Adams, M. (2013) *Land to the Rear of 84 High Street, Chatteris, Cambridgeshire*, British Archaeology Ltd, Stowmarket. http://www.britannia-archaeology.com/files/2614/3325/4086/R1019_Land_to_the_rear_of_84_High_Street_Chatteris_Cambs-_TT_V1Figs.pdf, accessed 30 June 2016.

Appleby, G., Bartlett, A. and Hutton, J. (2009) *Land off Downham Road, Ely, Cambridgeshire*, Cambridge Archaeological Unit Report 886, Cambridge.

Arnold, C. J. (1988) *An Archaeology of the Early Anglo-Saxon Kingdoms*, Routledge, London.

Aston, M. and Gerrard, C. (2013) *Interpreting the English Village*, Oxbow Books, Oxford.

Baines, A. (1996) 'The longevity of field-names: A case study from Sherington', *Records of Buckinghamshire* 38, 163–174.

Baker, J. (2006) *Cultural Transition in the Chilterns and Essex Region, 350 AD to 650 AD*, University of Hertfordshire Press, Hatfield.

Ballantyne, R. (2004) 'Islands in wilderness: The changing medieval use of the East Anglian peat fens, England', *Environmental Archaeology* 9, 189–198.

Banham, D. and Faith, R. (2014) *Anglo-Saxon Farms and Farming*, Oxford University Press, Oxford.

Barrow, M. and Hulme, E. eds (1997) *Climates of the British Isles, Past, Present and Future*, Routledge, London and New York.

Bassett, S. (1989) 'In search of the origins of the Anglo-Saxon kingdoms'. In *The Origins of the Anglo-Saxon Kingdoms*, ed. S. Bassett, 3–27, Leicester University Press, Leicester.

Bassett, S. (1997). 'Continuity and fission in the Anglo-Saxon landscape: the origins of the Rodings, Essex', *Landscape History* 19, 25–42.

Baxter, P. (2005) 'The east coast Big Flood, 31 January–1 February 1953: a summary of the human disaster', *Philosophical Transactions of the Royal Society* 363 (1831), 1293–1312. http://rsta.royalsocietypublishing.org/content/363/1831/1293.full, accessed 30 June 2016.

Behre, K.-E. (2007) 'A new Holocene sea-level curve for the southern North Sea', *Boreas* 36, 82–102.

Biddick, K. (1989) *The Other Economy. Pastoral Husbandry on a Medieval Estate*, University of California Press, Berkeley.

Biddle, M. and Kjølbye-Biddle, B. (1985) 'The Repton Stone', *Anglo-Saxon England* 14, 233–92.

Blair, J. (1992) 'Anglo-Saxon minsters: A topographical review'. In *Pastoral Care Before the Parish*, eds J. Blair and R. Sharpe, 226–66, Leicester University Press, Leicester.

Blair, J. (2005) *The Church in Anglo-Saxon Society*, Oxford University Press, Oxford.

Blinkhorn, P. (2005) 'Early to mid Saxon pottery'. In *The Saxon and Medieval Settlement at West Fen Road, Ely: The Ashwell Site*, eds R. Mortimer, R. Regan and S. Lucy, 62–65, East Anglian Archaeology 110, Cambridge.

Bolton, W. (1958) 'The Croyland quatrefoil and polychronicon', *Journal of the Warburg and Courtauld Institutes* 21 (3), 295–96.

Bond, C. J. (2004) *Monastic Landscapes*, Stroud, Tempus.

Bond, C. J. (2007) 'Canal construction in the Early Middle Ages'. In *Waterways and Canal-Building in Medieval England*, ed. J. Blair, 153–206, Oxford, Oxford University Press.

Brady, L. (2010) 'Echoes of Britons on a fenland frontier in the Old English *Andreas*', *Review of English Studies* NS 61 (252), 669–89.

Brandt, R., Van der Leeuw, S. and Van Wijngaarden-Bakker, L. (1984) 'Transformations in a Dutch estuary: Research in a wet landscape', *World Archaeology* 16 (1), 1–17.

Brather, S. (2005) 'Acculturation and ethnogenesis along the frontier: Rome and the Ancient Germans in an archaeological perspective'. In *Borders, Barriers and Ethnogenesis*, ed. F. Curta, 139–72, Brepols, Turnhout.

Brears, C. (1929) 'The fen laws of common', *Lincolnshire Notes and Queries* 20, 58–64 and 74–77.

Brew, D., Horton, B., Evans, G., Innes, J. and Shennan, I. (2015) 'Holocene sea-level history and coastal evolution of the north-western Fenland, eastern England', *Proceedings of the Geologists' Association* 126, 72–85.

Brugman, B. (2011) 'Migration and endogenous change'. In *Oxford Handbook of Anglo-Saxon Archaeology*, eds H. Hamerow, D. Hinton and S. Crawford, 30–45, Oxford University Press, Oxford.

Büntgen, U. *et al.* (2011) '2,500 years of climate variability and human susceptibility', *Science* 331 (6017), 578–82.

Burgen, S. (2015) 'US now has more Spanish speakers than Spain – only Mexico has more', *The Guardian*, 29 June 2015, https://www.theguardian.com/us-news/2015/jun/29/us-second-biggest-spanish-speaking-country, accessed 21 March 2017.

Burmeister, S. (2000) 'Archaeology and migration: approaches to an archaeological proof of migration', *Current Anthropology* 41, 539–67.

Cambridgeshire Historic Environment Record (HER), http://www.heritagegateway.org.uk/gateway/chr/herdetail.aspx?crit=&ctid=95&id=4759, accessed June and July 2016.

Cameron, K. (1979–80) 'The meaning and significance of Old English *walh* in English place-names', *Journal of the English Place-name Society* 12, 1–46.

Campbell, B. (2000) *English Seigniorial Agriculture, 1250–1450*, Cambridge University Press, Cambridge.

Campbell, B. and Bartley, K. (2006) *England on the Eve of the Black Death*, University of Manchester Press, Manchester.

Campbell, J. (1979) *Bede's Reges and Principes. Jarrow Lecture 1979*, J. and P. Bealls, Newcastle-upon-Tyne.

Campbell, J. (2005) 'Hundreds and leets: A survey with suggestions'. In *Medieval East Anglia*, ed. C. Harper-Bill, 153–67, Boydell and Brewer, Woodbridge.

Capelli, C. *et al.* (2003) 'A Y chromosome census of the British Isles', *Current Biology* 13, 979–84.

Charles-Edwards, T. (1972) 'Kinship, status and the origins of the hide', *Past and Present* 56, 3–33.

Charles-Edwards, T. (1979) 'The distinction between land and moveable wealth in Anglo-Saxon England'. In *English Medieval Settlement*, ed. P. Sawyer, 97–104, Arnold, London.

Charles-Edwards, T. (2013) *Wales and the Britons, 350–1064*, Oxford University Press, Oxford.

Cherry J. (2001) 'Pottery and tile'. In *English Medieval Industries: Craftsmen, Techniques, Products*, eds J. Blair and N. Ramsey, 189–210, Hambledon, London.

Clark, S. (2011) 'A more permanent homeland: Land tenure in Guthlac A', *Anglo-Saxon England* 40, 75–102.

Coates, R. (2005) 'Four pre-English river names in and around fenland: *Chater, Granta, Nene* and *Welland*', *Transactions of the Philological Society* 103(3), 303–22.

Coates, R. (2006) 'Names'. In *A History of the English Language*, ed. Richard Hogg, 312–51, Cambridge University Press, Cambridge.

Coates, R. and Breeze, A. eds (2000) *Celtic Voices English Places*, Shaun Tyas, Stamford.

Cole, A. (2007) 'The place-name evidence for water transport in early medieval England'. In *Waterways and Canal-Building in Medieval England*, ed. J. Blair, 55–84, Oxford University Press, Oxford.

Coleman, C. (1996) *Court Roll of the Manor of Downham 1310–1327*, Boydell and Brewer, Woodbridge.

Coles, J. and Coles, J. (1986) *Sweet Track to Glastonbury*, Thames and Hudson, London.

Cook, H. (2007) 'The hydrology, soils and geology of the Wessex water meadows'. In *Water Meadows. History, Ecology and Conservation*, eds Hadrian Cook and Tom Williamson, 94–106, Windgather, Macclesfield.

Crabtree, P. (1990) *West Stow. Early Anglo-Saxon Husbandry*, East Anglian Archaeology 47, Ipswich.

Crabtree, P. (2010) 'Agricultural innovation and socio-economic change in early medieval Europe: Evidence from Britain and France', *World Archaeology* 42 (1), 122–36.

Crowson, A., Lane, T., Penn, K. and Trimble, D. (2005) *Anglo-Saxon Settlement on the Siltland of Eastern England*, Lincolnshire Archaeology and Heritage Report 7, Lincoln.

Cummings, I. and Cutting, R. (2007) 'The effects of floating on plant communities'. In *Water Meadows. History, Ecology and Conservation*, eds Hadrian Cook and Tom Williamson, 82–93, Windgather, Macclesfield.

Cunningham, W. ed. (1910) 'Common rights at Cottenham and Stretham in Cambridgeshire', *Camden Miscellany* 12, 173–926.

Cutting, R. and Cummings, I. (2007) 'Drowning by numbers: The functioning of bedwork water meadows'. In *Water Meadows. History, Ecology and Conservation*, eds Hadrian Cook and Tom Williamson, 70–81, Windgather, Macclesfield.

Darby, H. C. (1934) 'The fenland frontier in Anglo–Saxon England', *Antiquity* 8, 185–201.

Darby, H. C. (1936) 'The Domesday geography of Cambridgeshire', *Proceedings of the Cambridge Antiquarian Society* 36, 35–57.

Darby, H. C. (1974) *The Medieval Fenland*, Cambridge University Press, Cambridge.

Dark, P. (2000) *The Environment of Britain in the First Millennium AD*, Duckworth, London.

Davies, A. and Dixon, P. (2007) 'Reading the pastoral landscape: Palynological and historical evidence for the impacts of long-term grazing on Wether Hill, Ingram, Northumberland', *Landscape History* 29, 35–47.

Davies, O. (2009) *Management Guidelines for Grassland in Environmental Schemes*, ADAS, Wolverhampton.

Davies, W. and Vierck, H. (1974) 'The contexts of Tribal Hidage: Social aggregates and settlement patterns', *Frühmittelalterliche Studien* 8, 223–93.

De Ridder, T. (1999) 'VLAK-Overdrukken Nr. 2. De oudste deltawerken van wes-Europa. Tweeduizend jaar oude dammen en duikers to Vlaardingen', *Tijdschrift voor Waterstaatgeschiedenis* 8(1), 10–22.

Dekker, W. and Beaulaton, L. (2016) 'Climbing back up what slippery slope? Dynamics of the European eel stock and its management in historical perspective', *ICES Journal of Marine Science* 73(1), 5–13.

Denman, D., Roberts, R. and Smith, H. (1967) *Commons and Village Greens: A Study in Land Use, Conservation and Management Based on a National Survey of Commons in England and Wales*, L. F. Hill, London.

Dodgshon, J. (1966) 'The significance of the distribution of English place-names in *-ingas, -inga* in south-east England', *Medieval Archaeology* 10, 1–29.

Douglas, D. C. (1927) *The Social Structure of Medieval East Anglia*, Clarendon Press, Oxford.

Dumville, D. (1977) 'Kingship, genealogies and regnal lists'. In *Early Medieval Kingship*, eds P. Sawyer and I. Wood, 72–104, University of Leeds, Leeds.

Dumville, D. (1985) 'The West Saxon genealogical regnal list and the chronology of early Wessex', *Peritia* 4, 21–66.

Dumville, D. (1989) 'Essex, Middle Anglia and the expansion of Mercia'. In *The Origins of Anglo-Saxon Kingdoms*, ed. S. Bassett, 123–40, Leicester University Press, London.

Dumville, D. (1993) *English Caroline Script and Monastic History: Studies in Benedictinism AD 950–1030*, Boydell and Brewer, Woodbridge.

Dyer, C. (1996) 'Lords, peasants and the development of the manor: England, 900–1280'. In *England and Germany in the High Middle Ages*, eds A. Haverkamp and H. Vollrath, 301–15, German Historical Institute and Oxford University Press, Oxford.

Ekwall, E. (1928) *English River-Names*, Clarendon Press, Oxford.

English Nature (2004) *Purple Moor-grass and Rush Pastures*, http://publications.naturalengland.org.uk/publication/76010, accessed 30 June 2016.

English Place-Name Society, *Key to English Place-Names*, www.kepn.nottingham.ac.uk, accessed 30 June 2016.

Ensor, B. (2011) 'Kinship theory in archaeology: From critiques to the study of transformations', *American Antiquity* 76(2), 203–27.

Environment Agency (2010) *Ecohydrological Guidelines for Lowland Wetland Plant Communities 2004, and Fens and Mires Update 2010*, Environment Agency, London.

Evans, C. (2003a) 'Britons and Romans at Chatteris: Investigations at Langwood Farm, Cambridgeshire', *Britannia* 34, 175–264.

Evans, C. (2003b) *Power and Island Communities: Excavations at the Wardy Hill Ringwork*, East Anglian Archaeology 103, Cambridge.

Evans, C. (2013) 'Delivering bodies unto the waters: A late Bronze Age mid-stream midden settlement and Iron Age ritual complex in the fens', *Antiquaries Journal* 93, 55–79.

Evans, C. and Hodder, I. (2006) *Marshland Communities and Cultural Landscapes From the Bronze Age to the Present Day, Volume 2*, English Heritage, Swindon.

Evans, C, and Serjeantson, D. (1988) 'The backwater economy of a fen-edge community in the Iron Age: The Upper Delphs, Haddenham', *Antiquity* 62(235), 360–70.

Evans, C. and vander Linden, M. (2009) *The Over Narrows* (Part III), Cambridge Archaeological Unit Report 878, Cambridge.

Evans, T.N.L. (2015) 'A reassessment of archaeological grey literature: Semantics and paradoxes', *Internet Archaeology* 40, http://intarch.ac.uk/journal/issue40/6/index.html, accessed 3 March 2017.

Faith, R. (1997) *The English Peasantry and the Growth of Lordship*, Leicester University Press, Leicester.

Faith, R. (2004) 'Cola's *Tūn*: Rural social structure in late Anglo-Saxon Devon'. In *Lordship and Learning. Studies in Memory of Trevor Aston*, ed. R. Evans, 63–78, Boydell and Brewer, Woodbridge.

Faith, R. (2012) 'Some Devon farms before the Norman Conquest'. In *Life in Medieval Landscapes. People and Places in the Middle Ages*, eds S. Turner and B. Silvester, 73–88, Windgather, Oxford.

Faull, M. (1975) 'The semantic development of Old English *wealh*', *Leeds Studies in English*, NS 8, 20–44.

Featherstone, P. (2001) 'The Tribal Hidage and the Ealdormen of Mercia'. In *Mercia: An Anglo-Saxon Kingdom in Europe*, eds M. Brown and C. Farr, 23–34, Leicester University Press, London.

Flinders Petrie, W. M. (1878) 'Proceedings at meetings

of the Royal Archaeological Institute, February 1, 1878', *Archaeological Journal* 35, 169–77.

Foard, G. (2001) 'Medieval woodland, agriculture and industry in Rockingham Forest, Northamptonshire', *Medieval Archaeology* 45, 41–95.

Fowler, P. (2002) *Farming in the First Millennium*, Cambridge University Press, Cambridge.

Fox, C. (1923) *The Archaeology of the Cambridge Region*, Cambridge University Press, Cambridge.

Frere, S. and St Joseph, J. K. (1983) *Roman Britain from the* Air, Cambridge University Press, Cambridge.

Friday, L. and Rowell, T. (1997) 'Patterns and processes'. In *Wicken Fen: The Making of a Wetland Nature Reserve*, ed. L. Friday, 11–21, Harley, Colchester.

Friday, L., Walters, S. and Lock, J. (1997) 'Carr and woodland'. In *Wicken Fen: The Making of a Wetland Nature Reserve*, ed. L. Friday, 82–97, Harley, Colchester.

Geary, P. (2002) *The Myth of Nations. The Medieval Origins of Europe*, Princeton University Press, Princeton.

Geary, P. and Veeramah, K. (2016) 'Mapping European population movement through genomic research', *Medieval Worlds* 4, 65–78.

Gelling, M. (1974) *Signposts to the Past*, Dent, London.

Gelling, M. (1992) *The West Midlands in the Early Middle Ages*, Leicester University Press, Leicester.

Gelling, M. (2010) 'Place-names and archaeology'. In *The Oxford Handbook of Anglo-Saxon Archaeology*, eds H. Hamerow, D. Hinton and S. Crawford, 1004–20, Oxford University Press, Oxford.

Gelling, M. and Cole, A. (2000) *The Landscape of Place-Names*, Shaun Tyas, Stamford.

Gibson, D. and Knight, M. (2006) *Bradley Fen Excavations 2001–2004, Whittlesey, Cambridgeshire*, Cambridge Archaeological Unit Report 733, Cambridge Archaeological Unit, Cambridge.

Glasscock, R. (1976) 'England c.1331'. In *A New Historical Geography of England before 1600*, ed. H. C. Darby, 136–85, Cambridge University Press, Cambridge.

Glasscock, R., ed. (1975) *The Lay Subsidy of 1334*, British Academy, London.

Godwin, H. (1940) 'Studies in the post-glacial history of British vegetation. III. Fenland pollen diagrams. IV. Post-glacial changes in relative land and sea-level in the English fenland', *Philosophical Transactions of the Royal Society of London* B230 (570), 239–304.

Godwin, H. and Clifford, M. (1938) 'Studies in the post-glacial history of British vegetation. I. Origin and stratigraphy of fenland deposits near Woodwalton, Hunts. II. Origin and stratigraphy of deposits in southern fenland', *Philosophical Transactions of the Royal Society of London* B229 (562), 323–406.

Godwin, H. and Vishnu-Mittre (1975) 'Studies of the post-glacial history of British vegetation: XVI. Flandrian deposits of the fenland margin at Holme Fen and Whittlesey Mere, Hunts.', *Philosophical Transactions of the Royal Society of London* B270(909), 561–604.

Goffart, W. (2006) 'The Barbarians in Late Antiquity and how they were accommodated in the West'. In *From Roman Provinces to Medieval Kingdoms*, ed. T. Noble, 235–61, Routledge, London.

Gooch, W. (1811) *A General View of the Agriculture of the County of Cambridge*, Philips, London.

Gray, A. (1911) 'On the late survival of a Celtic population in East Anglia', *Proceedings of the Cambridge Antiquarian Society* 15, 42–52.

Green, T. (2012) *Britons and Anglo-Saxons. Lincolnshire AD 400–650*, History of Lincolnshire Committee, Lincoln.

Härke, H. (2011) 'Anglo-Saxon immigration and ethnogenesis', *Medieval Archaeology* 55, 1–28.

Hall, A. (2012) 'The instability of place-names in Anglo-Saxon England and early Medieval Wales, and the loss of Roman toponymy'. In *Sense of Place in Anglo-Saxon England*, eds Richard Jones and Sarah Semple, 101–29, Tyas, Donnington.

Hall, D. (1977) '"Roman Bank" – A medieval sea-wall. II. The Sea Bank in Cambridgeshire', *Proceedings of the Cambridge Antiquarian Society* 67, 67–68.

Hall, D. (1987) *The Fenland Project, Number 2: Fenland Landscapes and Settlement between Peterborough and March*, East Anglian Archaeology 35, Cambridge.

Hall, D. (1992) *The Fenland Project, Number 6: The South-Western Cambridgeshire Fenlands*, East Anglian Archaeology 56, Cambridge.

Hall, D. (1996) *The Fenland Project, Number 10: Cambridgeshire Survey, The Isle of Ely and Wisbech*, East Anglian Archaeology 79, Cambridge.

Hall, D. (2000) 'Roman salt production in Cambridgeshire'. In *An Atlas of Cambridgeshire and Huntingdonshire History*, eds T. Kirby and S. Oosthuizen, 16, Anglia Polytechnic University, Cambridge.

Hall, D. and Coles, J. (1994) *Fenland Survey. An Essay in Landscape and Persistence*, English Heritage, Swindon.

Hallam, H. E. (1954) *The New Lands of Elloe: A Study*

of Early Reclamation in Lincolnshire, University of Leicester, Leicester.

Hallam, H. E. (1963) 'The fen by-laws of Spalding and Pinchbeck', *Lincolnshire Architectural and Archaeological Society Reports and Papers* NS 10(1), 44–56.

Hallam, H. E. (1965) *Settlement and Society: A Study of the Early Agrarian History of South Lincolnshire*, Cambridge University Press, Cambridge.

Hallam, H. E. (1988) 'Drainage techniques'. In *The Agrarian History of England and Wales. Volume 2. 1042–1350*, ed. H. E. Hallam, 497–507, Cambridge University Press, Cambridge.

Hamerow, H. (1997) 'Migration theory and the Anglo-Saxon "identity crisis"' in *Migrations and Invasions in Archaeological Explanation*, eds J. Chapman and H. Hamerow, 33–44, Noyes Press, Oxford.

Hamerow, H. (2002) *Early Medieval Settlements: The Archaeology of Rural Communities in North-West Europe 400–900*, Oxford University Press, Oxford.

Hamerow, H. (2012) *Rural Settlements and Society in Anglo-Saxon England*, Oxford University Press, Oxford.

Harley, J. B. (1989) 'Historical geography and the cartographic illusion', *Journal of Historical Geography* 15(1), 80–91.

Hart, C. R. (1966) *Early Charters of Eastern England*, Leicester University Press, Leicester.

Hart, C. R. (1971) 'The Tribal Hidage', *Transactions of the Royal Historical Society* Fifth Series 21, 133–57.

Hart, C. R. (1974) *The Hidation of Cambridgeshire*, Leicester University Press, Leicester.

Hart, C. R. (1992) *The Danelaw*, Hambledon, London.

Harvey, P. (1989) 'Initiative and authority in settlement change'. In *The Rural Settlements of Medieval England*, eds M. Aston, D. Austin and C. Dyer, 31–43, Oxford University Press, Oxford.

Haslam, J. (1982) 'The development and topography of Saxon Cambridge', *Proceedings of the Cambridge Antiquarian Society* 72, 13–19.

Hayes, P. P. and Lane, T. (1992) *The Fenland Project, Number 5: Lincolnshire Survey, the South-West Fens*, East Anglian Archaeology 55, Lincoln.

Hayes, P. P. and Lane, T. (1993) 'Moving boundaries in the fens of south Lincolnshire'. In *Flatlands and Wetlands: Current Themes in East Anglian Archaeology*, ed. J. Gardiner, 58–70, East Anglian Archaeology 50, East Dereham.

Higgitt, J. (2006) 'The inscriptions'. In *Corpus of Anglo-Saxon Stone Sculpture: South-West England, Volume 7*, ed. Rosemary Cramp, 63–68, Oxford University Press, Oxford.

Higham, N. (1992) *Rome, Britain and the Anglo-Saxons*, Seaby, London.

Higham, N. (1994) *The English Conquest. Gildas and Britain in the Fifth Century*, Manchester University Press, Manchester.

Hills, C. (2011) 'Overview: Anglo-Saxon identity'. In *The Oxford Handbook of Anglo-Saxon Archaeology*, eds H. Hamerow, D. Hinton and S. Crawford, 3–12, Oxford University Press, Oxford.

Hinton, A. (1995) 'Holocene tides of the Wash, U.K.: The influence of water-depth and coastline-shape changes on the record of sea-level change', *Marine Geology* 124, 87–111.

Holling, C. (2001) 'Understanding the complexity of economic, ecological and social systems', *Ecosystems* 4, 390–405.

Hollinrake, C. and Hollinrake, N. (2007) 'Glastonbury's Anglo-Saxon Canal and Dunstan's Dyke'. In *Waterways and Canal-Building in Medieval England*, ed. J. Blair, 235–243, Oxford University Press, Oxford.

Homans, G. (1953) 'The rural sociology of medieval England', *Past and Present* 4, 32–43.

Hooke, D. (1978) 'Early Cotswold woodland', *Journal of Historical Geography* 4, 333–41.

Hooke, D. (1998) *The Landscape of Anglo-Saxon England*, Leicester University Press, Leicester.

Hoskins, W. G. and Stamp, D. (1963) *The Common Lands of England and Wales*, Collins, London.

Hughes, S. *et al.* (2014) 'Anglo-Saxon origins investigated by isotopic analysis of burials from Berinsfield, Oxfordshire, UK', *Journal of Archaeological Science* 42, 81–92.

Hutton, J. (2010) *Walsingham Way, Ely. An Archaeological Evaluation*, Cambridge Archaeological Unit Report 927, Cambridge.

Insley, J. (1999) 'Gyrwe', *Reallexicon der Germanischen Altertumskunde* 13, 230–32.

Joint Nature Conservation Committee (2001) *National Vegetation Classification: Field Guide to Mires and Heaths*, English Nature, Peterborough.

Joint Nature Conservation Committee (2012) *Special Areas of Conservation: Habitat account – Raised Bogs and Mires and Fens*, http://jncc. defra.gov.uk/protectedsites/sacselection/habitat. asp?FeatureIntCode=H7210, accessed 30 June 2016.

Kelly, F. (1997) *Early Irish Farming*, Dublin Institute for Advanced Studies, Dublin.

Kelly, S. ed (2009) *Charters of Peterborough Abbey*, British Academy, Oxford University Press, Oxford.

Kershaw, J. and Røyrvik, E. (2016) 'The "People of the British Isles" project and Viking settlement in England', *Antiquity* 90 (354), 1670–80.

Kestner, F. (1975) 'The loose-boundary regime of the Wash', *Geographical Journal* 141(3), 388–414.

Kirby, D. (1965–66) 'The Saxon bishops of Leicester, Lindsey (Syddensis) and Dorchester', *Leicestershire Archaeological and Historical Society* 41, 1–8.

Kirkus, A. M. (1959) *The Records of the Commissioners of Sewers in the Parts of Holland 1547–1603, Volume 1*, Lincoln Record Society, Lincoln.

Lamb, H. H. (1985) 'Climate and Landscape in the British Isles'. In *The English Landscape. Past, Present and Future*, ed. S. R. J. Woodell, 148–67, Oxford University Press, Oxford.

Lavelle, R. (2003) 'The 'Farm of One Night' and the organisation of royal estates in late Anglo-Saxon Wessex', *Haskins Society Journal* 14, 1–37.

Leslie, S., Winney, B., Hellenthal, G. *et al.* (2015) 'The fine-scale genetic structure of the British population', *Nature* 519, 309–14.

Lethbridge, T. C. (1934) 'Investigations of the ancient causeway in the fen between Fordy and Little Thetford', *Proceedings of the Cambridge Antiquarian Society* 35, 86–89.

Lewis, C. (1993) 'The Domesday jurors', *Haskins Society Journal* 5, 17–44.

Lewis, C., Dyer, C. and Mitchell-Fox, P. (1997) *Village, Hamlet and Field*, Manchester University Press, Manchester.

Lucy, S. and Reynolds. A. (2002) 'Burial in early medieval England and Wales: Past, present and future'. In *Burial in Early Medieval England and Wales*, eds S. Lucy and A. Reynolds, 1–23, Society for Medieval Archaeology, London.

Lucy, S., Newman, R., Dodwell, N., Hills, C., Dekker, M., O'Connell, T., Riddler, I. and Rogers, P. (2009) 'The burial of a princess? The later seventh-century cemetery at Westfield Farm, Ely', *Antiquaries Journal* 89, 81–141.

MacKenzie, N. 2010. *Ecology, Conservation and Management of Aspen. A Literature Review*, Scottish Native Woods, Aberfeldy.

Mason, H. J. (1984) *The Black Fens*, Providence Press, Cambridge.

Masser, P. (2000) *Archaeological Evaluation at West Fen Road, Ely: The Cornwell Bungalow site*, Cambridge Archaeological Unit Report 373, Cambridge.

Mawer, A. and Stenton, F. (1926) *The Place-Names of Bedfordshire and Huntingdonshire*, Cambridge University Press, Cambridge.

McCarthy, M. (2013) *The Romano-British Peasant*, Windgather, Oxford.

Met Office (2015) January 2014 weather summary. http://www.metoffice.gov.uk/climate/uk/summaries/2014/january, accessed 30 June 2016.

Miller, E. (1951) *The Abbey and Bishopric of Ely*, Cambridge University Press, Cambridge.

Miller, S. and Skertchly, S. (1878) *The Fenland Past and Present*, Longmans Green, London.

Mills, A. D. (2011) *A Dictionary of British Place-Names*, Oxford University Press, Oxford/Online edition http://www.oxfordreference.com/view/10.1093/acref/9780199609086.001.0001/acref-9780199609086, accessed March 2017.

Mitchell, R. and Crook, D. (1999) 'The Pinchbeck Fen map: A fifteenth-century map of the Lincolnshire fenland', *Imago Mundi* 51, 40–50.

Moore, J. (1685) *The History, or Narrative of the Great Level of the Fenns, called Bedford Level*, Moses Pitt, London.

Morris, A. M. (2006) 'Forging links with the past: the twelfth-century reconstruction of Anglo-Saxon Peterborough', PhD dissertation, University of Leicester, Leicester.

Morris, R. (1989) *Churches in the Landscape*, Dent, London.

Mortimer, R., Regan, R. and Lucy, S. (2005) *The Saxon and Medieval Settlement at West Fen Road, Ely: The Ashwell Site*, East Anglian Archaeology 110, Cambridge.

Murphy, P. (1994) 'The Anglo-Saxon landscape and rural economy: Some results from sites in East Anglia and Essex'. In *Environment and Economy in Anglo-Saxon England*, ed. J. Rackham, 25–37, Council for British Archaeology Research Report 89, York.

Naismith, R. (2016) 'The Ely Memoranda and the economy of the late Anglo-Saxon fenland', *Anglo-Saxon England* 45. https://kclpure.kcl.ac.uk/portal/en/publications/the-ely-memoranda-and-the-economy-of-the-late-anglosaxon-fenland(803566da-ea29-44f8-99a4-ef341b8ba7dd).html, accessed March 2017.

Nash Briggs, D. (2011) 'The Language of inscriptions on Icenian coinage'. In *The Iron Age in Northern East Anglia: New Work in the Land of the Iceni*, ed. J. A. Davies, 83–102, British Archaeological Report 549, Archaeopress, Oxford.

Natural England (2008) *State of the Natural Environment 2008 (NE85): Chapter 3, Biodiversity*. http://publications.naturalengland.org.uk/publication/31043, accessed 30 June 2016.

Natural England (2013) *NE424. National Character Area (NCA) Profile: 46. The Fens*. http://publications.naturalengland.org.uk/publication/6229624?category=8005, accessed 30 June 2016.

Neilson, N. (1910) *Customary Rents*, Oxford Studies in Social and Legal History II, Clarendon Press, Oxford.

Neilson, N. (1920) *A Terrier of Fleet, Lincolnshire*, British Academy, London.

Neilson, N. (1925) 'Custom and the common law in Kent', *Harvard Law Review* 38(4), 482–98.

Neilson, N. (1929) 'English manorial forms', *American Historical Review* 34(4), 725–39.

O'Connor, T. (2009) 'Culture and environment: Mind the gap'. In *Land and People: Papers in Memory of John G. Evans*, eds M. J. Allen, N. Sharples and T. O'Connor, 11–18, Prehistoric Society Research Papers 2, Oxford.

O'Connor, T. (2011) 'Animal husbandry'. In *The Oxford Handbook of Anglo-Saxon Archaeology*, eds H. Hamerow, D. Hinton and S. Crawford, 363–78, Oxford University Press, Oxford.

Oosthuizen, S. (1998) 'The origins of Cambridgeshire', *Antiquaries Journal* 78, 85–109.

Oosthuizen, S. (2001) 'Anglo-Saxon minsters in south Cambridgeshire', *Proceedings of the Cambridge Antiquarian Society* 90, 49–68.

Oosthuizen, S. (2006) *Landscapes Decoded*, University of Hertfordshire Press, Hatfield.

Oosthuizen, S. (2008) 'Field-names in reconstructing late Anglo-Saxon land-use in the Bourn Valley, west Cambridgeshire'. In *Recent Approaches to the Archaeology of Land Allotment*, ed. A. Chadwick, 323–40, British Archaeological Report S1875, Archaeopress, Oxford.

Oosthuizen, S. (2011a) 'Anglo-Saxon fields'. In *Oxford Handbook of Anglo-Saxon Archaeology*, eds H. Hamerow, D. Hinton and S. Crawford, 377–401, Oxford University Press, Oxford.

Oosthuizen, S. (2011b) 'Archaeology, common rights, and the origins of Anglo-Saxon identity', *Early Medieval Europe* 19(2), 153–81.

Oosthuizen, S. (2012) 'Cambridgeshire and the peat fen: Medieval rural settlement and commerce, *c*.AD 900–1300'. In *Medieval Rural Settlement Britain and Ireland, AD 800–1600*, eds N. Christie and P. Stamper, 206–24, Windgather, Oxford.

Oosthuizen, S. (2013a) '"A truth universally acknowledged?" Morphology as an indicator of medieval planned market towns', *Landscape History* 34(1), 51–80.

Oosthuizen, S. (2013b) *Tradition and Transformation: Archaeology, Common Rights and Landscape*, Bloomsbury Academic, London.

Oosthuizen, S. (2014) 'Re-evaluating maps of Domesday population densities: a case study from the Cambridgeshire fenland', *Medieval Settlement Research* 29, 1–10.

Oosthuizen, S. (2016a) 'Beyond hierarchy: Archaeology, common rights and social identity', *World Archaeology* 48, published online July 2016 http://www.tandfonline.com/doi/full/10.1080/00438243.2016.1180261.

Oosthuizen, S. (2016b) 'Culture and identity in the early medieval fenland landscape', *Landscape History* 37(1), 5–24.

Oosthuizen, S. (2016c) 'Review article: Recognising and moving on from a failed paradigm: The case of agricultural landscapes in Anglo-Saxon England *c*.400–800', *Journal of Archaeological Research* 24(2), 179–227.

Oschinsky, D. (1971) *Walter of Henley, and Other Treatises on Estate Management and Accounting*, Clarendon Press, Oxford.

Östrom, E. (1990) *Governing the Commons. The Evolution of Institutions for Collective Action*, Cambridge University Press, Cambridge.

Owen, A. E. B. (1965) 'A thirteenth-century agreement on water for livestock in Lindsey Marsh', *Agricultural History Review* 13(1), 40–46.

Owen, A. E. B. ed (1977) *The Records of the Commissioners of Sewers in the Parts of Holland 1547–1604, Volume 3*, Lincoln Record Society, Lincoln.

Owen, A. E. B. (1981) *The Records of a Commission of Sewers for Wiggenhall 1319–1324*, Norfolk Record Society, Norwich.

Owen, A. E. B. (1982) 'A Fenland frontier: The establishment of the boundary between Cambridgeshire and Lincolnshire', *Landscape History* 4(1), 41–44.

Owen, A. E. B. (1984) 'Salt, sea banks and medieval settlement on the Lindsey coast'. In *A Prospect of Lincolnshire*, eds N. Field and A. White, 46–49, privately published, Lincoln.

Owen, A. E. B. (1986) 'Isle of Ely, Cambridgeshire,

and Holland Lincolnshire'. In *Local Maps and Plans from Medieval England*, eds R. Skelton and P. D. A. Harvey, 89–98, Oxford University Press, Oxford.

Page, F. (1929) '*Bidenties Hoylandiae*, a medieval sheep farm', *Economic History, the Economic Journal Supplement* 1, 603–13.

Page, F. (1934) *Estates of Crowland Abbey, A Study in Manorial Organisation*, Cambridge University Press, Cambridge.

Page, W., ed. (1906) *A History of the County of Lincoln: Volume 2*, James Street, London.

Parsons, D. (2011) 'Sabrina in the thorns: place-names as evidence for British and Latin in Roman Britain', *Transactions of the Philological Society* 109, 113–37.

Patterson, W., Dietrich, L., Holmden, C. and Andrews, J. (2010) 'Two millennia of North Atlantic seasonality and implications for Norse colonies', *Proceedings of the National Academy of Sciences* 107(12), 5305–10.

Penn, K. (2005) 'Discussion and conclusions'. In *Anglo-Saxon Settlement in the Siltland of Eastern England*, eds A. Crowson, T. Lane, K. Penn and D. Trimble, Lincolnshire Society for Archaeology and History, Heckington, 289–300.

Pfister, C., Luterbacher, J., Schwarz-Zanetti, G. and Wegmann, M. (1998) 'Winter air temperature variations in western Europe during the Early and High Middle Ages (AD 750–1300)', *Holocene* 8(5), 535–52.

Phillips, C. W. ed. (1970) *The Fenland in Roman Times*, Royal Geographical Society, London.

Pohl, W. (1997) 'Ethnic names and identities in the British Isles: A comparative perspective'. In *The Anglo-Saxons from the Migration Period to the Eighth Century. An Ethnographic Perspective*, ed. J. Hines, 7–40, Boydell and Brewer, Woodbridge.

Postan, M. (1973) *Essays on Medieval Agriculture and the Problems of the Medieval Economy*, Cambridge University Press, Cambridge.

Portable Antiquities Scheme, www.finds.org.uk, accessed 30 June 2016.

Prosopography of Anglo-Saxon England, www.pase. ac.uk, accessed 30 June 2016.

Pryor, F. (1998) *Etton. Excavations at a Neolithic Causewayed Enclosure near Maxey Cambridgeshire 1982–87*, English Heritage, London.

Pryor, F. (2001) *The Flag Fen Basin. Archaeology and Environment of a Fenland Landscape*, English Heritage, Swindon.

Raban, S. (1977) *The Estates of Thorney and Crowland. A Study in Medieval Monastic Land Tenure*, University

of Cambridge Department of Land Economy, Occasional Paper 7, Cambridge.

Rackham, O. (1987) *The History of the Countryside*, Dent, London.

Raftis, J. (1957) *The Estates of Ramsey Abbey*, Pontifical Institute, Toronto.

Ravensdale, J. (1974) *Liable to Floods*, Cambridge University Press, Cambridge.

Ravenstein, E. (1885) 'The laws of migration', *Journal of the Statistical Society of London* 48, 156–235.

Reaney, P. H. (1935) *The Place-Names of Essex*, Cambridge University Press, Cambridge.

Reaney, P. H. (1943) *The Place-Names of Cambridgeshire and the Isle of Ely*, Cambridge University Press, Cambridge.

Reynolds, S. (1983) 'Medieval *origines gentium* and the community of the realm', *History* 68(224), 375–90.

Roberts, B. K. (2008) *Landscapes, Documents and Maps*, Oxbow Books, Oxford.

Roberts, B. K. and Wrathmell, S. (2002) *Region and Place*, English Heritage, Swindon.

Roffe, D. (1993) '*On middan Gyrwan fenne*: Intercommoning around the Isle of Crowland', *Fenland Research* 8, 80–6.

Roffe, D. (2005) 'The historical context'. In *Anglo-Saxon Settlement in the Siltland of Eastern England*, eds A. Crowson, T. Lane, K. Penn and D. Trimble, 264–88, Lincolnshire Society for Archaeology and History, Heckington.

Rollason, D. (1978) 'Lists of saints' resting places in Anglo-Saxon England', *Anglo-Saxon England* 7, 61–93.

Rothero, E., Lake, S. and Gowing, D. eds (2016) *Floodplain Meadows – Beauty and Utility. A Technical Handbook*, Floodplain Meadows Partnership, Open University, Milton Keynes.

Rowell, T. A. (1986) 'Sedge (*Cladium mariscus*) in Cambridgeshire: Its use and production since the seventeenth century', *Agricultural History Review* 34(2), 140–48.

Royal Commission on Historical Monuments England (1972) *North-East Cambridgeshire*, HMSO, London.

Schiffels, S., Haak, W., Paajanen, P., Llamas, B., Popescu, E., Loe, L., Clarke, R., Lyons, A., Mortimer, R., Sayers, D., Tyler-Smith, C., Cooper, A. and Durbin, R. (2016) 'Iron Age and Anglo-Saxon Genomes from East England reveal British Migration Industry', *Nature Communications* 7, 10408, 1–9.

Schladweiler, J. (2016) *The History of Sanitary Sewers*, http://www.sewerhistory.org/grfx/components/pipe-wood1.htm, accessed 30 June 2016.

Schram, O. (1950) 'Fenland place-names'. In *The Early Cultures of North-West Europe*, eds C. Fox and B. Dickins, 427–41, Cambridge University Press, Cambridge.

Scull, C. (1993) 'Archaeology, early Anglo-Saxon society and the origins of Anglo-Saxon kingdoms', *Anglo-Saxon Studies in Archaeology and History* 6, 66–82.

Shennan, I. (1986) 'Flandrian sea-level changes in the Fenland. II: Tendencies of sea-level movement, altitudinal changes, and local and regional factors', *Journal of Quaternary Science* 1(2), 155–79.

Shennan, I. and Horton, B. (2002) 'Holocene land- and sea-level changes in Great Britain', *Journal of Quaternary Science* 17(5–6), 511–26.

Shennan, I., Bradley, S., Milne, G., Bassett, S. and Hamilton, S. (2006) 'Relative sea-level changes, glacial isostatic modeling and ice-sheet reconstructions from the British Isles since the Last Glacial Maximum', *Journal of Quaternary Science* 21(6), 585–99.

Schrijver, P. (2013) *Language Contact and the Origins of the Germanic Languages*, Routledge, London.

Silvester, R. (1985) 'West Walton: The development of a siltland parish', *Norfolk Archaeology* 19(2), 101–17.

Silvester, R. (1988) *The Fenland Project, Number 3: Norfolk Survey, Marshland and the Nar Valley*, East Anglian Archaeology 45, East Dereham.

Silvester, R. (1991) *The Fenland Project, Number 4: The Wissey Embayment and the Fen Causeway, Norfolk*, East Anglian Archaeology 52, East Dereham.

Silvester, R. (1993) 'The addition of more-or-less undifferentiated dots to a distribution map'? The Fenland Project in retrospect. In *Flatlands and Wetlands: Current Themes in East Anglian Archaeology*, ed. J. Gardiner, 24–39, East Anglian Archaeology 50, East Dereham.

Sims-Williams, P. (1983) 'The settlement of England in Bede and the Chronicle', *Anglo-Saxon England* 12, 1–41.

Skeat, W. W. (1901) *Place-Names of Cambridgeshire*, Cambridge Antiquarian Society Octavo Publications 36, Cambridge.

Skeat, W. W. (1902) 'Two Anglo-Saxon fragments of the eleventh century', *Proceedings of the Cambridge Philological Society* 61–63, 12–16.

Slater, A. (2011) *Walsingham Way, Ely, Cambridgeshire; An Archaeological Excavation*, Cambridge Archaeological Unit Report 993, Cambridge.

Smith, A. H., ed (1956) *English Place-Name Elements*, 2 volumes, Cambridge University Press, Cambridge.

Smith, C. (1980) 'The survival of Romano-British toponymy', *Nomina* 4, 27–40.

Smith, D., Zalasiewicz, J., Williams, M., Wilkinson, I., Redding, M. and Begg, C. (2010) 'Holocene drainage systems of the English fenland: roddons and their environmental significance', *Proceedings of the Geologists' Association* 121(3), 256–69.

Spufford, M. (1974) *Contrasting Communities*, Cambridge University Press, Cambridge.

Tabor, J. (2010a) *Land at King's Delph, Whittlesey, Cambridgeshire*, Cambridge Archaeological Unit Report 915, Cambridge.

Tabor, J. (2010b) *Archaeological investigations at Must Farm, Whittlesey, Cambridgeshire*, Cambridge Archaeological Unit Report 951, Cambridge.

Tabor, J. (2011) *Sutton Gault Irrigation Reservoir, Cambridgeshire*, Cambridge Archaeological Unit Report 1032, Cambridge.

Taylor, A. (1977) '"Roman Bank" – A medieval sea-wall. I. A culvert beneath the Sea Bank at Newton, near Wisbech', *Proceedings of the Cambridge Antiquarian Society* 67, 63–66.

Taylor, C. C. (1973) *The Cambridgeshire Landscape*, Hodder and Stoughton, London.

Taylor, C. C. (1983) *Village and Farmstead*, George Phillip, London.

Tester, A., Anderson, S., Riddler, I. and Carr, R. (2014) *Staunch Meadow, Brandon, Suffolk: A High Status Middle Saxon Settlement on the Fen Edge*, East Anglian Archaeology 151, Ipswich.

Thirsk, J. (1953a) *Fenland Farming in the Sixteenth Century*, University College, Leicester.

Thirsk, J. (1953b) 'The Isle of Axholme before Vermuyden', *Agricultural History Review* 1(1), 16–28.

Trent Foley, W. and Higham, N. (2007) 'Bede and the Britons', *Early Medieval Europe* 17, 154–85.

Tristram, H. (2007) 'Why don't the English speak Welsh?'. In *Britons in Anglo-Saxon England*, ed. N. Higham, 192–214, Boydell and Brewer, Woodbridge.

Van der Meer, W. (2009) 'Harvesting underwater meadows, use of eelgrass (*Zostera* spp.) as indicated by the Dutch archaeological record', *Journal of the Archaeology of the Low Countries* 1(1), 97–105.

Vancouver, C. (1794) *A General View of Agriculture in the County of Cambridgeshire*, W. Smith, London.

Victoria History of the County of Cambridge and the Isle of Ely, Volume IV (1953) ed. R. B. Pugh, Institute of Historical Research, Oxford University Press, London.

Victoria History of the County of Cambridge and the Isle

of Ely, Volume V (1973) ed. C. R. Elrington, Institute of Historical Research, Oxford University Press, London.

Victoria History of the County of Cambridge and the Isle of Ely, Volume IX (1989) eds A. P. M. Wright and C. P. Lewis, Institute of Historical Research, Oxford University Press, London.

Victoria History of the county of Cambridge and the Isle of Ely, Volume X (2002) eds A. F. Wareham and A. P. M. Wright, Institute of Historical Research, Oxford University Press, London.

Victoria History of the County of Huntingdon, Volume II (1932) eds W. Page, G. Proby and W. Inskip Ladds, Institute of Historical Research, Saint Catherine Press, London.

Victoria History of the County of Huntingdon, Volume III (1936) eds W. Page, G. Proby and W. Inskip Ladds, Institute of Historical Research, Saint Catherine Press, London.

Victoria History of the County of Northampton, Volume II (1906) eds R. M. Serjeantson and W. Adkins, James Street, London.

Victoria History of the County of Somerset, Volume II (1911) ed. W. Page, Constable and Company, London.

Waddelove, A. and Waddelove, E. (1990) 'Archaeology and research into sea-level during the Roman era: Towards a methodology based on highest astronomical tide', *Britannia* 21, 253–66.

Waller, M. (1994) *The Fenland Project, Number 9: Flandrian Environmental Change in Fenland*, East Anglian Archaeology 70, Cambridge.

Warner, P. (1988) 'Pre-Conquest territorial and administrative organisation in east Suffolk'. In *Anglo-Saxon Settlements*, ed D. Hooke, 9–34, Blackwell, Oxford.

Weale, M., Weiss, D., Jager, R., Bradman, N. and Thomas, M. (2002) 'Y chromosome evidence for Anglo-Saxon mass migration', *Molecular Biological Evolution* 19, 1008–21.

Webster, C. J. (1987) 'Ernest Greenfield's excavations at Exning Roman villa', *Proceedings of the Cambridge Antiquarian Society* 76, 41–66.

Wells, S. (1828–30) *The History of the Drainage of the Great Level of the Fens, Called Bedford Level: With the Constitution and Laws of the Bedford Level Corporation*, Pheney, London.

Whitelock, D. ed (1979) *English Historical Documents, c.500–1042*, Eyre Methuen, London.

Wilkinson, K. and Straker, V. (2007) 'Neolithic and Early Bronze Age environmental background'. In *The Archaeology of South-West England*, ed. C. J. Webster, 63–74, Somerset County Council, Taunton.

Williamson, T. (2010) 'The environmental contexts of Anglo-Saxon settlement'. In *Landscape Archaeology of Anglo-Saxon England*, eds N. Higham, and M. Ryan, 133–56, Boydell and Brewer, Woodbridge.

Yorke, B. 2000. 'Political and ethnic identity: A case study of Anglo-Saxon practice'. In *Social Identity in Early Medieval Britain*, eds W. Frazer and A. Tyrell, 69–90, Leicester University Press, London.

Index

Numbers in **bold** refer to Figures.